F

20

D1545754

HUMAN RIGHTS

NOMOS
XXIII

NOMOS

Lieber-Atherton, Publishers

New York University Press

NOMOS XXIII

Yearbook of the American Society for Political and Legal Philosophy

HUMAN RIGHTS

Edited by

J. Roland Pennock, Swarthmore College

and

John W. Chapman, University of Pittsburgh

New York and London • New York University Press • 1981

Human Rights: Nomos XXIII
edited by J. Roland Pennock and John W. Chapman
Copyright © 1981 by New York University

Library of Congress Cataloging in Publication Data
Main entry under title:

Human rights.

    (Nomos ; 23)
    Includes selected papers from meetings of the American Society for
    Political and Legal Philosophy and the American Political Science
    Association, held jointly Sept. 1978.
    Includes bibliographical references and index.
    1. Civil rights—Addresses, essays, lectures.
I. Pennock, James Roland.   II. Chapman, John William, 1923-
III. American Society for Political and Legal Philosophy.
IV. American Political Science Association.   V. Series.
JC571.H7683   323.4   80-21253
ISBN 0-8147-6578-5

PREFACE

The twenty-third volume of NOMOS receives its impetus and roughly two thirds of its substance from the meetings of the American Society for Political and Legal Philosophy, held jointly with those of the American Political Science Association in September 1978, in New York City. The subject could hardly have been more timely.

Resurgence of talk about rights and of assertions of rights is commonplace. Although the concept of "natural rights" has not been completely displaced, the expression "human rights" certainly has a greater popularity today than has been true of "natural rights" since the days of Tom Paine. But of course widespread appeal to and use of the concept does not mean that all understand it in the same way, as will clearly emerge from a reading of these pages. Moreover, people differ about the significance of the shift in terminology from "natural" to "human" rights. Is this shift merely terminological, or does it involve an effort to enlarge the category of fundamental rights? Or may it be that to speak of "human" rather than "natural" rights implies and fosters alteration of the original understanding of "fundamental" rights?

In the liberal philosophy of life, "natural" rights are fundamental in that they have to do with freedom, autonomy, and equality of opportunity. Indeed, it is arguable that the liberal conception of equality itself is derived from the supreme importance attached to human freedom. Today, however, security, both physical and psychological, seem to many more important than opportunity, and equality tends to displace rather than to derive from freedom. Hence the transition from "natural" to "human" may reflect a change in attitude toward the human condition, a change that some will welcome and others deplore.

Yet the book is not focused on controversy. Our authors deal with various aspects of the subject, taking up such problems as seem to them most important or most in need of analysis.

After an introductory overview by one of the editors, the essays have been classified, with only a modest amount of forcing, as dealing with the nature, the justification, and the scope of human rights. The first of the three groups of chapters following the introductory one displays considerable disparity of treatment. It opens with John Charvet's critique of the autonomist liberal theory of human rights. This theory is said to ground men's claims on man's own nature, and Charvet finds this theory radically incoherent. Having argued that neither Rawls nor Marx offers a satisfactory solution to the problem he detects, he proceeds to sketch his own theory of human rights, which he believes to be in accord with the truth about our nature. If we understand him correctly, this theory relies on a conception of man that is not, so to speak, natural, but rather social in that we are seen as the necessary product of our interrelations. Human psychology is inherently social.

Frithjof Bergmann, contrary to Charvet, finds no incoherence in the liberal theory of rights. Neither rights to freedom nor rights to equality can be unlimited. But, *pace* Charvet, this fact is not fatal to liberalism's emphasis upon the fundamental right to freedom. Bergmann goes on to outline a theory of his own. Like Charvet, he would not derive rights from human nature as such. Rather, he argues that we do not possess rights to freedom and equality in the early stages of social development. But, he says, "our rights are specific social measures designed to, step by step, bring about some delimited respects in which we will be somewhat free and a bit more equal" (p. 57).

Anthony Kronman devotes his discussion of the nature of rights to the notion of "talent pooling," especially as defended by John Rawls in his theory of society. He finds that Rawls's theory corrodes personal integrity; it assumes that a person's talents are not really his own, while still holding that his goals in life *are* genuinely his. And yet, Kronman concludes, fairness does call for a considerable amount of "talent pooling." A considerable amount but not complete, because moral attitudes "must somehow be accommodated to the contingent and irrational features of the human condition" (p. 77).

The question of the moral coherence of the liberal philosophy of life appears again in John Gray's essay that concludes the first part of the book. He contends, with subtle and complicated argument that defies capsulization, that many of the standard criticisms of Mill's *On Liberty* are mistaken. These objections — "objections in which the incoherence of the utilitarian theory of moral rights is taken for granted — are unfounded" (p. 112).

In the first chapter of the second part, Alan Gewirth performs the seemingly impossible feat of presenting the essence of his recent work on *Reason and Morality* in the compass of a single chapter. As does the "traditional" view, as Charvet calls it, Gewirth seeks logically to derive human rights from human nature, from the fact that we are rational and purposive agents. Gewirth's originality consists in his claim that the derivation is a matter of logic, not just a psychological matter of how we come to feel about ourselves. He insists that no one can deny the reality of human rights save on the pain of self-contradiction. For the rights to "freedom" and "well-being" are intrinsic to human nature as the conditions of human agency. Not surprisingly, Gewirth's logical audacity is not greeted with universal acquiescence. Richard Friedman, Arval Morris, and Martin Golding all rise in the spirit of Hume to challenge him. According to Friedman, morality is lurking in Gewirth's allegedly factual premises. Arguing that since the capacity for agency is a matter of degree, so it must be also with rights, Morris contends that Gewirth's theory is not egalitarian, not a theory of "human" rights. Rather, it is of necessity perfectionistic in its implications. Morris also attacks Gewirth's dialectically necessary form of reasoning. In similar vein, Martin Golding attempts to demonstrate that Gewirth's complex chain of reasoning to get from the "is" of the conditions of agency to the "oughts" of moral rights must fail the test of logical consistency.

Finally in this section, Jan Narveson bases his justification of human rights on a kind of contract theory, a more conventional theory than Rawls's, for Narveson would dispense with the "veil of ignorance." At the conclusion of his line of analysis, he says: "We are left, then, with a strong argument for negative rights, and a problematic argument for positive rights, or rather, for the right to engage in political processes possibly resulting in the acquisition of legal rights of the positive type; plus, of course, such 'administrative' rights as are entailed by these" (p. 195).

Kurt Baier leads off the third section with a work much of which might properly be included in the first section, for he deals with the

definition of rights and human rights. Baier holds that a right
(whether special, general, moral, legal, or human) *purports* to be
morally justifiable, and no more than this. The use to which he puts
this discussion of the nature of human rights, however, places it
squarely in this section. Baier applies his analysis to the determination of when the right to life begins. He distinguishes between the
negative right to retain life and the positive right to be provided the
necessities for life. The latter depends upon the capabilities of the
particular society in question. Fetuses, Baier concludes, fall in this
positive category, and hence their rights in a world of scarcity cannot
have high priority.

Susan Okin, basing her argument on the whole panoply of human
needs and capacities, not on any single characteristic or need of the
human person, defends economic and social rights, denies the priority of the classical liberal rights, and generally attacks the liberal
philosophy of life for insufficient enumeration of rights. For her, personal security is a crucial freedom of the individual.

Louis Henkin then moves to an appraisal of the international scene
and to the attempts that have been made to give some binding international legal quality to human rights. After discussing the various
philosophical perspectives and philosophies of life from which flow
the rights set forth in the "International Bill of Rights"—the Declaration and the Covenants—he considers the question of whether
these rights deserve their name (as *legal* rights) in view of the weakness of their sanctions. He points out that even domestic legal rights
are far removed from effective remedies in some situations. And he
suggests that the international rights, even when (as is the case with
the Covenant on Economic, Social, and Cultural Rights) they are expressed simply as obligations on states to do their best, may nevertheless be viewed as rights.

William Nelson concludes the volume with a paper that is elicited
by Henkin's essay. Nelson is concerned to examine the presumption
that, whereas human rights apply to all persons, the attendant obligations relate only to their particular governments. "Either universal
human rights have universal obligations," he declares, "or they don't
exist" (p. 283). But the rights may be protective to institutions, and
there may be no *general* answer to the question of who bears their
correlative obligations. In the case of many human rights, Nelson decides, the standard assignment of obligations to nation-states may indeed be adequate. Thus his philosophical analysis supports Henkin's

legal findings.

Around the turn of the century, inspired by belief in a "common good" infused with "harmony" and toward which "progress" was tending, L. T. Hobhouse and others began the transition from classical to collectivistic liberalism and a new reading of human mutual responsibility. Our current preoccupation with "human" rights springs from a noble aspiration in collision with adversity.

It is the editors' pleasure to acknowledge assistance without which this volume could not have come into being: to our contributors, of course; to Richard Flathman, the chairman of the program committee and the main architect of the program; and to Eleanor Greitzer, invaluable editorial assistant.

J.R.P.
J.W.C.

CONTENTS

CONTRIBUTORS

KURT BAIER
Philosophy, University of Pittsburgh

FRITHJOF BERGMANN
Philosophy, University of Michigan

JOHN CHARVET
Government, London School of Economics and Political Science

RICHARD B. FRIEDMAN
Political Science, State University of New York at Buffalo

ALAN GEWIRTH
Philosophy, University of Chicago

MARTIN P. GOLDING
Philosophy, Duke University

JOHN GRAY
Politics, Jesus College, Oxford

LOUIS HENKIN
Law, Columbia University

ANTHONY T. KRONMAN
Law, Yale University

ARVAL A. MORRIS
Law, University of Washington

JAN NARVESON
Philosophy, University of Waterloo, Ontario

WILLIAM N. NELSON
Philosophy, University of Houston

SUSAN MOLLER OKIN
Politics, Brandeis University

J. ROLAND PENNOCK
Political Science, Swarthmore College

1

RIGHTS, NATURAL RIGHTS, AND HUMAN RIGHTS—A GENERAL VIEW
J. ROLAND PENNOCK

I. HISTORICAL SKETCH

The phrase "human rights" or "rights of man" seems to go back no more than two centuries and has come into common parlance only since World War II. It has, however, obvious affinities to the older expression, "natural rights." In fact, some writers treat them as synonymous, as appears to be the case with Kurt Baier in his contribution to this volume. Although the term "natural rights" has a close blood relationship with "natural law," it is generally held that the distinction between the two marks a major turning point in the history of Western political thought. Leo Strauss remarks that "the premodern natural law doctrines taught the duties of man," whereas modern, liberal political theory "regards as the fundamental political fact the rights, as distinguished from the duties, of man."[1] For him this change marked a qualitative decline of major importance.

This shift from "law" to "rights" is said to have been first articulated (or at least first given definitive form) by William of Ockham.[2] Its significance, whether for better or worse, derives from the fact that the concept of rights is individualistic in the sense that it is a from-the-bottom-up view of morality rather than one from the top down, and from the related fact that it generally expresses claims of a part against the whole.[3] In its origin, and for most of its career, too, it has been used by persons to make claims on their own behalf, or on behalf of those with whom they identified. Thus, Strauss understandably thought of it as an egoistic doctrine, to be sharply contrasted with the classical doctrine of "natural right," the focus of which was on law, justice, duty, and the public interest. These points are important to the understanding of modernity. And the fact that the language of the ancient Greeks had no word to express our meaning of "a right" is undoubtedly significant.[4] Yet its importance must not be exaggerated. Even in Greek law, not to mention Roman law, if A owes B money and refuses to pay, B can claim it at law. B can also release A from the obligation, a characteristic of "option rights." Likewise, an owner of land can appeal to the law to prevent others from trespassing on it.[5] Although these are legal concepts, it is hard to see how they could fail to be paralleled by moral rights. Surely a person who was legally entitled, let us say, to the fulfillment of a contract must have felt that it was right for him to insist on fulfillments if he liked. The fact that he had no word to express it as "a right" may have prevented him from understanding the situation as clearly as we do, or at least from thinking of it in the same way as we do. Or perhaps it was the lack of clear conceptualization that kept him from inventing the word. But, in any case, as important as this may be for understanding significant difference between ancient and modern times, even a difference in *Weltanschauung,* if you like, it seems fair to say that the *idea* of "a right" was at least implicit and potential among the Greeks.[6]

When we come to Roman law, in addition to special rights growing out of the law of property and of contracts, the general right of all citizens to participate in the making of laws and other public functions was guaranteed. Now we are speaking, it will be noted, of rights against the state, not simply rights of one individual against another. This kind of right depends upon the recognition of a certain class of persons (citizens) as being, at least in one important respect, on a par with each other and as possessing sufficient status to be owed this kind of (participatory) privilege by the state. We are not yet speaking, to be sure, of either "natural rights" or "human rights." But Stoic and Roman "natural law" claimed universal applicability; and its relation to natural rights may properly be conceived of as cognate to the relation between law and rights sketched above. That is to say, law implies rights and natural law implied natural rights. That, at least, is my argument.

The move from natural law to explicit natural rights, *pace* Strauss, does not necessarily indicate a more self-centered, in the sense of selfish, point of view. Hobbes indeed did make the right of self-preservation fundamental; but not Kant. The Categorical Imperative demands universality and goodwill. Individualism and liberalism, in their origin, were indeed rebellions, but not against duty. They were rebellions against the failure of certain groups of individuals, and the institutions they controlled, to act in accordance with their duties (although the rebels generally expressed this behavior as a failure to respect rights). In short, it was the failure of rulers to respect natural law that led to the development of the rhetoric of natural rights. At first, it was the failure of kings to protect "right religion"—and indeed not to persecute religious dissenters—that gave rise to assertions of natural rights. Later, in the secular sphere, it was the violation by rulers of the principles of equality and nonarbitrariness, which had been central to natural law philosophy almost from the beginning, that provoked the rebellion. Whereas individualism stresses self-reliance, and natural rights philosophy may be used as a justification of self-help in the enforcement of natural rights (law), the appeal, at least in the early stages of natural rights claims, was normally for joint action in pursuit of joint (common) rights. (The origins of the contest out of religious persecutions almost guaranteed this outcome.) Even Hobbes, who was protesting against the anarchistic leanings, or at least rhetoric, of some Protestants, saw himself as pursuing interests that all hold in common; and Locke wrote to see that political power was exercised "only for the Publick Good."[7]

For at least three reasons, the doctrine of natural rights came upon hard times. It was frequently associated with metaphysical or theological doctrines that many liberals no longer found acceptable. Furthermore, it was traditionally cast in absolute terms: natural rights were claimed to be inalienable, absolute, and unalterable. As a consequence, claimed natural rights, unless confined to a single natural right, tended to come into conflict with each other. Of greatest importance for present purposes, however, most claims, certainly the classical lists, were confined to negative rights.[8] That is to say, they were essentially claims to be protected, by the state, against invasion of liberty or property. The claimed right to vote, to have an equal share in determining how they should be governed, was formally an exception to this rule, but it was the one exception believed essential to the defense of the other rights.

Not only was natural rights doctrine eroded by these weaknesses; it was also exposed to a powerful attack—that of utilitarianism. Bentham's assault on natural rights is notorious.[9] More generally, the utilitarian doctrines, which dominated much of the nineteenth and twentieth centuries, were inhospitable to doctrines that gave a fundamental position to the concept of rights, whether or not denominated "natural." Even J. S. Mill, in spite of his spirited defense of liberty, insisted that ultimately rights were founded on utility. (Whether or not this view involved him in incoherence is the subject of John Gray's essay in this volume.)

Some critics of the utilitarians were equally opposed, although for quite different reasons, to the idea of individual rights. Thus the British Idealist F. H. Bradley wrote: "The rights of the individual today are not worth serious criticism. . . . The welfare of the community is the end and is the ultimate standard. And over its members the right of its moral organism is absolute. Its duty and its right is to dispose of those members as it seems best."[10]

Nothing as extreme as Bradley's position ever became the dominant position (or reigning paradigm, if you will) in modern Western thought. It was rather the utilitarian position, quite capable of being applied in a collectivistic manner, but by its very nature flexible and relativistic, that provided the prevalent moral philosophy during the first part of this century.

A strong doctrine of rights, however, was not due for extinction. On the contrary, two developments brought about its revival: totalitarianism and the further development of democratic doctrine — the one by revulsion and the other by extension. The horrendous treatment of human beings by totalitarian governments during the second quarter of the present century occasioned a popular demand for constitutional protections in the forms of bills of rights and even judicial review. But this time around negative rights were not considered to be enough. Laissez-faire was dead, and the responsibilities of the state were steadily enlarging. Moreover, the democratic ideal of equality was extending its scope. And equality of opportunity was not enough. Hence an increasing demand for positive rights, for welfare rights. All of this found expression not only in constitutions but also in the Universal Declaration of Human Rights.

The popular demands expressed in these documents were also expressed in the thought of philosophers. Nazism and later the Vietnam War played a major role in bringing about a sea change in ethical theory. The horrors of human torture and genocide brought home the realization that it was impossible to do justice to our moral intuitions by any purely utilitarian or other consequentialist line of reasoning. Certain things are wrong, period. And human beings have *rights* to life, to respect, to decent treatment. Disagreements about theorists as to the extent of rights, even their definition and certainly their justification, abound. No single theory has achieved ascendancy, but the antiutilitarian nature of this general position is clear. It is well expressed by Ronald Dworkin's definition: "a right is a claim that it would be wrong for the government to deny an individual even though it would be in the general interest to do so."[11]

II. THE NATURE OF HUMAN RIGHTS

The fact that the Universal Declaration of Human Rights was adopted by the General Assembly of the United Nations with no dissenting votes indicates the widespread agreement that human beings as such have certain fundamental rights; but it must be noted that a countertendency is also at work. It will be recalled that Leo Strauss's condemnation of the shift from natural law to natural rights was because of his disapproval of the individualistic cast of the latter. Today we observe the phenomenon, not to say the anomaly, of a widely prevalent philosophy of anti-individualism combined, often in the same persons, with a philosophy of individual rights. The fact that these rights are referred to as "human" rights makes clear that they are general rights, in some sense equally possessed by all humans. But this cannot disguise the further fact that they pertain to individuals and are not, normally at least, to be subordinated to the general interest. Rights are one thing; interests are another; and when they collide rights are trumps.

This tension has by no means escaped notice. Richard Flathman, who arranged the program for the meetings that formed the starting point for this volume has himself discussed the question of whether the liberal conception of rights is antisocial.[12] Nor has it been overlooked by contributors to this volume. John Charvet's critique might be said to be solely devoted to this problem. Frithjof Bergmann's essay takes sharp issue with Charvet's position. In greater or lesser degree the problem is also discussed in these pages by John Gray and Susan Okin.

While philosophers grapple with this tension or contradiction, which to a considerable degree overlaps the liberty-equality tension that has been central to democratic theory from its beginnings,[13] it has manifested itself on the popular front in the form of vigorous assertions of the right to privacy and the right to "do your own thing," on the one hand, and, on the other hand, of the competing ideal of community.

This is not the place to deal with this issue in the large, but a few words on the subject are in order. Rights of course *are* social at the very least in the sense that they imply the existence of society and that their function relates to society. They are claims on the part of the individual against one, some, or all other members of society. They are claims about what is owed to them, about duties. They are moral concepts, having place only in a system of morality. (I believe that the same can be said of legal rights, but since human rights are a kind of moral rights that issue does not call for discussion here.) Do they derive from society, from its needs; or do they derive from man's needs, his powers, and the requirements for his development? Ultimately, these questions come down to a controversy over the nature of man: More specifically, does he have a "nature" or is he completely the product of society (i.e., other men in their mutual relations)? Perhaps even more precisely, the practical issue is whether it is believed that individuals should have a sphere within which each should judge for himself what is in his best interest, and if so how large this sphere should be, rather than having that judgment made by a community-formed consensus, or by the majority, or by some elite.

Specifically, what are "human" rights? They have much in common with the older concept of natural rights. Both claim universality, applicability to all persons and places.[14] (Universality as to time — eternal validity — is another matter, as will appear more fully below.) Inalienability (imprescriptibility) is also a part of both concepts. A person may not alienate a natural or human right, but he may forfeit it. Thus, whatever may be the case with respect to capital punishment, a person who kills in self-defense is not thought to have violated either a natural or a human right. But one cannot sell himself into slavery or, presumably, make a binding promise to obey a tyrant. (Hobbes, hardly a conventional natural rights theorist, would disagree.) Locke makes much of this point. Perhaps most important of all, the validity of both types of rights is held to be independent of government, although of course their enforcement normally is dependent upon the sanctions of law backed up by the power of the state.

How, then, do human rights differ from natural rights?[15] Human rights make no claim to be mutually exclusive. In the International Bill of Human Rights, the right to liberty rests alongside the right to education as supported by the proposition that primary education shall be compulsory.[16] Although the claim of mutual exclusiveness is not necessarily specified by natural rights philosophers, it seems generally to be implied or assumed. In any case, and this gets to the heart of the matter, natural rights are commonly said to be absolute, not subject to exception (once defined) or to be overridden. Human rights, on the contrary, are not normally so defined. Some call them *prima facie* rights. Others feel that this position is too weak. The rights persist, under all circumstances, these philosophers maintain, but in given circumstances they may be overridden (but not nullified) by stronger claims of right. Those who take this position, while it is stronger than the *prima facie* line, must nevertheless recognize that rights vary in degree, that some rights are stronger than others, or even that the same right may be stronger under certain circumstances than in others. In fact, some who insist on a strong position for human rights seem willing to admit that *in extremis,* rights must yield to other, consequential considerations.[17]

Whereas natural rights are claimed to be valid for all time, with no suggestion that new natural rights may emerge, be created, or be discovered, in the case of human rights it seems to be implied, even when it is not specified, that new human rights may come into being. This may come about because changed circumstances make possible the protection or advancement of interests, as of *right*, that could previously not be given this status because, for economic or technological reasons, their satisfaction was impossible or perhaps too difficult, too costly, to justify imposing them as duties.[18] Or it may come about because people have become sensitive to certain needs of all humans to which most people were hitherto oblivious. In either case, it is little more than a matter of semantics when it is said that new rights have come into being or that latent rights have now achieved recognition, transforming them from ideal to real rights. In the international human rights documents, commonly some of them are stated as aspirations, which states are bound to implement as it becomes possible (feasible?). This way of putting it, however, does not fit the case of new sensitivities, although, possibly, it could be argued that they, too, had always existed, like an undiscovered mathematical theorem.

III. JUSTIFICATION: PRELIMINARY
CONSIDERATIONS

What are the most important outstanding issues with respect to
human rights? Perhaps they can, for the most part, be brought under
one or another of the headings "nature," "justification," and "extent," the first of which has already been discussed. As to justification, in spite of the very widespread acceptance of the doctrine, utilitarians and other consequentialists have not given up the field. Perhaps unfortunately, however, the issue is not joined in these pages.
Among contemporary defenders of utilitarianism, in one or another
of its various forms, probably the best known are J. J. C. Smart and
R. M. Hare; but the recent publication of Richard Brandt's *A Theory of the Good and the Right* undoubtedly will place him in that
company.[19] The key question for critical thinking, says Hare, is
"What principles of justice . . . what attitudes toward the distribution of goods, what ascriptions of rights, are such that their acceptance is in the general interest."[20] Rights are not ruled out, but human rights would seem to be, and moral rights generally are placed
in a secondary, derivative position. That is to say, no list of universal
rights is to be given priority over all other considerations. A further
comment by Hare casts light upon his thinking and doubtless upon
that of others who support a similar position. He argues that to begin
with the question "What are my rights?" is a recipe for civil war.[21] It
is both the rigidity and, even more, the egoistic reference of philosophies that give priority to rights that bothers the critics of these doctrines. Are the rights of one or a few to be allowed to stand in the way
of tremendous benefits to all the rest of mankind? And, the practical
argument, are people to be encouraged to think more of their rights
than of their duties?

On the other side, the defenders of "rights" as a primitive concept,
or at least as one that takes priority over any arguments from consequences, fear the trade-offs that such reasoning appears to allow.
They insist that certain basic human concerns are not commensur-
able with any degree or extent of happiness or any other (for them)
lesser concern. More specifically, they hold that consequentialist reasoning, as Rawls argues, is no respecter of persons, allowing quantity
of good to prevail over differences in quality.[22] Presumably unsatis-
fied with even qualified consequentialism, and generally acknowledging some debt to Kant (as in the second passage quoted from

Rawls in note 22) they insist that interests must be subordinated to rights.

Perhaps in raising this issue that separates consequentialists from deontologists, with respect to the role of rights and their place in a moral system, a vital step has been omitted. Do such things as moral rights, in any but a derivative sense, exist? Is the concept itself essential? We may approach this problem by making a preliminary point: use of the phrase "moral rights" calls to mind the parallel construction "legal rights" and raises the question of their mutual relations. At certain stoplights I am entitled to turn right even if the light is red. This is a right—not merely a legal right but also a moral right, which is to say that to behave in this manner is not wrong. Clearly in *this* situtation it is the law that determines my moral as well as my legal rights; my moral right has no independent validity. But how different it is when we leave matters of moral indifference! Take, for instance, the law prohibiting murder. Here clearly it is the law that reflects and supports the moral standard. However, one must say "moral *standard*" rather than "moral *right*" to avoid begging the question. Rudolph van Jhering defined "a right" as "a legally protected interest,"[23] thus making legal rights dependent upon interests, without any reference to moral rights. So we still have the question, "Do moral rights exist?" It cannot be avoided by the simple device of deriving moral rights from legal rights.

Another preliminary must be dispatched. We are here discussing general rights, not special rights. The rights that derive from contracts, promises, or the ownership of property are not at issue. No one questions their reality. In no sense do they derive from man's mere existence; they are the product of interaction between the right-bearer and one or more other persons.[24]

IV. THE JUSTIFICATION OF GENERAL RIGHTS

A weak argument for general moral rights (of which human rights constitute a subclass) is simply to say that any moral system has to do with duties and that duties imply rights. If people have a general duty not to harm others without just cause, then all have the right not to be harmed by others unjustly, and so on. Against this position, it might be contended that the natural law tradition, and the ancient Greeks, had strong concepts of duties but not of rights. But this line of argument has already been discussed and found wanting. Even the Greek view does imply the existence of rights, in spite of the fact that it was not recognized as doing so; rights were at the very least latent in the system. More fundamentally, to recur to a point already adverted to, it is contended by supporters of general rights[25] in any but the weakest sense that to make rights derivative from duties is a conceptual error in that rights should be given priority over duties. It is by no means self-evident that this is true. Thus, John Plamenatz states that "a man (or an animal) has a right whenever other men ought not to prevent him from doing what he wants or refuse him some service he asks for or needs."[26] One trouble with this formulation is that it does not distinguish among different kinds of duties. Not all duties imply rights. If I am ill and in need of help, you, my neighbor, may rightly feel it is your duty to help me, within reasonable limits. But it would not normally be said that I had a right to your help. Perhaps more fundamentally, the concept of a right usually (but not always)[27] implies a choice on the part of the rightholder. If A owes B ten dollars, it is B's (special) right that A should pay him. But B may waive his right, thereby altering A's duty.[28] It thus seems to be implied, in the case of option rights at least, that they take priority over duties and so cannot be justified by reference to them. Other reasons for believing this to be the case will appear as we proceed.

1. INTUITION

What justifications then are offered for general rights? Some rely simply upon intutition. Other considerations apart, the weakness of this theory is that intuitions about rights are by no means in complete agreement. Of course supporters of other theories of rights may disagree among themselves about specific rights, but at least they have principles upon which to rely in advancing their arguments. Disagreements are likely to depend upon their understandings of the facts or of the way institutions are likely to operate, or the like. In the case of the intuitionist view, even though differences of the kind just referred to may underlie their differing assignments of rights, it is difficult to identify them. One is cut off at the pass by a flat statement of intuition.

2. SOCIAL CONTRACT

Another approach, attaining renewed popularity today, is that of the social contract, or what might better be called a social quasi contract. Readers of these pages will be well familiar with the variety of theories encompassed under this designation. They range from the radical individualism of Thomas Hobbes to the equalitarian liberalism of John Rawls. They may derive rights from what men, being what they are, would agree upon as rules of justice and sets of rights for their governance for evermore (as does Jan Narveson in his contribution to this volume), or from what rational men (perhaps, as in Rawl's case, deprived of much knowledge about their own self and situation) would agree upon. Depending upon what they take human nature to be, the lists of rights they deduce may differ considerably one from another, although their agreements — upon life, liberty, security of person, equality of consideration — are more striking than their differences. Some stress the individual person, in his agreement with others, as basic, while others emphasize the social progress, suggesting that human nature is itself formed in the process of human interaction. Yet again the differences seem to be more matters of emphasis than of fundamentals. A common strategy of members of this group is to argue from what they take to be human nature (innate or socially produced) to a system of justice, including a list of individual rights. Perhaps people would not come to agreement and form a viable society unless the rights that they claimed for themselves were recognized by their society; or perhaps their nature was such that they would agree upon rights that they saw as essential to social living. In either case, the results tend to be less divergent than might be thought.

Rawls seldom refers to rights but various rights can readily be derived from his theory of social justice. While he makes use of the contract device, it is important to note that his subject is narrower than the title of his book might suggest: it is confined to *social* justice. This theory deals with "the way in which the major social institutions distribute fundamental rights and duties and determine the division of advantages from social cooperation."[29] Emphasis is placed on the proposition that, in order to win the cooperation of all in which no one knew his or her specific abilities, it would be necessary to agree upon principles that gave great weight, in determining the distribution of goods, to the fact that society and its goods depend upon cooperation. Yet when it comes to explaining why a society accepting his theory of social justice would be stable, Rawls relies heavily upon a theory of human nature, especially on the idea of reciprocity, the tendency to which he says is "a deep psychological fact."[30] Although this method of justification fits the commonly enumerated natural and human rights, it is also more readily adaptable than some other approaches to the problem.[31]

3. CONVENTION

According to another mode of justification, rights are conventional; that is to say they originate as customs and attain binding force from the fact that people have voluntarily accepted them and have come to rely on them. They are rights by prescription. While this line of reasoning is most frequently used with respect to legal rights, it is applied to moral rights as well.[32] Obviously, the rights derived include those that appear on the historically accepted lists.

4. NECESSARY CONDITIONS FOR HAPPINESS

Finally, general rights may be defined as the necessary conditions of human happiness (or self-development, or self-realization, or satisfaction) and justified in those terms. In the light of what was said in the discussion of social quasi contracts, it should not seem strange that here again the differences in the mode of approach are greater than those in the conclusions reached. Here once more philosophers look to human nature. They speak of the "essence" of man (and they may consider this essence as fixed for all time or they may recognize the possibilities of change in this respcet) or simply of his "nature." The significant part of man's nature has been variously held to be rationality (itself subject to numerous definitions), dignity, self-respect (which, in turn, requires the respect of others), worth, and liability to pain, suffering, and violent death. To me, more persuasive than any of these, save rationality itself, which seems to be basic, is the fact that humans have the capacity and the tendency to develop a moral sense and to make judgments and choices reflecting that moral sense. A variant of this mode of justification of rights, and their priority, is that of Alan Gewirth, as explained in his essay in this volume and more fully in his book.[33] For him, rights are the necessary conditions for action, logically implied by human purposes. Philosophers in this general category frequently give to "needs" or, alternatively, well-being, an important role in the derivation of rights.

V. THE SCOPE AND SUBSTANCE OF GENERAL RIGHTS

What has been said above is very abstract. What are these general rights? What is their scope and substance (leaving aside for the moment the question of whether they are distinguishable from human rights)? Let us begin with the right to life. Whether one adheres to some form of contractualism or whether one derives rights directly from the nature of man, this right is fundamental. [34] But what does it mean? What is its extent? When does life begin and when does it end? (The problem of when life begins is the subject of Kurt Baier's analysis in this volume.) Does it entail bare existence? Or must it, more plausibly, be a life that admits of something beyond mere survival? If so, how much beyond? Surely, it would seem, it must be a good life. A happy life? What are the necessary conditions for happiness? Some are happy with very little; others are unhappy with a great deal. And I speak not only of material things. It is often claimed, in the words of the Universal Declaration of Human Rights, that "everyone has the right to a standard of living adequate for the health and well-being of himself and his family" (art. 25). A right that is expressed in such vague terms as "well-being" tends to become indistinguishable from an interest. [35] At that juncture, the whole point of specifying rights threatens to disappear. If one accepts Dworkin's definition of a right as "a claim that it would be wrong for the government to deny an individual even though it would be in the general interest to do so," what is its significance? If "well-being" means some basic minimum, without which an individual could hardly be a person, the proposition is understandable; but if it means anything that makes one's being better, then it is difficult to see why an individual should prevail over the generality, why an individual's well-being should have a right against the well-being of society. [36]

In short, to hold that life itself (at least "experiential" life, in Baier's phrase)[37] should prevail over the lesser interests of others, even though the latter be greater in number, at least makes sense. This is easily, and perhaps necessarily, extended to include the conditions for purposive behavior, for using one's reason to select his ends and the means by which to achieve them, for having some elbow room, some liberty, within which to exercise the resulting choices. It is also of vital interest to the individual that he have sufficient self-respect to stand up for his interests: and undoubtedly the concept of himself as a "rights-bearer" is of assistance in this regard.[38] Certain things, too, are so closely connected with life; with "dignity" (a more inclusive term, which I now substitute for "self-respect"); and with the opportunity ("liberty") to move about, to marry, to enjoy some privacy, and not to be treated arbitrarily, that to mark them off from other "interests" makes sense. Thus rights not to be tortured, to a fair trial, and others of the traditional fundamental liberties, appear to cause no problem of principle.

Going still further from our starting point, the right to participate in the selection of those who make public policy is now widely accepted. But even those who claim it as a right attribute varying degrees of fundamentality to it, and probably most would agree that it is not a universal right, without regard to conditioning factors. Here again, as with rights versus interests, we reach a borderline of indeterminacy, where matters of degree inevitably take over.

I shall say no more about the question of under what circumstances this interest may be properly called a right, but it wil be useful to point out that, when it is asserted as a right, the justifications are not always the same. The standard liberal argument rests heavily upon the proposition that it is best to let each adult judge his or her own interests. Careful adherents to this position do not say that each person is the best judge of his own interests, but they do say that each person has certain information about (insight into) his own interests that no one else is privy to. They also say that the individual is less likely than others to abuse or overlook his own interests. To these arguments, two others may be relied upon. Both relate to choice, and so to liberty. The first of these is that the act of choosing is part of what it is to be a rational being; or at least that to be rational without the capacity to choose would be completely stultifying. The second and closely related argument is that the act of choosing is essential to the development of human capacities. Joel Feinberg has put this argument in terms most obviously related to rights. He argues that "the activity of claiming [a right], . . . as much as any other thing, makes for self-respect and for respect for others, gives a sense of the notion of personal dignity."[39]

When we consider any rights, but perhaps especially those extensions of the right of the person that come under the heading of well-being, when we move from negative liberties to positive liberties (enablements), whether education, health care, or further means to the good life, our attention is called to another dimension of rights of which no mention has yet been made.[40] I refer to equality. Nothing in the concept of rights itself requires that they should be equal; and, in a feudal society, for instance, a person's rights are entirely dependent upon his rank or status. The ideology of natural rights, however, has from the beginning included the notion of equality of rights. Indeed, the natural law, from which they in large measure derived, embodies a notion of human equality. Historically, a variety of devices have been used to contain that potentially subversive ideas. But feudal rights were special rights, pertaining to particular groups. The modern concept of general rights (whether called natural, human, or whatnot) involves a kind of equality by virtue of their very generality. They are, by definition, rights that belong to all men, H. L. A. Hart, in a famous essay, maintained that if there are any rights at all there is one natural right, the *equal* right to liberty. [41]

Harking back to the previous discussion, it is worth noting that when Hart wrote this essay he argued that the liberty in question was a *negative* right. The rights in question, he declared, "are asserted defensively, when some unjustified interference is anticipated or threatened, in order to point out that the interference is unjustified."[42] More recently, however, Hart has enlarged his concept. (Although he is dealing with legal rights, what he says clearly has a bearing on moral rights.) Certain rights, he declares, "are not rights under the ordinary law but fundamental rights which may be said to be against the legislature, limiting its powers to make (or unmake) the ordinary law, where so to do would be to deny individuals certain freedoms and benefits now regarded as essentials of human well-being, such as freedom of speech and of association, freedom from arbitrary arrest, security of life and person, education, and equality of treatment in certain respects." For the constitutional lawyer, he now maintains, it is neither individual choice nor individual benefit that provides the core of the notion of rights but "basic or fundamental needs."[43] Both benefits and needs, even when preceded by the qualifier "fundamental," lack precision, and are indeed indefinitely expansible. Once more one notices the tendency for rights to tail off into interests, thus diluting the concept of moral (including human) rights.

To return to the theme of equality, the second dimension of rights, a few points must suffice. In the first place, at least in the beginning, the idea of equality as applied to rights is a formal concept, even as that of liberty is a substantive concept. If one person has a right not to be enslaved, so must all, if it is to be a general right. And so on down the line. Just what the right to life entails, as we have seen, is open to debate. What is not open to dispute, however, is that the right to life, whatever it is, is the same for all. Nor does this mean that old people or young children should be subject to drafting for military service. But it does mean that persons similarly situated should be similarly treated.

The last sentence opens a hornet's nest. No two persons or two sets of circumstances are exactly alike. Moreover, not all differences—color of hair or color of skin, for example—are relevant to considerations of rights. This is not the place to become deeply involved in the debate about what is relevant to the consideration of similarity in such matters, although one must acknowledge the existence and the difficulty of the problem and give some indication of how it may be approached, even though it is not dealt with explicitly in the chapters that follow.[44] Of course those who hold that humans are equal with respect to their rights need not do so because they believe all humans are equal with regard to any other ascertainable characteristic. In their strengths, their weaknesses, their physical and mental capacities, their sensitivities to moral considerations, their needs, their contributions to others—in all these things they differ one from another in great degree. It is sometimes alleged that men are equally capable of suffering and, conversely, of relief from acute pain. But "equally" here can mean no more than that all persons possess these capabilities *in some degree:* for it seems to be true that not only can some bear suffering more than others but also that some actually *do* suffer more than others under like circumstances. Perhaps the most significant point is that we cannot measure these differences.[45] In the final analysis, interpersonal comparisons appear to be impossible, except in a very rough and uncertain way. This fact itself may provide an argument for equal rights.

A second and perhaps equally persuasive point is the fact that, although human beings are not created equal, they are also not created fixed, set for all time. They have immeasurable potentialities for development, for attaining a happy life or a miserable one. If they are to develop their desirable potentialities, certain requirements must be met: their potential must not be prejudged; they must have a great deal of freedom of choice; and they must have certain material and social conditions for the exercise of this freedom.

Thus it appears that the formal approach to rights, via equality, brings us out at much the same place as does the substantive (life-liberty) one. Both open the way to rights to well-being, or "welfare rights." This position is accepted by Gewirth and argued for more fully by Susan Okin, both in this volume. It is the position assumed by the United Nations Declaration and Covenants. At the same time it has been sharply criticized by Maurice Cranston (against whom Susan Okin particularly levels her argument) and many others. [46] One can readily understand both the reasons for extending the concept and the objections to doing so. The latter derive in part from the vagueness of the line between rights and interests. At first glance, it appeared that the idea of equality would provide an answer to this objection, but on closer examination it is seen to be subject to the same problem of indefinite expansibility, and to a further watering down of the concept of rights to the point where they become indistinguishable from interests and where, for all practical purposes, the line between deontologists and utilitarians disappears. [47] Now yet another area of uncertainty must be added: What, formally, is being claimed when a right is asserted? Let us consider the following possibilities:

For A to have a moral right means:

(1) that it is not wrong for A to do X (where "doing X" includes doing nothing, or possessing property, or simply living, or possibly living well or up to some prescribed standard);

(2) that is not wrong for A to exert force to do X;

(3) that A's liberty to do X ought to be respected;

(4) that A's government ought to protect his liberty to do X; or

(5) that A should be enabled (provided with the necessary means) to do X.

It seems not unlikely that some of the differences of opinion concerning rights follow from this plethora of meanings that participants in debate may attach to the term, without always being careful to explain how they are defining the term or even to use it consistently with any given definition. [48]

However that may be and whatever definition of rights we adopt (save possibly the first and weakest of them all), it now appears that, though men may have equal rights, not all rights are created equal. Both the substantive (life-liberty) line of argument and the formal (equality) line lead to this conclusion. For liberty, the "top of the line" appears to be claimed by life itself, followed closely by the opportunity to make significant choices, to seek satisfaction of the most basic interests. On the equality side, a parallel position is occupied by the right to equal consideration of interests. For both, as we proceed from these starting points (which could easily be amalgamated as "the equal right of all to protect and pursue their most basic interests"), we encounter increasing difficulties. Not only does the distinction between rights and interests tends to become blurred, but also, as Jan Narveson makes clear in his contribution to this volume, emphasis on rights tends to make us overlook costs. Well-being in any degree enlarges liberty, makes purposive action more effective; but to grant it as a right entails the cost of accepting the duty of seeing to it that it is provided for others, which may entail giving up some of one's own well-being for the enhancement of that of others. To what extent is this essential for the attainment of the good life? To what extent would it be agreed to by persons behind "the veil of ignorance"? To what extent would it be included in "any moral code which I [or you], if I [you] were fully rational, would tend to support, in preference to all others or none at all, for the society of the agent, if I [you] expected to spend a lifetime in that society?"[49]

In spite of these difficulties, it would be unwise (as well as practically impossible) to give up the language of rights. Dworkin's definition of a right as "a claim that it would be wrong for the government to deny even if it would be in the general interest to do so," if properly understood, has much to commend it. By "general" interest he cannot mean "universal" interest, for then there would be no conflict. It is also true that Dworkin admits exceptions, in dire emergencies, to the dominance of rights over interests.[50] He is of course protesting against any general and easy trade-offs between the extremely important interests (of a kind possessed by all) of one or a few, on the one hand, and, on the other hand, almost any aggregation of lesser interests of a larger number of persons. He is using the concept of rights to defend against a conseqentialist's possible willingness to permit the interests of a majority to override the less essential interests of a minority. To accomplish this purpose, he places the latter in a class of what might be called "practical absolutes." Stated in this way, even many utilitarians would not be inclined to take issue.[51]

VI. HUMAN RIGHTS

The discussion in the preceding section has focused on rights generally and especially upon general rights. Certain issues have thereby been avoided. As we return to the subject of "human" rights, these issues should be brought to the surface, if only to call attention to them. One may grant, with Gewirth, that human rights are "rights that every person morally ought to have"; but numerous questions remain. For instance, are rights confined to persons? Anomalously, in view of the nomenclature, some argue that human rights are not confined to persons. Doubtless, though, they are conferred by humans and would have no existence in the absence of humans—but the same could be said for any rights. Thus, some philosophers would ascribe rights—even human rights—to animals, plants, and perhaps even inanimate objects. But none of the essays in this volume seems to do so.

Other questions: Are human rights claims *against* all persons, and only such claims? Do they imply duties for all persons? If the latter claim is adopted, either our duties are considerably enlarged beyond what they are usually considered to be or the scope of human rights is greatly restricted. It accords better with usage to say that human rights are possessed by all persons but that, in most instances, they imply duties only against one's own state or, at most, the state in which he or she is currently located. (And in the latter case they may be more restricted than in the former.) This is the position analyzed and defended by William Nelson in his contribution to this volume. An intermediate position is to hold that human rights are rights of all against all states, although with primary obligations resting upon the states in which the claimants reside, recognizing that a state's obligation gives rise to an obligation on the part of its citizens to use their power as best they can to direct its policy accordingly. This position appears to be the one assumed by the International Covenant of Economic, Social, and Cultural Rights. (Note especially Articles 2, 23, and 25.) The precise legal status of the rights asserted in the major international agreements regarding human rights is subject to varying interpretations, as Louis Henkin makes clear in his contribution to this volume. Henkin also argues persuasively that the legal status of these rights is not different in kind from that of other rights, even though the legal remedies provided are distinctly limited.

Finally comes the question: Are all general rights "human rights"? Or is that term to be reserved for only those general rights that are deemed "fundamental"? Kurt Baier takes the broader view, defining human rights as "those moral rights whose moral ground and generating factor are the same, namely, being human in some relevant sense" (p. 216). Joel Feinberg, on the other hand, defines human rights as "moral rights of a fundamentally important kind," to which he adds that they are "held equally by all human beings, unconditionally and unalterably."[52] One may of course define the term as one likes, and both of these definitions find wide support. Feinberg's restriction of the term has the advantage of ruling out certain claims, like that of vacations with pay, that have been the butt of much ridicule. It also has the advantage of minimizing those cases where one human right conflicts with another.[53]

The problem of conflicting rights can be handled in various ways. One way is simply to recognize conflict and leave the matter of which right is to prevail for ad hoc determination. This procedure has the advantage of permitting a rich contextual consideration of all relevant factors, but it does not give the kind of quasi absoluteness that is generally thought to constitute the advantage of rights analysis over consequentialism. For this latter purpose, some hierarchy or some fundamental guiding principle seems to be required. It is undoubtedly for this reason that several philosophers have attempted to argue for just one basic right, which might be called "natural," "fundamental," or "human." William Ernest Hocking, for instance, gives such status to the "natural" right to develop one's powers equally with others.[54] Hart's argument for "the equal right to liberty" has already been noted.[55] William Frankena has contended that the only natural right is the right to institutions that will protect *prima facie* or high-order goods.[56] This kind of right would fall under the fifth category of those enumerated above (p. 17) and is a second-order right in that it is not a claim for immediate protections and benefits but for what would lead to them. For A. I. Melden, the fundamental human right is the right of persons to pursue their interests as they see them.[57] Finally, although undoubtedly many other candidates could be added to the list, Ronald Dworkin, while arguing that all rights are "trumps," appears to consider "the right of each person to concern and respect as an individual" as that from which all others flow.[58]

Joel Feinberg might be said to go the single-natural-right philosophers one (or two!) better. He finds three kinds of rights that may be understood to be absolute and nonconflictable. First, he cites positive rights to "goods" that can never be in short supply. He suggests that the right to a fair trial, the right to equal protection of the laws, and the right to equal consideration fall under this heading. (It would appear to me that the last-named right might well encompass them all, and that it might as well be designated as a negative right not to be discriminated against unjustly.) The second candidate is "the negative right not to be treated inhumanely or cruelly, not to be tortured or treated barbarously." Finally, he declares: "A third possibility is the right not to be subjected to exploitation or degradation even when such subjection is utterly painless and therefore not cruel."[59] This degree of elaboration is certainly enlightening; and it may be exhaustive of those human rights that are, in Feinberg's words, "unalterable, 'absolute' (exceptionless and nonconflictable), and universally and *peculiarly* human."[60] Having said this, it may do no harm to remark that they all can be derived from the admittedly much blander statement that all persons are entitled to respect, equally.[61]

Many other "conditions of well-being" can be admitted as human rights only in a weaker sense, because, unlike Feinberg's "fundamental" rights, they are not "exceptionless and nonconflictable." Thus, we would have human rights of two senses—a strong sense and a weak sense. It is arguable that it would have been better to have reserved the term "human rights" for the strong sense, thus underlining its importance. Either way, something is gained and something is lost. The example of many of the countries—especially the communist countries—that have, in their constitutions, opted for the expanded view of human rights in order to elevate welfare rights in their hierarchy of values suggests that the price of that elevation may be the degradation of strong-sense rights—and without a clear improvement in the general welfare at that. However that may be, usage, given considerable cachet by the Declaration and the Covenants, has adopted the looser terminology. That being the case, it is important to maintain and emphasize the distinction between the strong and weak senses of the phrase and to keep clearly in mind which rights fall in which category.

Although it is true that various factors have weakened the potency of appeals to rights and deprived it of much of the precision that it once had to a greater degree, it would be a mistake not to remind ourselves of the benefits that may derive from "rights talk." I call attention to two of them. First, it serves as a reminder of the importance of human dignity and the centrality of the self. It enhances both self-respect and respect for others, for their liberty and their well-being. Second, at least in the intellectual milieu of the modern world, it provides a bias toward equality. This point in fact is implied by the first, but it is worthy of separate mention.

* * *

It is the nature of a dynamic society to move the spotlight of attention from one aspect of experience to another, to produce variety in philosophies, in world views. This phenomenon is well illustrated by theories of rights. The focus of attention alternates, for instance, between individual and society, between a vision of absoluteness and one of relativity or variety, and so on. For any given society and era, it is important to have frames of reference, paradigms, focusing now on clear rules and now on flexibility; but it is also important to recognize that these variations are all within the context of a larger unity within which a certain constancy remains, as in the Decalogue.

NOTES

1. Leo Strauss, *Natural Right and History* (Chicago: The University of Chicago Press, 1953), pp. 182, 181.
2. Martin P. Golding, "The Concept of Rights: A Historical Sketch," in Elsie L. Bondman and Bertram Bondman, eds, *Bioethics and Human Rights* (Boston: Little, Brown, 1978). pp. 44–50, p. 48.
3. The "part" in question might be a town or a rank rather than an individual.
4. J. Walter Jones, a leading scholar in the field, declares that "the Greeks never worked out anything resembling the notion of a legal right" (*The Law and Legal Theory of the Greeks* [Aalen: Scienta Verlag, 1977], p. 191).
5. It is true that the implied right was not the same as would be the case in modern Anglo-American law, and that from our point of view it would be less satisfactory. If a court adjudged that land belonged to A, it would take no steps to enforce its judgment. A must depend upon self-help. If, however, on entering the land he met resistance, he would then have a new actionable claim, this time of a penal character. This implies that the first judgment created (or recognized) a legal duty on the part of others than A not to resist his entrance upon the land. (See Jones, *Law and Legal Theory*, p. 203.) In short, if A's claim against B is adjudged legitimate, it entails a duty to A on the part of B. That meets the modern definition of a right, whatever the ancients may have thought.
6. To argue in this fashion is not to deny that the practical consequences of the Greek view and our own may differ. On the contrary, it would make no sense to the ancient Greek to argue, as we do, that one may have a right to do what is wrong (as we say that one has a right to spend money as one likes, although it is wrong to spend it frivolously, as in gambling).

    After writing these lines, I came across a fuller argument and documentation for the same point — that the concept of "a right" is by no means modern. See Alan Gewirth, *Reason and Morality* (Chicago: The University of Chicago Press, 1978), pp. 98–102. Also, Martin Ostwald makes the point that even the concept of equal (general) rights is at least closely approximated by the Greek *isonomia. Nomos and the Beginnings of the Athenian Democracy* (Oxford: Clarendon Press, 1969), p. 113, n. 1.

7. John Locke, *Two Treatises of Government,* ed. P. Laslett (Cambridge: Cambridge University Press, 1960), book II, sec. 3.

8. It is sometimes argued, as Susan Okin does in her contribution to this volume, that rights of this kind are "positive" because they call for action by the government. Whatever terminology we use, however, the important distinction to be noted is between governmental action against harmful actions against a person by others (including agents of the government) and the actual provision of goods and services (other than protection) by the government. Rights to the protection of rights are second-order rights.

9. "Anarchical Fallacies," in *Works of Jeremy Bentham,* ed. J. Bowring (New York: Russell and Russell, 1962), vol. II, p. 105. He wrote: "Natural rights is simple nonsense: natural and imprescriptible rights, rhetorical nonsense — nonsense upon stilts."

10. Quoted without citation by Maurice Cranston, *What Are Human Rights?* (New York: Basic Books, 1962), p. 5.

11. *Taking Rights Seriously* (Cambridge, Mass.: Harvard University Press, 1978), p. 269.

12. *The Practice of Rights* (Cambridge: Cambridge University Press, 1976), esp. chaps. 8-10. In part, Flathman resolves the problem by distinguishing between *private* individualism, and especially the related private rights of property and contract, and what he denominates *civic* individualism, with its attendant Great Rights, "freedom of speech, press, and association, habeas corpus, and perhaps the right to free and equal suffrage" (p. 203).

Eugene Kamenka has argued that the belief in natural or human rights (which he equates with each other) is quite contrary to the pre-individualistic ideas that prevailed universally before the growth of Stoic, Roman, and Christian ideas, and that in its developed form it is a product of the rise of individualism in modern times. "The Anatomy of an Idea," in Eugene Kamenka and Alice Erh-Soon Tay, eds., *Human Rights* (London: Edwin Arnold, 1978), pp. 5-7. (This of course is in accord with Strauss's position, mentioned earlier.) It is interesting to note in this connection and also in connection with Flathman's distinction between private and civic individualism that virtually all of the classical individualistic and negative eighteenth-century rights are incorporated in the Universal Declaration of Human Rights.

13. See J. Roland Pennock, *Democratic Political Theory* (Princeton: Princeton University Press, 1979), chaps. 2 and 3.

14. A possible exception with regard to human rights: some would say that they apply only to persons living under organized politics — not in practice a very significant exception.

15. Some authors use the terms interchangeably. Kurt Baier, in this volume, appears to do so, and so also does Maurice Cranston. For Cranston's view, see his "Human Rights: A Reply to Professor Raphael," in D. D. Raphael, ed., *Political Theory and the Rights of Man* (Bloom-

ington, Ind.: Indiana University Press, 1967), pp. 95-100. But the distinctions enumerated below follow the general usage.

16. Universal Declaration of Human Rights (art. 3), and International Covenant on Economic, Social, and Cultural Rights, (art. 13).

17. Ronald Dworkin, while distinguishing between rights in the strong sense and rights in the weak sense, acknowledges than even the former may be overriden "to prevent a catastrophe," (*Taking Rights Seriously*, p. 191).

18. D. D. Raphael has remarked that "the gradual extension of the scope of rights means that the concept of justice gradually takes over more of what formerly came under the concept of charity" (*Political Theory and the Rights of Man*, p. 117). Note also Article 22 of the Universal Declaration of Human Rights, which reads: "Everyone, as a member of society, has the right to social security and is entitled to realization, through national effort and international co-operation and *in accordance with the organization and resources of each state*, of the economic, social and cultural rights indispensable for his dignity and the free development of his personality, [italics mine]."

19. J. J. C. Smart and Bernard Williams, *Utilitarianism: For and Against* (London: Cambridge University Press, 1973), pp. 3-74; R. M. Hare, *Freedom and Reason* (New York: Oxford University Press, 1972) and "Ethical Theory and Utilitarianism," in H. D. Lewis, ed., *Contemporary British Philosophy* (London: Allen and Unwin, 1976); and Richard B. Brandt, *A Theory of the Right and the Good* (New York: Oxford University Press, 1979).

20. R. M. Hare, "Justice and Equality," in John Arthur and William H. Shaw, eds., *Justice and Economic Distribution* (Englewood Cliffs, N.J.: Prentice-Hall, 1978), pp. 116-31, 130.

21. Ibid.

22. Two passages are especially relevant. First, "Utilitarianism does not take seriously the distinction between persons." And second, "In justice as fairness one does not take men's propensities and inclinations as given, whatever they are, and then seek the best way to fulfill them. Rather, their desires and aspirations are restricted from the outset by the principles of justice which specify the boundaries that men's system of ends must respect," (John Rawls, *A Theory of Justice* [Cambridge, Mass.: Harvard University Press, 1971], pp. 29 and 31). Recall also Ronald Dworkin's statement, quoted above, note 11.

Jan Narveson has contended that the utilitarian theory of J. S. Mill distinguishes between "harm" and "good" in a way that bars the justification of harming a person by any amount of consequential good to others. *Morality and Utility* (Baltimore: The Johns Hopkins University Press, 1967), chap. 6. T. M. Scanlon has recently argued for a broadly consequentialist view of rights in a nonmaximizing fashion that limits the trade-offs between harms and goods in somewhat the same way proposed by Narveson. He points out that "the case for most familiar rights—freedom of expression, due process, religious toleration—seems to be more concerned with the avoidance of particular bad consequences than with promoting maximum benefit." His position is more complicated than can be set forth here, and the quotation above is qualified in its sequel. "Rights, Goals and Fairness," in Stuart Hampshire, ed., *Public and Private Morality* (Cambridge: University Press, 1978), pp. 92-111; quotation at p. 104.

23. *Law as a Means to an End,* trans. I. Husik (New York: Macmillan, 1924), p. 50, quoted in Golding, "The Concept of Rights: A Historical Sketch," p. 50.

24. To be sure, the rights to make promises, to negotiate contracts, and to acquire property are general rights and are at least arguably to be included among human rights. The last-named of these is proclaimed by the Universal Declaration of Human Rights (art. 17).

25. Thenceforth the word "rights," in this discussion, means "general rights," unless otherwise specified.

26. "Rights," in *Proceedings of the Aristotelian Society,* Supplement, vol. 24, pp. 75-82, p. 75. Also Charles Fried argues that rights are second-order concepts: we have a right to pursue our own good so long as we meet our obligations and do no wrong. *Right and Wrong* (Cambridge, Mass.: Harvard University Press, 1978), p. 9.

27. See Geoffrey Marshall, "Rights, Options, and Entitlements," in A. W. B. Simpson, ed, *Oxford Essays in Jurisprudence,* second series (Oxford: Clarendon Press, 1973), vol. IX.

28. This example, to be sure, is taken from the class of special rights and duties. Presumably it is true of general rights as well with the important exception of those general rights that are denominated "natural" and "inalienable" rights. Generally speaking, most of the "freedom rights," such as the right to move about or leave the country, are "option rights."

29. John Rawls, *A Theory of Justice* (Cambridge, Mass.: Harvard University Press, 1971), p. 7.

30. Ibid., p. 494.

31. See Charles R. Beitz, "Human Rights and Human Justice," in Peter G. Brown and Douglas MacLean, eds., *Human Rights and U.S. Foreign Policy* (Lexington, Mass.: D. C. Heath), pp. 45-63, p. 59.

32. It would be readily derivable, for example, from Henry Sidgwick's theory of justice. *The Methods of Ethics* (London: Macmillan, 1922), Bk. III, Chap. 5. See also David K. Lewis, *Conventions: A Philosophical Study* (Cambridge, Mass.: Harvard University Press, 1969) especially chap. 1, for a sophisticated discussion of the logic of conventions. Although Lewis does not discuss rights, and some modifications of his discussion would be required to fit an analysis of rights to his treatment of conventions, it is fairly clear how this might be done.

33. *Reason and Morality* (Chicago: The University of Chicago Press, 1978). Richard Friedman, Martin Golding, and Arval Morris all take issue with Gewirth's position in their contributions to this volume.

34. I am not arguing that it is absolute in the sense that it cannot be forfeited. The right I am discussing is not incompatible with capital punishment, compulsory military service, and killing in self-defense.

David Ritchie's discussion of this subject is still worthy of attention. He argues that "the principle that there is an inalienable and imprescriptible right in all men to preserve their lives, however much social utility may demand the sacrifice of their lives . . . would bring all regulated actions to a standstill, and would lead to a rapid disappearance of the civilized men who adopted such a principle before the barbarians who did not." (*Natural Rights* [New York: Macmillan, 1924] p. 120).

35. Gewirth also includes "well-being" as a basic right.

36. Speaking of the inflation of rights-talk and of its degeneration into mere political sloganeering, John Kleinig cites the example of Nan Berger's *Rights: A Handbook for People Under Age,* which proclaims "the right to a tobacco-free job," "the right to sunshine," and "the right to a sex-break" ("Human Rights, Legal Rights, and Social Change," in Kamenka and Tay, *Human Rights*, p. 40, n. 12).

37. Below, p. 219.

38. See Norman E. Bowie and Robert L. Simon, *The Individual and the Political Order* (Englewood Cliffs, N.J.: Prentice-Hall, 1977), pp. 77–85, esp. p. 78.

39. "The Nature and Value of Rights," in Richard E. Flathman, ed., *Concepts in Social and Political Philosophy* (New York: Macmillan, 1973), pp. 456–68, 468.

40. I am considering all of the rights so far discussed as pertaining to the dimension of liberty—more accurately described as "life-liberty."

41. "Are There Any Natural Rights?" *Philosophical Review,* 64 (1955): 175–91.

42. Ibid., p. 187.

43. "Bentham on Legal Rights," in Simpson, ed., *Oxford Essays in Jurisprudence,* pp. 198, 201.

44. David Lyons argues that the formal concept of equality is vacuous. "The Weakness of Formal Equality," *Ethics,* 76 (1966): 146–48. I believe this is an overstatement. The requirement of even formal equality calls for the establishment of judicial or other machinery for the determination of the issue of relevance and that machinery tends to have a powerful effect in cabinning the concept of similarity. For a fuller treatment of this problem, see Pennock, *Democratic Political Theory,* pp. 143 ff.

   "Equality" was the subject of *NOMOS IX* (New York: Atherton, 1967) and has been the subject of an extensive bibliography since then. For this and other references relevant to the present volume, see Rex Martin and James W. Nickel, "A Bibliography on the Nature and Foundation of Rights, 1947–1977," *Political Theory,* 6 (1978): 395–413.

45. This last argument is borrowed from Richard Wasserstrom, "Rights, Human Rights, and Racial Discrimination," *Journal of Philosophy,* 61 (October 29, 1964): 628–41; reprinted in David Lyons, *Rights* (Belmont, Calif.: Wadsworth, 1979), pp. 46–57, 54–55.

46. Maurice Cranston, *What Are Human Rights?* (New York: Taplinger, 1978).

47. In fairness, it should be noted that both Rawls and Gewirth deal with this problem, at various points, by ordering priorities. Rawls not only gives top priority to equal liberty but also, in dealing with economic matters, favors the least advantaged over all others. But the identification of the least advantaged remains a problem. Gewirth, although insisting that liberty does not necessarily take priority over well-being, has his own system of priorities, but also his own vague categories ("basic needs") and admitted judgments of degree. See especially *Reason and Morality*, pp. 338–54.

48. John Stuart Mill's definition, although it would rule out the weakest of these definitions, remains vague. It reads that to have a right is "to have something that society [he does not say "government"] ought to defend me in the possession of," ("Utilitarianism," chap. 5, par. 25).

49. The veil of ignorance formulation of course refers to Rawls. The following formula, with its quotation, is taken from Richard B. Brandt, *A Theory of the Good and the Right* (Oxford: Oxford University Press, 1979). See especially chap. 10, sec. 3.; the quotation is at p. 194. Brandt generally shies away from the language of rights, but in the section just cited, on "The Definition of 'Morally Right,' " he does say that " 'has a moral right' can be defined in terms of 'morally ought' " (p. 195). Brandt's theory and that of Narveson in this volume bear an obvious kinship.

50. See above, note 17.

51. For a statement of a modified consequentialist position that attempts to give the deontologists their due, see T. M. Scanlon, "Rights, Goals and Fairness."

52. Joel Feinberg, *Social Philosophy* (Englewood Cliffs, N.J.: Prentice-Hall, 1973), p. 85.

53. Another distinction worthy of note is that between rights that can be presently realized and those that must be treated as aspirations. The latter are sometimes denominated "ideal rights."

54. *The Present Status of the Philosophy of Law and of Rights* (London: Oxford University Press, 1926), pp. 70–73.

55. See above, note 41.

56. "Natural and Inalienable Rights," *Philosophical Review*, 64 (1955): 212–232, esp. p. 231.

57. *Rights and Persons* (Berkeley: University of California Press, 1977), p. 167.

58. See his chapter on "Liberalism," in Hampshire ed., *Public and Private Morality*, quotation at pp. 133–134. At least the position attributed to him in the text appears to be Dworkin's view in this essay. In some of his earlier writings, notably "Taking Rights Seriously," it is not obvious that he considers any one right as fundamental above all others, nor is it completely clear how his rights are derived. *Taking Rights Seriously* (Cambridge, Mass.: Harvard University Press, 1978), pp. 184–205. In that essay, however, he does say "it makes sense to say that a man has a fundamental right against the government, *in the strong sense,* like free speech, if the right is necessary to protect his dignity, or his standing as equally entitled to concern and respect, or

some other personal value of like consequence. It does not make sense otherwise [italics mine]," p. 199.

59. Feinberg, *Social Philosophy,* p. 97.
60. Ibid.
61. It is important to phrase the right this way, rather than in the more common form, "equally entitled to respect," in order to stress the fact that persons as such are entitled to respect, absolutely, not just equally.

THE NATURE OF
HUMAN RIGHTS

2

A CRITIQUE OF HUMAN RIGHTS
JOHN CHARVET *

In the first and major part of this paper I present what I take to be
the essential idea of a theory of human rights, which grounds men's
claims on each other not in any external source, such as God's will or
a transcendental natural law, but in man's own nature. I argue that
this idea involves radical incoherence. I consider briefly the possibility that the difficulty I discern can be resolved by the discovery of
neutral or objective subordinate principles and show that such principles would not help and do not exist. In the second part I sketch in
what I understand to be the positive implications of this negative critique for a conception of the ground of men's rights.

I

1. The view of human rights that I shall be criticizing, then, holds
that men have rights as men, that is by virtue of something about their
nature as human beings. Since whatever it is that establishes the right
is something pertaining to the individual's pure humanity, all such
beings have the same basic rights.

The right is to be understood in broad terms as a claim each man
has on other men to the satisfaction of his particular life, his needs,
desires, and purposes. Let us not worry here about the undefined nature of this claim to satisfaction of particular life. The point to be
made is simply that the claim the individual has against others by virtue of his human right must be a claim in respect of his particular life,
and his particular life is composed in broadest terms of needs, desires, and purposes. The basic idea of the view of human rights that I
am elaborating, then, is that this claim to the satisfaction of particu-

lar life is grounded in the fact that it is the particular life of a human individual. Needs, desires, or purposes have moral worth in so far as they are the needs, desires, or purposes of human individuals.

One cannot, therefore, say that it is the satisfaction of desire or wants as such, or the giving of pleasure and avoidance of pain, in themselves that has moral worth, for this would not accommodate the basic idea that it is the human individual who bestows moral worth on particular desires by their being *his* desires. Given that desires arise in human beings as they do in other living beings, and that it is not desire as such that contains moral worth, there must be something that the individual does to the desires that arise in him through which moral worth is created. This something is the fact that the human individual is a self-conscious and self-forming being. He acquires the capacity in the course of his development to reflect on the desires that arise in him and to order these desires into a preference system with a view to realizing in his life some desires rather than others. Thus, he comes to conceive his life as a whole in terms of the realization in it of purposes that he has formed in a self-reflective and evaluative way.

This individual may be said to form or determine himself, since he creates in his life an order of his own choosing. It is this self-determination of the human individual that bestows moral worth on particular life. Whatever an individual wills for his life has moral worth, simply because he wills it. Thus, the human rights view I am considering is committed to the fundamental claim that the source of moral value lies in a self-determining being. Man is a self-determining being insofar as he forms his particular life for himself. The basic human right, then, is the right of the human individual to determine his particular life for himself. And he has the right because he is a self-determining being.

This idea can be put in another way. On premodern views of the source of moral value, the particular choices of men had moral worth only insofar as they conformed with an external validating will or pattern, God's will or natural law. On the modern view the particular choices of an individual have moral worth if they conform with that individual's own will, that is, if they are genuinely the product of his own self-determination.

On this conception of the fundamental content and ground of human rights it is necessary that the individual can be meaningfully conceived as determined neither by his neurophysiological mechanisms nor by his social existence. With regard to the latter, the individual must be understood as capable of reflective evaluation of the influences on him of his social environment and of engaging in the same ordering process through which he commits his will to a certain pattern of particular values, encompassing his relations to others, to be realized in his particular life.

2. It follows from the above account of the source of moral value that an individual's particular purposes have moral worth only if they are genuinely his and not another's. His choices for his life must be authentic choices. In the first place, then, an unreflective life that the individual has not chosen for himself but has simply grown into has no moral worth. Second, however, there are lives that appear to be chosen by the individual for himself but that are inauthentic because what the individual chooses is a life that another wants him to live, not one that he really wants for himself. It is true that the individual wants indirectly to lead the life he does, but it is the indirectness of the want for that life that makes it inauthentic. He chooses nothing directly for his particular life but elects another to choose his life for him. An authentic choice must be an unmediated one. But this does not mean that the choice cannot absorb the impact on the individual of the desires and purposes of others. However, the individual must rise above them and choose a life for himself having regard only to what *he* wants, not what others want, for *his* life.

Another way of putting this is to say that for a choice of a particular life to be authentic, it is necessary that the individual have himself as the *only* end for himself. The individual is an end for himself insofar as his ultimate aim in his choice of particular life is to please or satisfy himself rather than another. He may, of course, have to please another as a means to attain his own purposes for his life, but he does not thereby treat the other as an ultimate end for him. He may also as part of his choice for his life, having regard only to himself as ultimate end, desire the good of particular others. He has benevolent desires towards others, and the fulfillment of these desires enters into his conception of the life he wishes to lead. Since his aim is to contribute to their welfare, it must include a desire that they should be pleased or satisfied with his efforts. But the choice of this life is not made because these others want him to lead that life, and it is not made ultimately to please them because they are ultimate ends for him, but solely because this life of benevolence is one that in reflecting on his life he wishes for himself.

Again, an individual may choose a life that involves relations of a
certain kind with others. He may particularly value the practice of
monogamous marriage and desire to realize that value in marrying X.
Relations of a particular sort with X, therefore, enter into his conception of the life he desires. But X does not thereby become an ultimate end for him. For he does not desire that particular life with X
because wholly or in part X wants him to live that life, and he wants
(inauthentically) to live as X wants him to live. X may be supposed to
have views on how they should live together, but these must be absorbed into the individual's reflection on the life he desires for himself,
and insofar as they reappear in the individual's authentic decision,
they do so having received the imprimatur of his purely self-determining will.

The authentic self-determining individual, then, must not have
others as ultimate ends for him but treat himself at *the particular
level* as his only end. I emphasize the particular level, because at this
point we are concerned with individuals who are determining themselves or being determined by others in respect of the particular values they seek to realize in their lives. In respect of moral values,
others are, of course, ultimate ends. But they are ends for the individual because they are *ends in themselves,* independently of his
choice of them as ends. This distinction between the moral and the
particular level is crucial, and I will return to it shortly.

3. There is no reason to think of these self-determining individuals, who have in respect of their particular life only themselves as
their end, as egoists. As indicated above, an individual may authentically choose for himself a life of benevolence toward others and
otherwise may desire to live in relations of various kinds with others.
Perhaps it will be said that since authentic choice requires the individual to choose a benevolent life or whatever having regard ultimately only to himself as his end, benevolence and every other
"good" relation to another is thereby absorbed into an all-encom-
passing egoism. Maybe this is so. But egoism would, then, be a characteristic of the individual's overall attitude to his life; it would not
be a characteristic of the particular values he seeks to realize in it.

One can, following Williams,[1] distinguish between I-desires and
non-I-desires. I-desires are desires for states of oneself that can always
be expressed in the form: I desire that *I* have, possess, or enjoy something, whereas non-I-desires are desires for states of other beings
where what I desire is that X have, possess, or enjoy something, and

this desire cannot be reduced to a means to the attainment of some further I-desire. A benevolent life, then, involves, in the first instance, the having of non-I-desires. For what I desire is some state of another which is not a means to the bringing about of some particular state of myself. And yet, on the view I have been presenting, ultimately my non-I-desires for others receive the imprimatur of my will because they form part of the conception of my life as a whole that I desire that *I* enjoy. But although being part of a comprehensive I-desire for my life, they are not means to particular I-desires, and so should not be deprived of their relatively nonegoistic nature.

4. I have so far been arguing that a view of human rights is committed to understanding the source of moral worth to lie in the individual's relation to himself, which requires that his life be genuinely the product of his own will. The idea is that each individual bestows moral worth on himself insofar as he is genuinely self-determining. The important point here is that the individual does this in a relation with himself without the mediation of others. The moral value of each lies in himself, and not through his relation to others.

However, that by virtue of which the individual establishes his claim against others establishes in others an equal claim against him. The right of the individual to determine his own particular life is necessarily an equal right of all such individuals. Hence, the particular choices of the individual are morally valid, now, not only by being authentically his choices, but by not infringing the limits imposed on him by the rights of others.

There is no reason to suppose that these two requirements will produce results that coincide. What an individual desires authentically may be irretrievably frustrated by some state of the world legitimately enjoyed by others. The belief that the two requirements will coincide provided that we first remove the distorting structures of state, private property, or indeed any established institution is the fantasy of revolutionary anarchist thought. Their idea is that only inauthentic desires conflict and that the presence of inauthentic desires in men is not the consequence of some original fault in their taking on particular life but of the limiting social and moral structures whose function it is to discipline, and in their view thereby to distort, particular desire.

Given that there is no reason to suppose that the authentic particular desires of men will spontaneously harmonize with each other, and so within a structure of equal rights, a potential conflict can be seen to arise in the individual between the demands of his particular self for its authentic self-realization, and the requirement to respect the rights of others. This is the point at which the incoherence that I perceive in the view of human rights that I am considering emerges.

One might hold that the individual's right is only a *prima facie* right and that conflicts between such rights are to be resolved through the elaboration of neutral, subordinate principles, which all can agree to in their own interest. This idea I will come to in a moment. My claim, now, is that on the view of the source of moral worth discussed above the individual is conceived as forming his own particular life "egoistically" or with himself as his sole end, for it is only insofar as he does this that his particular life has moral worth. Hence, in respect of his particular life he cannot be concerned with the rights of others and cannot have any interest in limiting his choice of life by respect for those rights. If the individual is to be able to respect the claims of others, we must attribute to him a new dimension to his personality, a moral self whose specific object is the equal worth of all particular selves. But this creates within the individual a split between his particular self and his moral self. It is the necessity within this view of human rights for the introduction of a divided self that constitutes the incoherence of that conception.

In order to understand better how this "gap" arises within the individual, it is necessary to go back over some of the above ground. The basic idea of the theory is that the individual, insofar as he forms his own particular life, creates moral value. But it is clear that we can conceive of the individual forming himself without at the same time conceiving of the moral value that is supposed to be created in that process of self-formation. It is not self-evident that a being that forms itself creates moral value. We need, in order to endorse this identity, to accept the prior claim that a being that forms itself creates moral value.

My claim is that we can without difficulty identify one individual as forming his own particular life without attributing any moral quality to that life. For in forming his life in the manner specified he treats himself necessarily as an end for himself, and his life as a value for *him*, but he is not committed to claiming, and we do not have to see him as claiming, that he is an end *in* himself, and his life a value for anyone. Whether we see him as claiming only subjective value for his life or as claiming objective value, what he does *in forming his life* is the same. The only difference between the two cases is the additional claim in the latter that a self-determined life is a value for anyone. But this has to be added on to, for it is not contained in the description of the subjective, nonmoral worth of the individual's life.

Insofar as we can make the distinction between the subjective and the objective descriptions of the self-determining will, we must do so. The source of moral worth cannot lie in the self-determining will understood subjectively, and because of this we have to conceive of moral worth as an objective validation of what is in the first instance determined subjectively by each individual for himself. The moral claim is that whatever the individual chooses for himself subjectively, that is, as valid for him, is morally valid. These quite separate determinations of the subjective and objective worth of the individual's choice insure that they must be represented in the individual in two quite separate motivational structures: on the one hand, a particular will concerned with the choice of a particular life which is only subjectively valid, or in which the individual has only himself for his end; on the other hand, a moral will concerned with the equal moral value of all particular wills. [2]

Because the moral will of the individual is, so to speak, a separate self within him, quite unrelated to his particular self, it appears as an impersonal will which has as much reason to value the satisfaction of the authentic particular will of another as the satisfaction of his own. In this way individuals as moral agents become valuers of each other's particular lives and so treat each other as ends. But because of the separation of particular and moral selves, this having of others as ultimate ends for one does not conflict with the requirement of authenticity at the particular level—namely, that one *not* have another as one's end. For it is the impersonal moral self that values the other as end, and this being independent of the particular self leaves that self free to determine itself in accordance with the demands of authenticity.

The conflict between particular and moral will lies, however, in their opposed natures, the one directing the individual to self-consideration only (as his ultimate aim), and the other directing the individual toward equality. [3] But this becomes an open war only when conflict occurs between the particular purposes of different individuals. For were it the case that each individual's purposes for his life harmonized with the purposes of all the others, the moral will would have no constraining work to do to get the particular wills to respect the rights of others. The moral will need only passively endorse the fortunate state of affairs brought about by particular striving. But once not all particular aims can be satisfied together, one man's satisfaction can be obtained only at the expense of another's and hence by an infringement of his rights. And this immediately brings the individual's particular and moral will into conflict.

5. Let us now consider the possibility that these conflicts can be dealt with by the elaboration of secondary or subordinate ordering principles. I have so far been considering human rights in the most abstract, general way, and at this level the right of each individual to determine his particular life for himself will most likely conflict with the right of others. Hence, subordinate principles for ordering such conflicts are absolutely necessary if sense is to be made of the equal right of each. A requirement of such principles is that they are neutral as between the particular claims of different individuals. They must carry through into their operation the fundamental claim to equality contained in the notion of human rights. One way of conceiving of this requirement is in terms of what principles all men could agree to as in their own interests whatever their particular interests are.[4]

The discovery of such neutral principles would not in itself provide an answer to the fundamental issues raised above about the separation and opposition of the particular and moral will. For the subordinate principles would take the primary principle for granted, and the trouble stems from the primary principle. Hence, whether neutral, subordinate principles exist or not might be considered irrelevant to the claims that I have so far been making. Yet, were such principles to exist, they would constitute an embarrassment to my argument. For despite the continued unsatisfactoriness of the primary principle, we would then have secondary principles derived from it that would appear to give us an objective and effective way of ordering our social life. Furthermore, insofar as we see these principles as one that all particular wills could agree to in their own interest, we would seem to have bridged the gap between particular will and moral principles in a way deemed by me to be impossible. It will, therefore, be convenient for my argument if I can show that no one interpretation of the primary principle either has, or could have, gained universal acceptance.

The primary principle here is the equal right of individuals to determine their particular lives for themselves, and one can immediately point to the two extreme interpretations of this equal right. On the one hand is what might be called the classical liberal view to be found in Locke in the early modern period and in Nozick today, which defends the right of the particular to freedom at the expense of inequality and on the other hand is the egalitarian view that defends equality at the expense of freedom. Rawls's theory, like many others, can be seen as a compromise between these two extremes.

The issue concerns the individual's entitlement to the control of the resources necessary for him to exercise his right to determine his particular life. The classical liberal view typically holds that the entitlement of the individual arises out of the individual's own activity in his de facto appropriation of parts of the earth's surface and not through an initial grant of resources from some morally authoritative source. To avoid the difficulty of competing claims for scarce resources, the starting point for private appropriation is usually placed in a state of nature characterized by abundance. But this disguises the fact that an initial grant to individuals from a moral will is inevitably involved. The individual's de facto appropriation is rightful only because of an initial grant of a right by a moral authority, and this right is an *equal* right of individuals to appropriate in accordance with their needs; hence, the right of one man is limited by the right of every other. Inevitably, therefore, the starting point of the classical liberal position involves an egalitarian grant.

Let us represent this starting point in terms of an equal distribution of resources, for the crucial conflict between the classical liberal and the egalitarian interpretations of the primary equal right principle can be brought out by concentrating on what the individual's right is in respect of the use of the resources initially granted to him.

The liberal view emphasizes particularly the right of individuals to use their resources in any way they think fit, so long as no one is made worse off than he was in the starting position. The right to use one's resources is held to carry with it the right to use them in exchange with others, in such a way as to increase the amount of resources that one controls, to accumulate indefinitely. The result at any rate must potentially be a world in which some people control large quantities of resources and others have not advanced much, if at all, beyond their original baseline position. The justification of this inequality consists in the impossibility of overruling any particular transaction that brings about an inequality by reference to the fundamental principle of the right to freedom to which all adhere. If one denies individuals the right to make such transactions, one must deny them the right to improve their position even though they are not harming anyone else, and so deny the fundamental notion of the right to freedom, since this notion involves the *prima facie* equal right of individuals to do what they want provided that they do not injure others. The transactions envisaged satisfy this requirement and so cannot legitimately be forbidden.

Now, it is necessary to show that the fundamental principle of equal rights also requires the opposite thesis, namely that resources be distributed equally at all times. This thesis denies the freedom to make gains for oneself in which all do not share. What is wrong with an unequal command over resources is that it constitutes unequal means for individuals to form and realize their projects. It is proportionate equality that is required — a distribution of means that is the same in proportion to the different needs of individuals relative to their ends. This inequality is not acceptable from the point of view of the moral agent as opposed to the point of view of particular life. The self now in its capacity as moral agent must treat everyone's right to realize his projects as of equal value. From this point of view it looks clearly enough as though no one could have a right to greater means than any other, however he came by such means.

It is no use arguing to the moral self that the greater means of one person to realize his projects are, let us say, the result of his greater natural skills, or greater enterprise, hard work, or imagination in the use of his resources, for natural inequality of skill and capacity are irrelevant from the moral point of view, irrelevant to the question of the worth of each agent. From the moral point of view each agent has an inherent claim to as great an amount of resources relative to his demands as anyone else. It is true that this viewpoint of the moral self supposes that all resources are available to it to distribute in accordance with its own criteria, and that resources are not to be seen as already attached to particular persons, who in producing them have a natural right to decide on their disposal before the machinations of the socialistic moral self can redistribute them. It sees the question purely in terms of allocation, ignoring entirely the rights that producers may have.[5] But this is the attitude that the moral self must take up. For the rights of producers are the rights of the particular self to use its capacities and entitlements as it thinks fit, so long as it does not make anyone worse off in terms of his baseline position. It is the right of the particular to give himself the preference, to pursue *his* values, and not to have to treat the other's claims as of equal value with his own.

The moral self has to acknowledge the right of the particular to make substantive choices for his life having regard to his life only, since the moral self cannot make these choices itself, indeed any at all of a substantive nature; nevertheless, it must dissociate this right of making choices, the determination of projects for the self, from the acquisition of resources or exercise of skills or capacities that are means for the realization of these projects. Since the moral self must see the assets available in the world for the realization of human projects as in principle a collective asset the distribution of which it is for the moral self and not the particular self to determine, individuals from this point of view have no right to use their own capacities as they think fit for their private ends. As a collective asset of mankind, they must be used to produce resources available for an equal distribution. Individuals must continue to form for themselves their private projects, but this function of private willing must be divorced from the willing of individuals that involves the active use of their capacities to produce goods and services. Particular willing here must be identical with moral willing, on the assumption that the moral will had complete control or possession of the means of particular willing, namely the ability of individuals.

It is obvious that the consequence of the legislation of the moral self for an equal distribution of the means to self-development is an infringement of the rights of the particular self to its freedom. The rule of equality requires that no one be able to acquire through his own enterprise and virtue a superior position to any other, even if such individual enterprise is the result of transactions that make no one worse off. But it is irrational for the moral self to forbid transactions that make some people better off and no one worse off. This defines a Pareto-optimal position, and it is widely considered irrational not to be in such a position. Pareto-optimality may be attacked on the grounds that it refers to the rights of the particular self to secure the best position for itself so long as it does not infringe certain moral restraints, and it may then be argued that the definition of these restraints must have priority over what is permitted to the particular self. If a move to a Pareto-optimal position infringes some definition for moral restraints, for example, the equality of means to self-development requirement — then in terms of that criterion the Pareto-optimal position is illegitimate. It carries no rational weight and is of no importance if not met. But this merely begs the question as to the legitimacy of the Pareto criterion. Of course, in terms of the egalitarian principle a Pareto-optimal position that infringes it is illegitimate. But the problem arises because the primary principle, of which egalitarianism is an interpretation, bestows a right on particulars to make choices for their lives having regard to their own lives, the right of private will. The right of the private will must include the right to make choices for itself that make it better off so long as it does not make anyone else worse off. If the egalitarian principle requires the rejection of this right, then, it undermines itself, since this right is a corollary of the primary principle from which the egalitarian principle is derived.

The only way this result might be avoided is by the redefinition of what is involved in making another worse off. The individual's shifting relative position, not his absolute starting position, would determine whether another had harmed him or not. This would insure that one individual's gain in resources that left others' absolute position unchanged would make him relatively worse off and so count as harming him. But to make sense of this situation, it would have to be the case that the individual allows the value of his life to be determined, not by himself alone in accordance with the requirements of authentic choice, but from an external standpoint. The individual's purpose, on the realization of which his well-being would depend, would consist in his having superior, or not having inferior, control of resources to others — let us say simply his aim is to be superior, or not to be inferior, to others as evaluated according to some standard. This means that the individual is valuing his life as it would be valued by someone who valued a collection of individuals solely in accordance with their relative position in a whole order. The value of his life is not, therefore, ultimately value for himself, and thus something he determines by and for himself alone, but is something determined from a standpoint external to him. Insofar as the individual, in respect of his particular life, values himself ultimately from this standpoint, he values himself inauthentically.[6]

Thus, whether we reinterpret the no-harm principle to cover the relative standing of individuals or not, the egalitarian interpretation of the primary principle is incompatible with the specification of the primary principle itself. As we have seen, the classical liberal interpretation also produces results that are incompatible with the inherently equal worth of men as choosers as seen from the moral point of view. This incoherence in the subordinate principles that are supposed to be derivations from the primary principle is the result of the incoherence in the primary principle itself. For that principle was shown to contain two different points of view, being those of the moral and the particular self, which are not integrated with each other but are actually quite separate standpoints within the individual. A system of subordinate principles would have to include elements of both points of view, expressed as the rights of the particular self and those of the moral self. The right of the particular self is its right, given an initial equal distribution, to pursue its ends minding only its own business. The right of the moral self is, however, the right to be concerned with everybody's business.[7].

We must, however, consider briefly the sort of argument designed to reconcile the claims of freedom and equality, recently given elaborate expression by Rawls. The reconciliation proceeds through the positing of an equal distribution of resources as a basic norm, and allowing only those departures from this norm that bring about improvements in everybody's position. Rawls purports to derive these principles from an agreement between independent persons in an original position, but he designs the original position, as he admits, so that it will produce conclusions coincident with our actual moral intuitions.[8] The appropriate fundamental moral intuition here is that it is unacceptable for social arrangements to be designed in such a way that better-endowed persons gain advantages from their superior abilities.[9] This rules out the liberal interpretation of the initial freedom and equality of independent persons in an original position and commits us to the egalitarian interpretation as a basic norm.

Rawls has a special version of the formula for departures from the basic distributive norm of equality — the difference principle. The difference principle should be seen as that principle which involves the least possible departure from strict equality, provided we do not count inequality itself as a cost, which it would be irrational to do.[10] The question is whether, as a departure from the strict equality position, the difference principle gets over the incoherence of strict equality and achieves a reconciliation of the claims of freedom and equality. In effect, this approach, or some version of it, is much more popular than strict equality, but it is a compromise that contains the vices of both the liberal and the egalitarian positions. It is a compromise in that it starts with the egalitarian principle, as we have seen, but compromises with the liberal view of freedom insofar as it allows individuals to enter into transactions through which they can make gains for themselves provided that these work out to the long-term advantage of the worst-off sections of the community. Thus, liberal freedom has some scope. But, of course, the difference principle does not satisfy the Pareto criterion, for it forbids transactions that would make some people better off while leaving the worst off in an unchanged position. Thus, in this respect it is no better than the strict equality principle itself. But from the other side it offends the sensibilities of the moral self. It allows in principle for very large gains to some, provided that they satisfy the difference principle, and thus very large inequalities of means for individuals to attain their ends. Rawls tries to direct attention away from this by distinguishing a special range of rights called the equal liberties, which are to be held of equal value despite differences in individuals' command over resources. The equal worth of individuals is to be understood in terms of these equal liberties and not in terms of amounts of holdings. [11] But this *is* the liberal position that treats the equal worth of persons as embodied simply in their equal right to pursue their ends within the constraints of the no-harm principle, and thus potentially manifest in great inequalities of wealth. This is what is offensive to the moral self.

6. The separation and consequent opposition of particular and moral life in the theory of rights that I am considering can also be understood as an alienation of the particular self from its community insofar as the community stands here for those general relations between particulars that hold them together by defining their relative rights and duties. The theories of a Hegel or a Marx can be seen to be directed toward solving this problem by the overcoming of alienation. Before getting on to the final section of this chapter, I shall refer briefly to some of Marx's formulations of this problem, as they quite closely resemble my own, and in pointing to the inadequacy of his solution I will lead more easily into my own.

Marx's identification of alienation in the terms I have been using occurs most clearly in his early writing, for instance in the essay "On the Jewish Question." [12] His critique in these writings is of the idea of a purely political emancipation of man, the realization of freedom at the general level of equal citizenship only and not at the level of particular interest also. In the liberal theory of the state according to Marx, man leads a double life, a life in the political community where he is valued as a communal being and one in civil society in which he is active as a private individual and where he treats other men as means to his own private ends and allows himself to be degraded into a means to the ends of others. This double life in the liberal conception is I presume clear enough, but Marx assumes that it is obviously self-contradictory. The idea of man's communal being as equal citizen is merely an abstract, ideal conception. It cannot be realized, because the free play of private interest in civil society insures the dominance of some of those interests over others at the general level. Marx clearly rejects the liberal interpretation of the common good as a structure of rights that is neutral as between individual's interests. Marx presents the individual in civil society as egoistic, but as we have seen this is not a necessary interpretation of the liberal view.

Marx's proposals for the true emancipation of man involve the idea of the reintegration of the abstract citizen with individual material life, the creation of a unity of state and civil society. The individual man in his individual work and relationships must become a species being. He must see his individual forces, not as private ones, but as directly social forces. He must not separate social from individual forces.

This unity of individual and society is supposed to be such that the ends the individual pursues are at the same time social ends, and the ends of "society" are always instantiated in the particular ends of individuals. The individual is the ideal totality.[13] No possible tension can exist between what one particular wants for himself for his self-development, what he wants for others, and what others want from him, and hence between the particular level at any point and the social or general level.[14] This constitutes the "utopianism" of Marx, but in my view it makes no sense. For in denying the potential gap between the particular individual and his society (in some future condition), Marx denies that there is any difference between individual and social consciousness — any difference, that is, between the points of view of the particular individual and of society — and so makes the notion of individual consciousness impossible to understand. The human rights theory that I have been discussing clearly recognizes these different points of view but separates them from each other and fails to hold them together in a coherent relation of interdependence.

II

1. I come now to the sketch of a view of the relation between particular and moral life that I believe avoids the problems discussed above. The starting point for such a conception presupposes much that is contained in the view of human rights that I have been criticizing — in particular the understanding of the individual as a self-forming being.[15] But it is essential to begin with this notion of the individual as self-forming being in its purely subjective form, according to which the individual, in coming to form his own life, treats himself as an end *for* himself, and so does not claim that in forming himself subjectively, he is an end for others because he is an end in himself. It is this confusion between, or identification of, the subjec-

tive and objective ideas of self-determination that produces much of
the trouble. If we start with the clear notion of the individual as subjective end for himself and refuse to allow that the objective idea can
be in any way contained in, or derived from, that subjective formulation, we will be in a position to see how the moral or general dimension to particular lives can be introduced without positing it in the
abstract and separate form that it has in the notion of human rights.

The meaning of this starting point in which the individual conceives himself as an end for himself is as follows: the immature human being is of course formed by, and in relation to, a specific community and sees himself initially solely in relation to that community.
But at some stage in his development to maturity he partitions himself off in thought from its community, by coming to see that his life
is not necessarily and essentially contained in that community. The
individual sees that he could lead other lives than the one presently
organized by relation to his community and comes to hold that any
life that includes claims on him by others must satisfy *him*. Thereby
he affirms that in the first place he is an end for himself. Any arrangement with others through which rights and duties are created
must, if it is to be acceptable to the individual, allow for his pursuit
of particular ends.

Since we deny that, in this first move of the individual, in which he
alienates himself from his community, any objective or moral element can be perceived, it follows that this element cannot arise in the
individual as an independent being. It cannot be through some relation of the individual to himself, unmediated by a relation to others,
that the moral worth of his particular life is created. Hence, the
moral element can arise only through the relation to the other, and
the other can be said to participate in the creation of the moral worth
of the individual's particular life.

But it cannot be any other, or the other as such, who participates
in this creation. For the other, understood in that way, is simply the
abstract moral self whose will is an impersonal one identical with
one's own will as a moral being. Hence, the other here is not a mean-
ingful other. He is one's own will in its impersonal form. Determination by the other is identical with *self*-determination. This is the classic move whereby the relation to the other, which is obviously necessary, purports to be satisfied, but at the same time is shown not to
cancel the individual's sole dependence on himself. [16]

Insofar as the other in his capacity of creator of one's moral worth
is conceived abstractly and impersonally, then the value for him of

one's particular life is value for him as this pure moral being and is quite independent of *his* particular life. Furthermore, since his moral will is identical with one's own moral will, the value for him of one's particular life is identical with value for oneself. This is seen in the fact that he is committed to treating whatever one authentically chooses for oneself as having moral worth. He replicates, merely, the individual's own relation to himself, through which the individual bestows moral worth on his life.

The other, then, as value of one's life, must be concrete. The other is *this* person or *these* people with specific aims and potentialities. This concreteness of the other means that the value for him of one's particular life is value for him understood in a way that includes *his* particular life. He bestows moral value on one's life as that life is related in some way to his own particular life.

Insofar as the concrete other is creator of one's moral worth, one's particular life must satisfy him as well as oneself. One is no longer solely an end for oneself; the other is also an end for one. And this means that one forms one's life to please him as also to please oneself. One cannot, therefore, be authentically self-determining, in accordance with the requirement of the notion of human rights discussed in part I of this chapter. This is because, since the other is a real other, other-determination is not identical with self-determination.

The crucial requirement for the avoidance of the alienation of particular and moral life is that the individual should always form projects for his life only insofar as he thinks of these projects as lived in some concrete relation to particular others, and hence only insofar as he thinks of them harmonizing with the particular projects of these others within some communal structure creating the rights and duties of its members. This is not to say that one is committed to any particular relative identity — the one, for instance, that one is born into; since one may, finding this too limited in particular satisfaction, seek to change one's place, or later some or all of the terms of communal association, or find some other more congenial community within which to live one's particular life. It is say, however, that one's imagined possibilities of existence must contain an idea of one's particular place in a communal structure uniting one with other particular individuals seeking their satisfaction.

Each individual seeks some structured relation of his life to the other through which the other's valuation of his life can harmonize with his own valuation of it, and with his valuation of the other's life and the other's self-valuation. This multiplicity of perspectives on each other's lives through the terms on which particular lives are to be related and harmonized entails the perpetual possibility of conflict, of particular dissatisfaction with the terms of association. But this conflict is not a cause of *theoretical* imperfection, since the theory being sketched does not attribute to individuals apart from their relation any rights to particular satisfaction. Insofar as this relation of being ends for each other comes into existence, each makes himself the valuer of the other's particular life and so grants the other in relation to himself a claim to the satisfaction of his particular life. But since it is a claim that has no validity in itself, but only in relation to one's particular life, it involves no commitment to value him on his own terms, but only a commitment to find some terms through which each can be fulfilled. Thus an ideal of a perfect harmony of particular lives in mutual association is involved, but the falling short of the ideal in actuality does not call the theory into question.

The terms on which individuals' lives are to be related and harmonized constitute the general dimension of their lives, that which they share, their common good. It determines the value the particular life of each has for the others. The opposition between particular and general life is overcome, then, because the various particular values and the common good are always identified in relation to each other. In choosing terms of association, one chooses that which will harmonize such and such particular lives in a certain way, whereas in thinking of particular ends for oneself one thinks of them always in terms of an association harmonizing one's end with those of one's others.

Men associated in terms of a common good have a common identity consisting in their membership of the same association. Although each values the other as a particular according to his position in the association, the whole association is grounded in the wills of its members through which each constitutes the others as ends for him, and so as codeterminer of his life. This creative will is that which brings into existence the moral relation between persons. Each as end for the other lives to please the other, and this can be understood to involve in the most general and abstract way a commitment to each other's prosperity; hence a negative duty not to harm them and a positive duty to help them attain their ends. But this highly general formulation of what is necessarily involved in the fundamental commitment of individuals to each other as members of an association cannot itself yield any more specific rules of association. The specific determination of the general moral principles to a particular form given in the actual organization of a community has to be done not through a process of rational deduction but by the choice by a community of a substantive form for itself appropriate to its circumstances, traditions, and the particular aspirations of its members.

Insofar as the association is grounded in the will that creates the moral community, one might think of this will as a pure will, to be distinguished from a man's particular will in just the same sort of way as I criticize in the theory of rights. But its purity here consists in one's talking of it as a power to bring into existence concrete moral relations. It cannot have actuality other than as a will that creates those particular others in a substantive moral relation to itself through which their particular lives are harmonized. It can have actuality only as a unity of particular and moral will.

In making the other one's end one gives him a legitimate power over one's particular life and makes oneself dependent on him, not in respect of the means necessary to attain one's particular ends, but in respect of one's particular ends themselves. But if this is incompatible with freedom on the human rights view, it is still the case that it is oneself who gives the other this power over one. The other is one's own creation and so in a sense one's other self; at the same time, oneself is the creation of the other. This mutual creation as moral beings is nevertheless not the bringing into existence of a higher self by its nature opposed to the particular self, since it does not create the other for one as pure moral being, but as a particular being at the same time. It is this particular person with his particular life who becomes an end for one now for the first time. The coming into existence of the moral dimension between persons is necessarily instantiated in a definite relation between their particular lives.

2. In this sketch of what it is for men to be ends for each other without engendering the antinomies of freedom, I have discussed only the subjective side, and in doing so I have no doubt given the impression that the moral relation between persons is ultimately a matter of arbitrary choice, as to whether to treat this or that other as an end for one or not. The cost involved in avoiding the attribution of a moral claim to men in themselves and thus of tying the moral relation into our particular lives would, then, be very high. So, finally, in a few brief remarks aimed at pointing the way to the overcoming of this arbitrariness, I shall introduce the objective side of the story. I have been describing an explicit moral will, which I take to be implicit in all social relations insofar as these are relations of interdependence. Relations of interdependence are relations through which necessarily and objectively each completes and so helps to define the existence of

the other. My particular life is defined, whether I consciously will it or no, in terms of the exchange relations I have with other particulars through which I am enabled to attain my ends, whatever they are. The other on whom I am dependent necessarily contributes to the determination of the values realized in my life, a determination by the other that I can escape only insofar as I renounce social life altogether. It is, then, true that if this is an option for me, moral life, because social life, is ultimately a matter of arbitrary choice for the individual. But to the extent that I pursue my ends in a context of relations of dependence on others, my will is implicitly committed to treat those others as ends for me. I can act in a way that is contrary to this implicit commitment of my will, by seeking to obtain from the other by systematic coercion his contribution to my particular life, without offering him anything in return. The fact that I coerce the slave into giving me his contributions does not free me from dependence on him. Since I am dependent on him, I must desire his continued effectiveness as a contributor to my existence, just as I must desire this for any thing on which I am dependent. However, the slave is not a thing but a being with a conscious will, and this by my continued coercion of him I deny. The underlying self-contradiction consists in the fact that my coercion of him involves both denying that he has a will of his own and asserting that he is rather a thing, and yet by having to coerce him acknowleding that he has a will that I seek to make completely my own. Or I may think that I am acting in a purely self-interested way in my relations with others, and indeed obtain a better position for myself by so doing, but I will be deceiving myself insofar as my actions have to be undertaken in the context of interdependence that brings it about that I am contributing to the other's existence and he to mine independently of my conscious will. It is the will implicit in objective relations of interdependence, which becomes explicit or self-conscious as the moral will, through which we acknowledge each other as ends in the manner described above.

* I wish to thank the editor for his helpful comments on an earlier version of this essay.

NOTES

1. Bernard Williams, "Egoism and Altruism" in *Problems of the Self* (Cambridge: Cambridge University Press, 1973).

2. Of course, the history of moral philosophy is full of attempts to bridge this gap and to show how the two wills are related, but I think it is fair to say that none carries very much conviction. For a recent attempt, which is particularly relevant to the argument of this chapter, see Alan Gewirth's contribution to this volume.

3. The writers in whose work this conflict appears most clearly are Rousseau and Kant. My claim is, however, that any writer who commits himself to the first steps of the above view of human rights can be forced to acknowledge this conflict.

4. This, of course, is the way that John Rawls purports to derive the required subordinate principles. See *A Theory of Justice* (Oxford: Clarendon Press 1972), Pt. I.

5. I follow Nozick's argument against Rawls and Williams here. Robert Nozick, *Anarchy, State and Utopia,* (Oxford: Basil Blackwell, 1974), pp. 228-35.

6. Rousseau's account of human corruption in part II of the "Discourse on Inequality" should be read in this way. See John Charvet, *Social Problem in the Philosophy of Rousseau* (Cambridge: Cambridge University Press, 1974).

7. The moral self has at the same time a duty to be concerned with everybody's business.

8. Rawls, *A Theory of Justice,* pp. 19-20.

9. Ibid., p. 72.

10. To count inequality as itself a cost would be to hold that someone is made worse off by the improved position of another, although his own absolute position remains unchanged. This would be to make the individual's worth inauthentically dependent on his relation to others. See above, p. 33.

11. Rawls, *A Theory of Justice,* pp. 543-47.

12. D. McLellan, ed., *Karl Marx: Early Texts* (Oxford: Basil Blackwell, 1971).

13. Ibid., p. 151.

14. Ibid., p. 202.

15. See above, p. 32.

16. For example Rousseau's famous aim in *The Social Contract,* book I, chap. 6, to find a form of association in which each, while uniting himself with the others, obeys no one but himself.

3

TWO CRITIQUES OF THE TRADITIONAL THEORY OF HUMAN RIGHTS

FRITHJOF BERGMANN

In this chapter I shall argue first that Professor Charvet's critique of the traditional theory of human rights is only an ineffectual slap, and then I shall attempt to deliver a few blows of my own.

In essence, Professor Charvet wants to place the theory of rights on a new basis. He directs his arguments against the derivation of rights from human nature and proposes an alternative foundation. His critique can be compressed into the single charge that grounding rights on human nature generates a "radical incoherence" between the right to freedom and that to equality. It is naturally all-important to understand in precisely what this "radical incoherence" in fact consists, and a first question one might ask to that end is: Is it simply that the two rights cut across each other, that the gains of one will be the losses of the other, so that we must choose and cannot have all of freedom and all of equality at the same time? But if so, would this constitute a serious flaw, for why should rights *not* limit one another? Indeed, what sort of entity (if that is the right word) could possibly set bounds to rights if not another right or the right of another? Surely rocks cannot fence them in. Moreover, can any theory of rights be at all imagined in which this bounding of various rights could be avoided? And yet again: Could one conceive of any world where the rights of one person would not under certain circumstances become the boundary of the rights of others? And also, what of the comparison to moral codes? If a moral code enjoins me to be kind and also to tell the truth, then these principles will certainly at times conflict. (Perhaps the writing of this essay may even be a case in point.) Yet surely this does not show such a moral code to be defective. Yet if not then why should the analogous occurrence be an objection to a theory of rights?

So the sheer fact that freedom and equality do infringe on each other is no serious embarrassment to any theory of rights, and if this were the thrust of Professor Charvet's argument it would not even make a scratch. Yet it is far from clear whether this is all that is on Professor Charvet's mind. On the contrary, we made this thought explicit only to isolate it and move the actual issue into sharper focus. If the charge cannot be simply that freedom and equality encroach upon each other, then the accusation more likely is that the conflict is somehow exceptionally harsh — or maybe even total — or that it somehow cannot be softened or toned down or mitigated, or again that it is peculiarly so constituted that it occurs not between two but inside one and the same person and splits that individual in half.

To the objection so interpreted one could retort:

1. To imagine that the conflict divides (or alienates) the person shows that a metaphor has been read too literally. In truth, all that can be asserted is that the two rights have their grounds in two different attributes of man (whether this is self-consciousness, the capacity to be self-forming, or some other quality that generates all of man's moral being does not affect the issue) and that it is of course the case that man cannot be both completely free and completely equal. But clearly the conflict between these rights does not tear the individual apart, and it in not way suggests that man cannot quite comfortably possess both of these attributes on which these right are founded.

2. It certainly is not flatly self-evident that freedom and equality really are "radically" or totally set against each other. Not every increase in equality comes at the expense of a decrease in freedom; some equalities that we receive make us simultaneously more free, and clearly some of our democratic freedoms are equalities at the same time. So the relationship between freedom and equality is far more complicated and surprising then the image of a teeter-totter would suggest, and the degree to which they really do conflict would still have to be established.

The objection that Professor Charvet (at least on my reading) really means to press can now be isolated. It charges that the theory cannot provide a reconciliation of the conflict we have been discussing. Some answers to this form of the objection might run as follows:

a. Even if the conflict were really "radical," one just conceivably could adopt the attitude that this does not so much count against the classical theory of human rights as it does against the hapless actual world. The point to be brought into the open is that this conflict does not constitute a logical "contradiction" or "incoherence" of the *theory*. Its meaning is merely that the claims of both rights cannot be fully satisfied, and someone simply could insist that the claims are nonetheless legitimate and that man does have these rights all the same. (Imagine someone saying to Kant that almost no one could ever perform an act from considerations of morality alone — and Kant responding that this merely proves that many men had never performed a single moral act in their entire lives.)

b. But one could also say that it is again a good stretch from the obvious that the theory must reconcile that conflict, that this obligation falls upon the theory, and that it is seriously flawed if it cannot perform this feat. We are back to the comparison to moral or even legal codes. Must the theory itself arbitrate the conflict, or could one not maintain that the adjudication of how the satisfaction of both these rights can best be maximized is a far more menial affair, that undeniably depends on no end of changing circumstances (we accept restriction on freedom, e.g., in times of war, etc.), and that this has to be left to all kinds of technicians but falls far below the tasks to which philosophers need to stoop?

c. Most directly, one could of course point out that the failure of Rawls's attempt at a reconciliation proves very little, that the conflict is actually reconciled in all sorts of specific ways, through an unending process of pragmatic adjudication, so that when all is said and done there simply is no problem.

d. This still leaves out several other questions and objections, which we shall merely list. Is it to start with clear that anyone *has* a right to "complete" equality or "complete" freedom, and could anyone specify at all clearly what (in heaven's name) this means? Can these rights really be derived, not just from the attributes of human beings mentioned by Professor Charvet, but from any facts at all concerning human nature? What in the end is the logical connection between being self-forming and having a *right* to freedom?

Yet there is still another, deeper meaning that one might attach to the notion of this conflict between equality and freedom, though this third level is not touched in Professor Charvet's essay. Here the affinity to some Hegelian ideas becomes pronounced. The issue might be neither the sheer existence of the conflict nor the claim that the theory itself does not provide a basis for the adjudication. At stake might be instead a cardinal claim sometimes advanced in the name of liberalism. Very briefly, the idea is that it is in the very nature of rights (not of a theory of rights, but of rights themselves) to dissolve conflicts; that rights are designed to give moral and rational definition to the claims each individual has, so that disputes no longer need to be settled through violence and force but can now be arbitrated through arguments and words. The transformation of social life from a war into a calm discourse is thus the envisioned hope. This, so one might say, is why any conflict between the right to freedom and to equality is far more serious than are similar conflicts in other moral or aesthetic theories, for if that clash exists, and if it cannot be rationally settled, then this expectation is in vain.

In response to this formulation one could ask: Is anything like this picture of the lamb reasoning with the lion really a condition that the institution of rights could bring about, or is this seventeenth-century arrogance and wishful thinking? No anthropologist examining the immensely complicated structure of rights and privileges in tribal or communal cultures would, I think, get the impression that this is their function or their highest goal. On the contrary, one easily could turn the tables and dream up an exact reversal: among animals conflicts take place on the plain of force, and there a pecking order relatively soon reduces open battles to a minimum. Rights represent a new dimension that cuts across the biological with the effect that very often the less powerful feel nonetheless entitled to large dues and that duality and crossed-purposeness, far from abolishing conflicts, actually protracts them and renders them interminable.

If one chose to one could add that the constitutional enactment of our basic rights runs parallel to this development, that here too the indignation of the oppressed was placed on a new foundation, and that this also did not resolve the existing conflicts but, on the contrary, gave them more fuel. It is thus quite true that neither the theory of rights nor rights themselves have either the capacity to dissolve conflicts nor to raise them from a physical to a rational and moral level. Yet to concede this in no way admits that either the theory of rights or the concept of rights is bankrupt or beside the point. It merely means that one pretension which should never have been raised has now been dropped.

So far we have tried to show that the objection Professor Charvet brought against the theory of rights, that equality and freedom are in conflict with each other, does not possess much force. Yet it does seem to me that there are several other serious criticisms to which the theory as conceived traditionally is really vulnerable, and these should be made.

The first of these concerns the meaning of the right to freedom. If one introduces the idea of obstacles, one question presents itself at once, namely whether the right to freedom grants that one can pursue one's own values (or wants or pleasures or whatever) without having to face any obstacle at all, or whether it alternatively vouchsafes only that one of course can do these things, though perhaps only in the face of almost insuperable difficulties. Clearly, the second would be a too easy empty promise, and the first holds out far more than any social system can ever hope to keep. How could anyone ever guarantee that nothing will stand in my way? Yet this is precisely the expectation the word "freedom" raises, and if so the promise of a right to freedom will often be deceptive.

A second problem can here be only touched; it concerns the relationship that rights have to institutions. The theory of rights generally has assumed that our basic or natural rights constitute a standard against which social arrangements, and above all the state, can be assessed. (This is still done by Rawls and Nozick.) But there is another, quite different way in which one can think about rights: in the family we all have very many rights that entitle us to a great deal. My children can expect much support and even help with their college education, and I think this is their right and my obligation. But they expect of course much less from the most remote stranger, though they of course still have claim to some minimal consideration. So one can imagine a set of concentric circles: the most abstract and universal rights are also the weakest (the largest and thinnest circles); they represent the minimum that every human being owes to every other. As we move progressively toward the more specific and concrete, from mankind to the state, to a city, to a university, to one father and one daughter, the rights by degrees become more numerous and stronger.

Against this backdrop two thoughts can now be quickly sketched. For one, the theory of rights has always been almost exclusively preoccupied with the damage that the *state* might do to our rights. But the wealth of rights that existed in most prepolitical cultures were largely destroyed by a set of forces quite *different* from the state—primarily by the powers of technology and of industrialization. In many so-called primitive societies everyone has a right to sustenance.

We did not lose this right because the state became too strong. That right disintegrated when the communal culture broke apart. So the theory of rights stood guard against the state at the front door while a different set of thieves carried our rights out through the kitchen and back porch.

In the second place, the theory of rights may have been far too modest in its demand that our natural rights must be preserved. Our natural rights may well be very flimsy, but in tribal cultures we were protected by a host of rights. So why should we not have far more in the state than we possess by nature? To measure the state against our natural rights is a little like being satisfied with our schools because they do not increase the natural ignorance of our children by too much. Why not rise from the poverty of the minimal state and demand a set of institutions that will compensate us for the rights we once possessed but that we lost as we became a mobilized and modern culture?

My third disagreement with the theory of rights as we have known it is still more drastic. Should one really endeavor to derive rights, not just from human nature, but should they be derived at all? My concern is not only that one may have to leap over gaps from "is" to "ought" in this procedure. Rather, I wonder whether we must lay down certain rights in the beginning as if they were axioms and must then go on in a more or less deductive manner? Why not reverse the picture and move upward from below?

If we start from a basic right to freedom or to equality we may be asked to prove their existence. But that is difficult, for although we know how to prove the existence of black swans, what are the criteria that settle disputes over the "existence" of a right? Yet what hope is there to lay a firm foundation if even the criteria by which the basic building blocks are to be measured are mired in deep controversy? Why not say instead that we were of course to begin with swamped in inequality and unfreedom and that our rights are specific social measures designed, step by step, to bring about some delimited respects in which we will be somewhat free and a bit more equal?

To thus construe rights not as first postulates but to see in them instead one set of tools in a not very systematic, piecemeal, and haphazard struggle against outrage and indignity—that not only measures the distance we must travel from the traditional theory of rights but at the same time gives us a first outline of the different and new theory of rights we must construct.

4

TALENT POOLING
ANTHONY T. KRONMAN

At several points in *A Theory of Justice,* John Rawls suggests that the difference principle represents "an agreement to regard the distribution of natural talents as a common asset and to share in the benefits of this distribution whatever it turns out to be."[1] Put differently, Rawls views the principle as expressing a commitment to the idea that individual talents and capacities should be treated as part of a common fund or pool from which each has the right to draw an equal share, regardless of what his own endowment happens to be (the only exception being where everyone can be made better off if some are given larger shares than others). I shall refer to this idea as talent pooling.

Whatever its philosophical merits, the idea of talent pooling is surely one of the least intuitive features of Rawls's theory of justice, and indeed seems inconsistent with the considerable freedom normally allowed individuals—both by the law and customary morality—in exploiting their own natural gifts. To be sure, we all recognize limits on the use a person can make of his talents or natural capacities. Those with physical strength, for example, are not at liberty (in either a legal or a moral sense) to exploit their natural superiority by simply taking what they wish from the weak. Talent pooling goes well beyond anything these limitations require, however, and imposes a positive duty to share the whole sum of one's talents (or more precisely, the opportunities and advantages they represent) with the other members of society. Perhaps because the idea of talent pooling is so counterintuitive, Rawls never develops its implications in detail, and although he explicitly argues that the difference principle applies to natural as well as social inequalities,[2] he largely restricts his own discussion in *A Theory of Justice* to inequalities of the latter sort.[3]

Despite the fact that it lacks intuitive appeal, the idea of talent pooling nevertheless follows in a natural way from the premises of Rawls's theory. It is also an idea of practical significance: recent statutes such as the Architectural Barriers Act[4] (which requires various structural modifications in buildings to make them accessible to the handicapped) evidence some acceptance of the idea that a person's natural abilities and disabilities should be treated as part of a common fund in which all share equally. To a lesser extent, the same can be said of our progressive income tax, since a person's income is partly a function of his talents. In short, the idea of talent pooling occupies a prominent place in both the theory and the practice of the modern welfare state.

This paper explores the idea of talent pooling in greater detail. In the first part, I attempt to set out a Rawlsian argument for talent pooling and to show the connection between this idea and the elementary principles on which Rawls's theory of justice rests. I call the argument Rawlsian to indicate that although it captures the main features of Rawls's own view, it is never presented by Rawls himself in precisely the form in which I present it here. In the second part, I consider a variety of practical objections to talent pooling, objections based on the difficulty of actually implementing such a program, and conclude that these objections show talent pooling to be impracticable on anything but a limited scale but do not demonstrate its defectiveness as a moral ideal. In the third and final part of the chapter, I describe the conception of the self that I believe underlies the idea of talent pooling and argue that this conception is too simple and ignores an important dimension of personal identity. Although I do not reject the idea of talent pooling entirely, I conclude that there are moral and not merely practical reasons for limiting the socialization of individual capacities that talent pooling requires.

I. THE ARGUMENT FOR TALENT POOLING

Rawls imagines the principles of social justice to be the solution to a choice problem presented to individuals in what he calls the original position. As Rawls recognizes, the moral legitimacy of the principles adopted in the original position depends entirely upon how the original position itself is described. The most important feature of Rawls's description is the so-called veil of ignorance. The veil of ignorance operates as a filter or screen on the sorts of information available to persons in the original position and establishes the background against which their choice of principles is to be made.

As Rawls conceives it, the veil of ignorance is not merely a mechanical device but expresses a moral ideal as well. According to Rawls, the veil screens out information that ought not to be considered in arranging the basic structure of society, allowing to pass through only those facts that *are* relevant from a moral point of view. In this respect, the veil of ignorance performs both a negative and a positive function: the former by eliminating considerations that have no moral relevance to the problem at hand, the latter by focusing our attention more sharply on those considerations that do.

Among other things, the veil of ignorance screens out all information regarding the natural endowments of those in the original position. Rawls's view, stated repeatedly throughout the book, is that the advantages and disadvantages of natural endowment are distributed in a way that is morally meaningless, since no one can ever give a justification for the distribution that actually exists (at least without making strong theological assumptions).[5] Rawls several times compares the distribution of natural talents to a lottery,[6] in which, of course, no one has participated voluntarily. Since a person's natural endowment is wholly arbitrary, it cannot by itself provide a morally acceptable justification for either increasing or decreasing his share of the goods whose allocation is to be determined by the principles of social justice. Consequently, according to Rawls, a person's talents should not be permitted to influence his choice of a basic social structure, and the veil of ignorance, in its negative aspect, assures that they will not.

The positive function of the veil is more difficult to describe. Lowering the veil of ignorance leaves individuals in the original position with very little information about themselves or the society they are to enter. Certain facts about the nature of human behavior and social organization pass through the veil, but these general facts do not permit individuals in the original position to distinguish themselves from one another or to choose principles adapted to their own natural endowment or plan of life.

In addition, and more importantly, the veil of ignorance does not deprive those in the original position of the knowledge that they are beings of a particular sort, beings with a capacity for forming a conception of the good (expressed in more or less abstract terms) and en-

dowed with a sense of justice.[7] Put differently, individuals in the original position know that they all have certain general capacities, but
none know how these capacities have been (or will be) actualized in
their own case. This expresses Rawls's deep conviction that an individual's right to insist upon fair treatment from others derives entirely from the fact that he is a being endowed with these general
powers or capacities and does not depend upon the particular way in
which he chooses to exercise them.[8] It follows that in assessing the
justice of a society's basic structure, only one characteristic of its individual members is relevant from a moral point of view — the equal capacity of each to frame and then pursue a conception of the good.
This, or something like it, is the positive core of Rawls's moral theory, an idea he frequently expresses in shorthand form by describing
the veil of ignorance as a way of representing the freedom and equality of persons generally.[9] Rawls himself, of course, explicitly associates this notion with Kant's theory of moral personality.[10]

What does the Kantian idea of personality have to do with talent
pooling? One might think the connection between these two ideas is
an obvious one in light of Rawls's assertion that individuals choosing
principles of justice behind the veil of ignorance would choose his two
principles — the second of which he interprets at an agreement to
treat individual talents as the common property of society. However,
Rawls's derivation of the difference principle is based almost entirely
upon the self-interest of those in the original position and consequently fails to illuminate the moral argument for talent pooling and
its relation to the principle of equal respect for persons.

In fact, an argument of this sort is more difficult to construct than
one might suspect. As I have already indicated, the aim of talent
pooling is to equalize the share of each individual in the fund of resources represented by the sum of everyone's natural endowment.
Since the talents a person has influence his chances of achieving his
ends or plan of life, pooling may be viewed as a way of equalizing the
chances or opportunities of different individuals — their chances for
happiness, if we equate happiness, as Rawls does,[11] with the achievement of one's ends. But what is the moral justification for requiring
equality in this respect? The idea that all individuals are free and
equal persons does not by itself entail that they also have a moral
right to equal opportunities for happiness. Indeed, if a person's
chances for happiness are largely determined by factors, including
his natural endowment, which have no significance from a moral

point of view, it might seem that any distribution of such chances, including the one resulting from the natural lottery, would be consistent with the moral equality of persons and that a redistribution
through talent pooling could only change things but not improve
them in any morally relevant respect. [12]

In fact, Rawls's argument for talent pooling cannot be derived
solely from the principle that all individuals are entitled to equal respect as moral agents. To construct an argument for pooling, the
Kantian principle of equal respect must be supplemented by a second principle, drawn from a different philosophical tradition and
most clearly evident, in Rawls's own writings, in his discussion of the
nature of the good in the third part of *A Theory of Justice.* Stated
simply, this second principle is that happiness (which Rawls conceives, in a rationalistic fashion, to consist in the achievement of
one's ends) is an intrinsic good, something good for its own sake and
not merely because it leads to or promotes some other state of
affairs. [13] The notion that happiness has intrinsic worth is a key premise of Rawls's theory of the good and conflicts sharply with the
view, expressed by Kant, [14] that nothing can be good in itself except a
good will.

Despite its un-Kantian flavor, however, there is no inherent conflict between Rawls's second principle and the idea of a natural lottery that he uses to explicate his (Kantian) conception of the moral
equality of persons: the latter idea is merely a way of emphasizing the
lack of any moral justification for the difference in natural starting
points that gives some a greater chance for happiness than others; it
implies nothing about the status of happiness itself, about the *kind* of
good it is. Indeed, Rawls's second principle, that happiness is an intrinsic good, is not only consistent with the principle of equal respect
for persons but is in an important sense prior to it. It is this priority
that must be grasped if the moral argument for talent pooling is to be
understood.

Happiness, according to Rawls, consists in the achievement of
one's own ends, in their *actual* fulfillment. But it is the capacity to
formulate ends and design a plan of life—the *potential* for happiness, or at least happiness of a particular sort—that in Rawls's view
makes one a moral being—and establishes the equality of persons. If
one attaches moral significance, as Rawls does, to a capacity for the
kind of happiness that is achieved by fulfilling one's ends—if one
thinks of being endowed with such a capacity as subject to special

rights and duties— then it would seem that moral significance must also be attached to the condition for which this is a capacity, that is, to happiness itself.

But if this is so, then it must matter from a moral point of view whether a person is happy in Rawls's sense of being "in the way" of successfully executing his plan of life. *A fortiori,* it must also be a matter of moral concern whether a person has many or few opportunities for happiness and therefore how the various things that determine his chances for happiness are distributed. In short, if one defines a person as a being who can form a plan of life and be made happy by its achievement, the distribution of those instrumental goods that determine a person's chances of success itself becomes a moral problem, a problem that requires a solution acceptable from the moral point of view.

From a moral perspective, however, there is only one permissible answer to the question, How should opportunities for happiness be distributed among different individuals? Any principle of distribution must point to or invoke some morally relevant characteristic of the individuals involved, and on Rawls's view the only characteristic of this sort is the capacity to form and pursue a conception of the good. Since each person possesses this capacity to the same extent as every other (ignoring the complications raised by infancy and insanity), the only reason a person can give for having a right to participate in the distribution of opportunities is a reason everyone else can give as well. Consequently, one person's claim to a share is as strong as another's, and the only distribution that will not result in the unjust preferment of some is a distribution that assigns equal shares to all (with the uncontroversial proviso that inequalities will be allowed if they work to everyone's benefit). Any other distribution must involve differences in treatment that cannot be justified on moral grounds. From this general argument, the principle of talent pooling immediately follows, since a person's talents are one of the things that determine his chances of fulfilling his life plan. (The same argument also implies that political rights should be distributed equally, since these, too, are of instrumental value in pursuing one's conception of the good.)[15]

To summarize: Rawls's argument for talent pooling combines two different principles. The first, which Rawls associates with the Aristotelian tradition in moral philosophy,[16] is that happiness is an intrinsic good and consists in the fulfillment of a person's plan of life.

The second, claimed to be of Kantian derivation, is that a person's capacity to form such a plan is almost wholly independent of his natural endowment and alone establishes his status as a moral being and his right to be treated fairly by others. By dissociating this capacity from an individual's natural endowment, Rawls distinguishes his own theory of moral personality from Aristotle's;[17] by defining it as a capacity to form a conception of the good — and not merely as a capacity to act rationally, that is, in accordance with the conception of a rule — Rawls differentiates his theory from Kant's.[18] His peculiar combination of Kantian and Aristotelian premises, reflected in the argument for talent pooling, gives Rawls's theory of justice its distinctive character and represents an important and original contribution to moral philosophy.

II. PRACTICAL DIFFICULTIES

I want now to consider some practical difficulties that any attempt to implement the principle of talent pooling would be likely to involve. Although some of these difficulties are serious, they do not, in my view, point to a moral infirmity in the idea of talent pooling itself but merely suggest that its application may be more limited than one might think. Before discussing these genuine difficulties, however, I would like to dispose of two unpersuasive objections to talent pooling, each of which is misguided in a different respect.

The first objection, developed by Robert Nozick and derived from Locke's theory of property rights,[19] is that talent pooling necessarily violates people's entitlements by forcibly depriving them of the right they have to their own natural capacities. On Nozick's view, the fact that attributes come into the world already tied to particular individuals gives those individuals a proprietary interest in the attributes they happen to possess, an interest that legitimates their exploitation of the attributes for their own personal benefit. This is a conclusory argument, however, that assumes what is in question — whether individuals do in fact have the right to exclude others from the enjoyment of their own natural gifts. The appeal of the argument derives from our tendency to conflate possession and ownership. For example, if we see a cow in Smith's pasture, we are inclined to assume that the cow belongs to Smith and that it would be wrong for Jones to take it. But if we are told that Jones has temporarily left the cow with Smith, or has purchased and paid for it, we view the situation differently: although Smith happens to possess the cow, he does not own it—Jones does. Possession and ownership are, so to speak, divided between the parties.

The concept of talent pooling invites us to think about individual attributes in the same way. Although a person obviously possesses his own attributes, it does not necessarily follow that he is also their owner, with the right to exploit them, within limits, for his own benefit. It is the law's protection that transforms a possessory interest into a proprietary one, and the principle of talent pooling simply denies that a person ought to be given a protected interest of the latter sort in his own talents and capacities. To pursue the legal analogy one step further, the pooling idea requires us to view every individual as a kind of trustee, who holds his own attributes for the benefit of the community as a whole and who owes to his fellow citizens a fiduciary duty to manage his talents in accordance with the conditions of the trust, that is, in accordance with the principles of social justice that define what share each member of society is to have in the talent pool—in Rawls's theory, in accordance with the difference principle. In the first part of this chapter, I presented a Rawlsian argument for talent pooling. However great its inadequacies, the argument cannot be disposed of by simply asserting that the possession of one's natural talents implies their ownership as well.

A second objection to talent pooling that may be summarily dismissed turns on the impossibility of actually redistributing natural capacities, of transferring them from one individual to another. If Jones has an excess of musical talent and Smith a surplus of brains, no transfer will make Jones smarter and Smith a better pianist: however unfair it may be that each enjoys the particular advantages he does, there is no way (yet) of reshuffling the deck so as to equalize the distribution of desirable attributes. This objection, however, misconceives the nature of the redistribution a pooling program would entail. Treating Jones's talent as a communal asset does not mean that the talent itself must somehow be carved up into portions and distributed to the members of Jones's community (how could this be done?), but only that Jones must be prohibited from exploiting his gifts in a way that does not benefit others equally—that he must be prohibited, in other words, from selfishly using his own talent to make himself better off than his neighbors. The object of pooling is not to achieve an equal distribution of attributes but rather to equalize the advantages and disadvantages that result from the natural endowments different individuals happen to have. This requires only that

the well endowed make a compensatory payment of some sort to the
handicapped — a payment that may take the form either of a direct
income transfer or a transfer of in-kind services. A compensatory
payment of this kind of course represents only a second-best solution:
it may be that no income transfer from Jones to Smith will ever enable Smith to realize his dream of becoming a concert pianist (something Smith might be able to do if we could simply give him a portion
of Jones's talent). But it does not follow from the fact that we cannot
redistribute talents themselves that we should not require the well endowed to share the benefit of their talents by making a compensation
payment to those who have been less fortunate in the natural lottery.
In essence, then, what pooling requires is a system of forced transfers
(a tax system) that will counterbalance the effect of the initial and arbitrary distribution of talents among individuals.

Since, as a practical matter, talent pooling represents nothing
more than a system of taxation, it is not surprising that the difficulties involved in its implementation can all be characterized as problems concerning the design of an appropriate tax scheme (problems
already familiar, in other contexts, to welfare and public finance
economists).[20] The first of these difficulties concerns the definition of
fair shares in the talent pool: how much must the well endowed be required to give up before the overall distribution of benefits and burdens may be characterized as a fair one? It will not do, of course, simply to maintain people at the same (money) income level, since the
well endowed can do more with their dollars than those who are
poorly endowed. The only truly fair distribution is one that equalizes
the cost to every individual of achieving some specified set of ends — a
distribution that is likely to entail considerable inequality in the dollar incomes of different persons. But which ends would these be?
They cannot be simply the ends that people in fact choose to pursue,
since some may deliberately choose costly ends in order to claim a
disproportionate share of their society's wealth. In establishing a
standard by which to measure the fairness of a particular distribution, it makes more sense to select a set of ends — for example, the
achievement of a certain minimum level of physical health and the
acquisition of basic skills like reading and writing — that are likely to
be prerequisites for the fulfillment of almost any plan of life.[21] One
might then say that a distribution is fair if it equalizes the cost of
achieving these ends. Of course, this measure is a rough one and will
not equalize the cost of achieving higher-order ends (like becoming a

concert pianist), but it does provide a sufficiently workable standard to permit talent pooling on a limited scale.

A related difficulty—although one that it may be misleading to characterize as practical in nature — concerns the shares of the acutely disadvantaged.[22] If applied uncompromisingly, the principle of talent pooling would require that enormous resources be devoted to the care and education of the most severely handicapped individuals, leaving little for the better-endowed members of society. Although there may be no moral justification for stopping short of the strictly egalitarian regime that talent pooling requires (even if such a regime would result in a very low level of well-being for everyone), it is unlikely, for both political and psychological reasons, that any society would ever pursue the principle of talent pooling to this extreme. It is possible, however, to limit the principle's reach by placing a ceiling on the subsidy payment any individual is allowed to receive. A limited redistributive scheme of this sort (similar, in many ways, to the idea of a guaranteed minimum income) would represent an important step toward achievement of the moral ideal expressed by the pooling concept while avoiding the embarrassment caused by the claims of the acutely disadvantaged.

A third difficulty in redistributing benefits to compensate the poorly endowed for their disadvantages involves the measurement of income received by those with wealth-generating attributes. Not all of the income that Jones receives from his musical talent comes in the form of money: Jones's wealth is also increased by the admiration and respect he receives from others and by the pleasure he takes in the exercise of his own capacities (a pleasure that may be more intense than other people's precisely because of his greater gift for musical expression). Since these, too, are benefits that flow from his natural endowment, an ideal pooling scheme would require that Jones share them as well—would require, in other words, that they be included in his income for purposes of determining what tax Jones should pay into the fund for the naturally disadvantaged. (The same is true of the man whose physical attractiveness significantly increases his erotic opportunities: whether he exploits it or not, an advantage of this sort should also, in principle, be taxed.)

In most instances, however, the cost of identifying and measuring these hidden forms of income will be prohibitive—largely because the party receiving it is the only one in a position to say how much income he has actually received.[23] Unless the tax collector has a pleasure meter that can be attached to the back of Jones's head, there is no way in which he can accurately measure the amount of pleasure that Jones receives from his own playing (or anything else for that matter), a difficulty that is aggravated by the fact that Jones will have an incentive to conceal whatever pleasures he does experience and thus avoid taxation. Consequently, absent a technology that would permit the measurement of things like pleasure or respect, individuals who have attributes that produce pleasure and command respect will receive income that escapes taxation and hence makes them better off than their less well endowed neighbors. It only follows from this, however, that there are limits (in this case, technological limits) to pooling and that some important inequalities cannot be eliminated by even the most thorough pooling program.

An especially interesting aspect of the problem of measuring income concerns the individual who possesses a talent but refuses to utilize it. Suppose that Jones, despite his musical gifts, wants only to be an automobile mechanic. If Jones forgoes the opportunity to give concerts in order to pursue a career as a mechanic, the income he receives as a mechanic must exceed his expected income as a musician, even though it takes a different form (immediate pleasure in the performance of the activity rather than dollars). Ideally, assuming we could measure it accurately, Jones should be taxed on his true income: if the tax exceeds the small salary Jones makes as a mechanic, then Jones must choose between refusing to pay the tax (a crime, let us assume, for which he will be imprisoned) and changing careers. Although Jones may regard this as a harsh choice, it is perfectly appropriate, from a moral point of view, that he be required to make it. If Jones's musical talent really belongs to the community as a whole, then it is just as clearly an act of theft for Jones to refuse to perform as it would be for him to perform, and refuse to share the proceeds.[24] The only thing that distinguishes these two cases is the relative cost of preventing each sort of theft. If Jones can conceal the fact that he has any musical talent, it may be prohibitively expensive for society to determine how much real income he receives from being an automobile mechanic. By contrast, if he openly exploits his gifts, by giving concerts and piano lessons, the difficulties of measuring his income and deciding what tax he should pay are not likely to be as severe.

An opponent of pooling is certain to point out, however, that if Jones knows in advance that his income from concerts and lessons will be taxed away, he may have an incentive to devote himself to other activities — like repairing automobiles — and to deliberately conceal his musical talents. If this is true, and if Jones will be socially more productive as a musician than as a mechanic, in order to give him an appropriate incentive to utilize his most valuable skills, it may be necessary to reduce the tax on the income he receives from giving concerts. Quite clearly, this will require society to tolerate an inequality that has no moral justification, since Jones is in a position to insist upon preferential treatment only because he can control the flow of information about his own attributes and determine their use. (If Jones's talents are readily apparent to everyone, he can simply be ordered to perform and, if he refuses, prohibited from doing anything else. Although it may be impossible to make Jones play as well as he is able, he will have a strong incentive to give at least the appearance of doing so if the alternative is imprisonment.)[25]

Nevertheless, even if Jones must be given a morally unjustified advantage in order to induce him to reveal his talents, it would be irrational to deny him preferential treatment if he can make a greater contribution to the wealth of society by giving concerts than he can by repairing cars. If things can be arranged so that citizens less well endowed than Jones benefit from this increase in social wealth (something that may itself require a fairly complicated system of transfer payments), both Jones and his disadvantaged comrades will be better off than they would otherwise be — although the difference in their relative prosperity may now be even greater than it was before. Assuming the gain they realize from Jones's special treatment is not offset by feelings of envy, the poorly endowed members of Jones's society should prefer this distribution to a more strictly egalitarian one and there is no reason why their preference should be ignored.

A fourth difficulty in implementing the idea of talent pooling is linked to the questionableness of an assumption, implicit in all I have said so far, regarding the nature of human talents. In my discussion, I have assumed a talent to be a kind of capital asset that generates a stream of income over a period of time, talent pooling being merely a scheme for diverting this income stream to other, less well endowed members of society. This image is a misleading one, however. Most talents require time and effort to develop: they are not assets that are fully in place from the moment of birth. Even if Jones enjoys a natural gift for music, evident from his earliest days, his musical skills will not have blossomed overnight or without deliberate cultivation.

Jones's developed abilities (which are of course what people admire and pay to hear him exercise) are attributable, in part, to his native gifts, but also, in part, to the investment he has made in developing them and to character traits like perserverance and ambition. However, if this is so, it would be unfair to make Jones share all of his income with those who are less fortunate: fairness requires that he share only that portion which can be attributed to his natural endowment. But is it ever possible to divide someone's income up in this way — assigning part of it to native gifts, and the rest to things like industry, ambition, and good luck? And, if not, isn't talent pooling a hopelessly impractical ideal?

Several considerations blunt the force of this objection to talent pooling. In the first place, it is by no means clear that character traits like patience and resoluteness — or even ambition, for that matter — ought not themselves to be treated as part of a person's natural endowment (or at least as the developed product of some innate and fixed disposition). If we view character traits in this way, then it is obviously possible to assign a larger share of any person's successes and failures to his native endowment and therefore to regard them as essentially undeserved. An advocate of pooling is likely to regard this conception of character traits as a mixed blessing, however. On the one hand, it reduces considerably the difficulty of determining what portion of a person's achievements may properly be attributed to his natural gifts; on the other hand, it threatens to make the concept of voluntary action unintelligible and thus to undermine the Kantian notion of individual autonomy on which the argument for talent pooling is based.

Second, even if Jones will be overtaxed in case he is made to share all of his measurable income with those who are less well endowed, this injustice is mitigated by the fact that Jones is also likely to receive various hidden benefits — such as the respect and admiration of others — which will escape taxation altogether. On balance, it is unclear whether Jones's own share of the total benefits generated by his endowment is likely to be larger or smaller than the share to which he is actually entitled (the share he would receive under a perfectly administered pooling program).

Finally, although it may be impossible to decompose a developed talent into its constituent parts (native endowment, industry, ambition, etc.), there are some attributes, such as the general soundness of a person's physical constitution, that can be determined at or shortly after birth and that profoundly affect the life chances of any particular individual: at the very least, pooling requires that the advantages and disadvantages that flow from the possession of attributes of this sort be evened out by compensatory payments to the handicapped. Although payments of this kind may carry us only a small way to the sort of pooling program that would fully embody our moral ideals, they do not require, for their justification, any subtle analysis of the factors contributing to human achievement. There is no excuse, a pooling advocate might argue, for refusing to take this first important step.

I have now considered a number of objections to the idea of talent pooling and have attempted to meet them in the way a proponent of the idea himself might. Although these objections require numerous practical concessions, none directly challenges the soundness of the moral conception that underlies the idea of talent pooling. It is true, an advocate of pooling might say, that people can conceal their talents or refuse to exercise them and that material incentives may be needed to draw them out; that we cannot easily determine how much of any achievement is attributable to a person's native gifts or monitor the income he receives in the form of respect and gratification; and that we will probably never be able to equalize the cost, to different individuals, of achieving various higher-order ends (like becoming a concert pianist). But, he would quickly add, all of these things are true only because we are human beings with limited capacities of understanding and sympathy, and it would be a mistake to abandon our effort to redress the capricious inequities of the natural lottery simply because some unfairness is bound to remain.

III. TALENT POOLING AND PERSONAL INTEGRITY

Whatever its practical limitations, the idea of talent pooling expresses a powerful moral vision that may be derived, as I have attempted to show, from attractively simple premises. However, despite its appeal, Rawls's argument for talent pooling implicitly presupposes a conception of the self that in my view fails to reflect the complexity of the activity that Rawls himself places at the center of our moral life. In this section I shall develop and then criticize this conception of the self in order to show that there are moral, as distinguished from merely pragmatic, reasons for limiting the extent to which individual capacities may be treated as the common property of society.

According to Rawls, a person is entitled to respect as a moral agent because of his ability to frame and pursue a conception of the good. To have such an ability, however, a person must also have some distinguishing attributes of either a physical or psychological sort. If he lacked all such characteristics, a person could not reidentify himself from one moment to the next nor think of himself as following a rule over time—a thought entailed by any life plan regardless of its content.[26]

However, although a person must have some attributes that are uniquely his if he is to distinguish himself from other persons and know that he is following his own life plan rather than someone else's, the specific attributes that he happens to possess—his physical strength and appearance and the degree of his intelligence—have no bearing on his status as a person in the sense that he would be just as much a person, although a different one, if he had another set of equally determinate characteristics. On Rawls's view, someone is a person *with* a particular set of attributes; he is not a person *because* he has the attributes he does.

This conception of moral personality, which underlies Rawls's argument for talent pooling, imagines the self to be composed of two distinct parts.[27] One part of the self sets ends and decides which rules of conduct to follow. It is this choosing or planning part of the self that establishes a person's status as a moral agent entitled to respect and fair treatment from others. Everything else about a person—including his natural endowment—belongs to the second part of his self. This part of a person's self, unlike the first, has no bearing on his identity as a moral being: nothing belonging to the second part of his self can increase or decrease his stature as a person or affect his right to respect. The second part of a person's self does, however, contain resources, including his natural attributes, which the first or choosing part is likely to find useful in implementing the plans it adopts. The second part of the self is a storeroom to which the first part turns after it has chosen its ends and is searching for the means to achieve them.

If everyone had the same natural attributes—the same stock of storeroom goods—talent pooling would not be needed. But people do not have the same attributes and consequently some have a greater chance than others of realizing their conception of the good. To insure that all have a roughly equal chance of success, the arbitrary distinctions created by the natural lottery must be eliminated by a redistribution of opportunities from the well endowed to the handicapped. However, to think that such a redistribution will not violate the moral integrity of those whose attributes are being pooled, one must accept the concept of a bifurcated self—a self divided into one part that sets ends and another that contains the means to realize them. If one *does* believe the self can be divided in this way, pooling will not be thought to pose a threat to moral integrity, since it communalizes only that part of the self having nothing to do with an individual's status as a moral being. Put differently, if the self is assumed to be divisible into two independent and detachable parts, a person's natural attributes can be treated as the common property of his community without at the same time destroying his separate moral identity and transforming him into a dependent organ of society itself.[28] But if the concept or image of a bifurcated self is a misleading one—if the moral integrity of a person is built around and interwoven with his natural attributes in complex ways that this concept fails to express—it becomes much harder to see how an individual's attributes can be pooled without infringing his integrity as a moral being.

One respect in which the idea of a bifurcated self seems badly misleading concerns the role a person's natural attributes play in his choice of ends and design of a life plan. In fact, the ends a person chooses to pursue are often importantly influenced by the attributes he happens to possess. Because people generally find pleasure and satisfaction in exercising their capacities, a person's natural attributes are likely to play a significant role in determining which activities he enjoys and which he does not—and this, in turn, is likely to influence his choice of ends, since people also tend to value or esteem those activities they find the most enjoyable. It would be unusual, for example, if a person were to build his life around the pursuit of intellectual ends but have no aptitude for intellectual work himself. Although there are exceptions, those who attach a high value to thinking and devote themselves to it are more likely to be talented thinkers themselves and to find pleasure in exercising their intellectual skills (skills that must be ascribed, at least in part, to natural endowment). This, or course, is not to say that a person's choices are unalterably fixed by his natural constitution but only that his attributes provide the gravitational field within which he must work out his own personal destiny.

In addition to influencing his choice of ends, a person's attributes also function as means and can be used to realize whatever ends he may have chosen. The concept of a bifurcated self is plausible, however, only if we ignore the way in which a person's attributes help to determine his choice of ends and focus exclusively on their subsidiary role as means. But if someone's natural characteristics influence his values and ends in the way that I have suggested, it would be a mistake to consign them to the storehouse of means, to a part of the self that is wholly independent of the choosing or planning part and that can therefore be detached from it without violating a person's sense of identity or moral integrity. Instead of imagining an individual's moral personality to be localized in a part of the self whose integrity can be preserved even if we strip him of his natural characteristics, it is more appropriate to think of a person's autonomy (if I may use another spatial metaphor) as the interstitial space constrained by his attributes. Since they define the space in question, it is no more possible to deprive a person of his attributes while preserving his autonomy than it would be to remove the walls of a room without destroying the room itself.

At this point, a proponent of talent pooling is likely to caution us against the dangers of argument by metaphor and remind us that pooling is, after all, only meant to equalize the differential opportunities attributable to natural endowment — a redistributive program perfectly consistent with the view that an individual's ends are likely to be influenced by the particular characteristics he happens to possess. After all, he might say, the fact that a person's values are shaped by his native endowment does not automatically mean that he must be allowed to use his own attributes as he sees fit. It is true that if a person is permitted only a *pro rata* share of the benefits flowing from his talents, he may decide to pursue different ends than he would otherwise — but how, a pooling advocate might ask, does this infringe his autonomy or give him a claim to more than his fair share of the talent pool?

There are two reasons why the ultimate connection between a person's ends and his natural attributes should encourage us to proceed with caution in implementing the ideal of fairness expressed by the notion of a talent pool. In the first place, if ends and attributes are closely linked in the way I have suggested, there is reason to think that talent pooling will sometimes aggravate rather than cure the inequities of the natural lottery (or, more precisely, that it will merely substitute one inequity for another). Suppose that someone has an end that can be achieved only at great expense (he wants, for example, to achieve a high degree of self-awareness and believes this can be done only by undergoing a long and costly psychoanalysis). Suppose, in addition, that he also has a valuable talent (an operatic voice) that he would like to exploit in order to finance his own analysis. If he is allowed to keep for himself only a *pro rata* share of what he could earn by giving concerts, he may have to forgo more expensive pursuits (like psychoanalysis) in favor of less expensive ones. The fact that his means are limited may not alter his values and ambitions, but it is likely to influence which of them he elects to pursue, and if the ends our opera singer is required to abandon because of his limited budget are those he values most intensely, talent pooling is certain to make him less happy than he would be if he were free to exploit his capacities for his own benefit. To the extent that the singer's appetite for self-awareness has been shaped by his intellectual and somatic endowment, the unhappiness he experiences in being unable to achieve a valued end may just as legitimately be attributed to the accidents of the natural lottery as the unhappiness of those to whom the lottery has given insufficient means in the first place. The redistribution of opportunities achieved by pooling talents may ease the latter sort of unhappiness—but in some cases, only by increasing the former sort at the same time. For this moral dilemma to be visible at all, however, one must accept the notion that a person's attributes shape his ends as well as provide the means for realizing them.

A second reason we quite properly have reservations about talent pooling involves the important but elusive concept of personal integrity.[29] To a considerable extent, a person's identity depends upon the ends he chooses to pursue. By adopting a particular set of ends and integrating them in a coherent plan of life, a person acquires a character and thus a sense of his own integrity (i.e., some notion of which actions are—and which are not—consistent with his values and aspirations). Personal integrity is of great importance in our moral life, for without a sense of who he is, a person can feel shame, pride, responsibility, and accomplishment only to a diminished degree.

In my view, any attempt to implement the idea of talent pooling systematically would be likely to corrode individual integrity. Talent pooling is intended, of course, merely to equalize the means each individual has for pursuing his own freely chosen ends, and this might seem to be perfectly consistent with the view that a person's ends are themselves largely shaped by his attributes. But the argument for talent pooling assumes that a person's attributes are not really his own and do not form a part of his moral personality properly so called. If this is true, however, it is difficult to understand how a person whose talents have been pooled can be secure in believing that his ends are his own either — at least insofar as he is unable to dissociate his ends from the particular attributes he happens to possess. We can, of course, simply tell him that his ends *are* his own, however closely tied they may be to his natural characteristics, but reassurances of this sort are likely to be unconvincing when combined with a pooling program that treats these same characteristics as a collective asset belonging to no one in particular. For a person to have a sense of integrity, he must to some extent experience his own ends as constraints that limit what he can and cannot do. By encouraging people to think of their attributes as the common property of society, talent pooling is more likely to weaken than confirm this sense of constraint: if a person has no right to think of his characteristics as his own, what reason is there for him to feel bound by them or by the conception of the good from which they cannot be dissociated?

These considerations help to explain why we are likely to have equivocal feelings about any really significant effort to implement the idea of talent pooling. There is always a risk that pooling will create as many inequities as it eliminates; more important, when carried beyond a certain point, the socialization of individual attributes threatens to undermine the sense of personal integrity required for a fully developed moral life. It does not follow, however, as some libertarians maintain,[30] that no degree of coerced talent pooling is ever justified. Although I have attempted to point out the dangers associated with a redistributive program of this sort, I do think the basic idea of fairness underlying the notion of a talent pool retains much of its attractiveness even after these dangers have been taken into account. It is unfair that people's fates should be determined, to a considerable extent, by a natural lottery. The natural lottery offends us because it treats moral beings as if they were natural objects, and the idea of talent pooling represents an agreement (as Rawls might put it) to affirm our moral status in the face of nature's own indifference. Any attempt to do this, however, must also accept the fact that our moral personality cannot be neatly disengaged from the natural attributes that it is our accidental fate to possess. In this respect, the ambivalence we feel about talent pooling reflects a general tension inherent in the moral point of view: although morality requires us to look at human affairs from the timeless standpoint of reason itself, its prescriptions must somehow be accommodated to the contingent and irrational features of the human condition.

Of course, merely noting this general tension provides no guidance in determining the degree of talent pooling that can be justified on moral grounds. Perhaps a more developed theory of moral integrity — one that explained in greater detail how different sorts of attributes enter into the construction of an individual's moral personality, and how moral integrity is related to other dimensions of personal identity — would help us to decide how much and what kinds of talent pooling are morally acceptable. On the other hand, these may be questions that have only practical answers, toward which we must muddle without the guidance of any principles other than those of an unhelpfully general sort.

NOTES

* An earlier version of this paper was presented at a joint meeting of the American Political Science Association and the American Society for Political and Legal Philosophy, in New York City on August 31, 1978. I am grateful to Bruce Ackerman, Guido Calabresi, Joshua Cohen, Ruth Gavison, Paul Gerwirtz, Donna Patterson, Richard Posner, and Adina Schwartz for their helpful comments on a previous draft.

1. John Rawls, *A Theory of Justice* (Cambridge, Mass.: Harvard University Press, 1971), pp. 101, 107, 179, 278.
2. Ibid., pp. 72–75, 278.
3. In a recent paper, Rawls has retreated even further from the idea of talent pooling, but this represents, in my view, merely an ad hoc concession to his critics that Rawls cannot consistently make without reworking or at least elaborating the Kantian foundations of his theory. See John Rawls, "The Basic Structure as Subject," in A. I. Goldman and J. Kim, eds., *Values and Morals* (Dordrecht, Holland: Reidel Pub. Co. 1978), p. 65.
4. 42 U.S.C. §§ 4151–56, as amended March 1970 and October 1976. See also Rehabilitation Act of 1973, 29 U.S.C. §§ 701 et seq., as amended, November 1974 and March 1976.
5. Rawls, *A Theory of Justice,* pp. 72, 74–75, 100–103.
6. Ibid., pp. 74–75.
7. Ibid., pp. 12, 396–97.
8. Ibid., pp. 252–53. See also Rawls, "The Basic Structure as Subject,"

p. 63; Rawls, "Reply to Alexander and Musgrave," *Quarterly Journal of Economics*, 88 (November 1974): 639–43; and Rawls, "A Kantian Conception of Society," *Cambridge Review*, 96 (February 1975): 94–99.

9. Rawls, *A Theory of Justice*, pp. 252–53.
10. Ibid., pp. 251–57.
11. Ibid., pp. 409, 548.
12. This may have been Kant's view. See Immanuel Kant, *Critique of Practical Reason* (1788), ed. Thomas Abbott (London: Longmans, Green, Reader, and Dyer, 1873), pp. 126–27.
13. Rawls, *A Theory of Justice*, p. 549.
14. Immanuel Kant, *Fundamental Principles of the Metaphysic of Morals* (1785), ed. Thomas Abbott (London: Longmans 1873), p. 9.
15. Rawls, *Theory of Justice*, pp. 62–63.
16. Ibid., p. 549, n. 15.
17. Aristotle, *Politics* 126a 5–20, ed. Ernest Barker (Oxford, 1946), pp. 35–36.
18. Kant, *Fundamental Principles of the Metaphysic of Morals*, pp. 28–30.
19. See Robert Nozick, *Anarchy, State and Utopia* (New York, 1974), pp. 213–31; John Locke, *Two Treatises of Government* (1690), ed. Peter Laslett (Cambridge: Cambridge University Press, 1960), II, 27.
20. See, for example, Edmund S. Phelps, "Taxation of Wage Income for Economic Justice," *Quarterly Journal of Economics*, 87 (August 1973): 331–54; Robert Cooter and Elhanan Helpman, "Optimal Income Taxation for Transfer Payments Under Different Social Welfare Criteria," *Quarterly Journal of Economics*, 88 (November 1974): 656–70.
21. This is the role played by the notion of primary goods in Rawls's theory of justice. See *A Theory of Justice*, pp. 62, 90–95, and also John Rawls, "Fairness to Goodness," *Philosophical Review*, 84 (October 1975): 540–42.
22. This difficulty is discussed by Kenneth Arrow in "Some Ordinalist-Utilitarian Notes on Rawls's Theory of Justice," *Journal of Philosophy*, 70 (May 1973): 251.
23. For a general discussion of the ways in which control over information can facilitate opportunistic behavior, see Oliver Williamson, *Markets and Hierarchies: Analysis and Antitrust Implications* (New York: Free Press, 1975), pp. 31–37.
24. On this view, for example, it would be fair to tax a law professor on the income he could earn if he were engaged in the private practice of law. The dollar difference between what he actually earns and what he could earn is presumably smaller than the value a law professor attaches to his freedom and leisure: if he is taxed only on the salary he makes, he gets the latter benefits tax free.
25. See, for example, the famous case of the opera singer who refused to perform, *Lumley v. Wagner*, 1 DeG., M. & G 604, 42 Eng. Rep. 687 (ch. 1852).

26. See Peter Strawson, *Individuals* (London: Methuen Co., 1959), pp. 31-38.

27. Compare Kant's distinction between the autonomy of the pure will and the heteronomy of nature, *Fundamental Principles of the Metaphysic of Morals,* p. 73.

28. Rawls, in *A Theory of Justice,* criticizes utilitarianism for failing to take seriously the "distinction between persons" and for treating separate individuals as if they were "so many different lines along which rights and duties are to be assigned and scarce means of satisfaction allocated" (p. 27). Talent pooling is subject to the same criticism unless one assumes the self to be divided into two independent parts, in which case one part can be communalized without violating the distinctness of the other.

29. Others, like Charles Fried, have also argued that the notion of personal integrity requires us to think of individuals as the owners of their own capacities. See Charles Fried, *Right and Wrong* (Cambridge, Mass.: Harvard University Press, 1978), pp. 100-104. Fried, however, tends to view the argument for talent pooling (and its analogue in the economic theory of property rights) as an essentially utilitarian one and fails to appreciate that a justification for pooling can also be constructed from Kantian-Rawlsian premises. While Fried invokes the idea of personal integrity in his attack on talent pooling, his own theory of moral entitlements rests upon assumptions similar to those which I have attributed to the argument in favor of pooling. In this respect, although Fried and I arrive at similar conclusions, we do so by traveling along different routes.

30. Nozick, *Anarchy, State and Utopia,* pp. 172-73.

5

JOHN STUART MILL ON LIBERTY, UTILITY, AND RIGHTS

JOHN GRAY

I. MILL'S PROBLEM

According to a standard interpretation, the problem Mill poses in *On Liberty* is insoluble. Mill affirms that his aim there is to defend a single principle regulating interference with individual freedom of thought and action: "One very simple principle," as he famously puts it, "as entitled to govern absolutely the dealings of society with the individual in the way of compulsion and control."[1] His description of the principle that he seeks to defend as "entitled to govern absolutely" the liberty-limiting interferences of state and society with individual activity suggests that Mill intends the principle to be applicable exceptionlessly in all societies save those covered by his clause excluding "those backward states of society in which race itself may be considered as in its nonage."[2] In specifying the sorts of argument that he will adduce in justfication of assent to his principle, Mill declares that they will appeal only to utilitarian considerations: "It is proper to state that I forgo any advantage which could be derived to my argument from the idea of abstract right, as a thing independent of utility."[3] Those who uphold this common view are in no doubt that the enterprise to which Mill commits himself in these statements is so misconceived as to be virutally incoherent. Let us give this interpretation a good run for its money.

The Mill of *On Liberty* is a utilitarian attempting the impossible (but perennially attractive) feat of squaring the circle: his object is the thoroughly wrongheaded one of developing a utilitarian theory of moral rights, in which priority attaches to the right to liberty. Such an enterprise is doomed to failure for at least three major reasons. First, it is unclear how Mill can subscribe to two principles, each of which is supposed to make a strong claim on action, when one of them is stipulated to be the supreme principle in his theory of morality. As his own avowals make clear, the author of *On Liberty* subscribes to two principles or considerations, each of which is intended to supply a sufficient reason for acting, and to apply unabridged in the circumstance of a civilized society. What reason could there be for thinking of the values of liberty and happiness as being always complementary and mutually supportive, when naturally we think of them as rivals or competitors with one another in many of the dilemmas of civilized life? True, no formal inconsistency is involved in assenting to two exceptionless principles such as "Always act so as to maximise happiness" and "In the absence of harm to others, never restrict liberty." But Mill's problem is the hopeless one of showing how assent to one exceptionless principle (his principle of liberty) is dictated by adherence to another such principle (the principle of utility). After all, Mill has proclaimed himself a utilitarian: Why does he need an extra principle about liberty? Can he (more important) afford another? The object of Mill's inquiry, apparently, is a principle that, though *distinct* from the utilitarian principle, is in some sense an implication of it. The liberty principle cannot (it is supposed) be merely a *reiteration* of the principle of utility; if it were, it could not do the job Mill intends for it: it could have no bias in favor of liberty. Nor, so long as he retains his overall utilitarian commitment, can Mill's liberty principle have a force and weight that overrides its contribution to utility. But an exceptionless principle about the conditions under which liberty may rightly be limited will be extensionally equivalent with the principle of utility only on very questionable assumptions about the predictability and regularity of human affairs. On any realistically plausible view of man and society, serious disutilities must sometimes result from uncompromising adherence to such a principle. An exact coincidence of the predicates of the two principles must be judged to be marvelously unlikely. Given that his principles incapsulate distinct and sometimes divergent values, what reason could Mill give for refusing to allow his supreme principle to override the liberty principle wherever the two conflict? Even in the favorable circumstance of a civilized society, no utilitarian argument can adequately support political principles having a typical liberal force and content. Such principles characteristically assign a priority to liberty over all other political values, and they stipulate that the right to liberty belongs equally to all men. Now, if having a right means anything, it means being able to invoke a moral constraint on the pursuit of general welfare. Utilitarian arguments are always reversible, however: they will never give indefeasible support to liberal principles. Utilitarianism enjoins us to bring about the maximum good: What reason could we have for assenting to any principle that restricts us to the means we may adopt to achieve this end? For a utilitarian, according to G. E. Moore, "it must always be the duty of every agent to do that one, among all the actions which he can do on any given occasion, whose *total consequences* will have the greatest intrinsic value."[4] This is to say that, for a utilitarian, obligation and rightness are indistinguishable: the only duty anyone ever has is to bring about the best consequences. How can it ever be right for a utilitarian, then, to forgo the promotion of utility for the sake of liberty?

Second, whether utility be conceived in terms of attainment of some state of mind or in terms of the satisfaction of preferences;[5] utilitarianism cannot plausibly be supposed to embody any special tenderness toward liberty. The happiness of many men is bound up with the attainment of illiberal ideals, by which their preferences are informed and shaped, and policies guided solely by concern for the promotion of happiness or the satisfaction of preferences will not normally conform to liberal principles. Indeed, if liberalism is itself defined as a doctrine dictating that preferences be maximally satisfied, regardless of any ideals other than those expressed in men's preferences, then (as Barry, who conceives liberalism in this fashion, has perceived)[6] liberalism will have a self-defeating effect. How might Mill avoid the conclusion that liberty should be restricted, whenever this is necessary to satisfy preferences informed by illiberal conceptions of the good life? Only by redefining utility so that its promotion cannot conflict with respect for liberty. For, unless liberty and utility are one and the same, or liberty is given an infinite weight as one of the components of utility, a utilitarian cannot have sufficient reason for ascribing to liberty that absolute priority over other values that it enjoys in all liberal philosophies (whenever certain background conditions have been met). If utility is thus reinterpreted, however, it is hard to see how Mill can *argue for* adoption of liberal principles: his defense of them starts to look like a piece of circular reasoning. Or, if his reasoning lacks this character of circularity, then arguably Mill's appeal must finally be to a specific conception of personal excellence; but in this case, the neutrality often claimed for liberalism in respect of competing conceptions of the good life[7] is compromised, and Mill's liberalism might come to resemble the caricature of it elaborated by those who see him as a moral totalitarian.[8] A utilitarian argument can guarantee support for liberal principles, it seems, only at the cost of question-begging circularity, or, perhaps, of appealing to a partisan ideal of the good life.

Third, even supposing the previous objections could somehow be circumvented, it is plain that nothing in Mill's utilitarian argument allows him to give good reason why his liberty principle should be cast in a negative form licensing liberty limitation only in cases where "harm to others" is in question rather than in a positive form requiring that liberty be restricted whenever a net benefit will thereby result. And this is only a result of the crucial point, that the aggregative form of Mill's utility principle prevents it from supporting liberal requirements about the *distribution* of political goods. Mill cannot hope to show, for example, that basic civic and political rights are to be held equally by all; he cannot give good reason why the rights and interests of some should not be sacrificed if a gain to the general welfare can be produced in no other way. Mill's utilitarian commitment is in competition, not only with the priority he attaches to liberty, but with the value he attaches to the equal distribution of liberty and of other primary political goods. This is only to say that liberal principles cannot be supported adequately by appeal only to aggregative considerations such as those embodied in the principle of utility: Mill's liberalism, like any other, must embody a principle of justice. That Mill's overriding utilitarian commitment thus excludes any distributive principle of this sort serves to clinch the common argument that no utilitarian theory of moral rights is viable.

II. A REVISIONARY INTERPRETATION

This standard view endorses a number of commonplaces of political theory, and it draws on what John Rees has called "a common story"[9] about the history of nineteenth-century English political thought. It takes for granted that moral theories may be divided neatly into two categories, variously distinguished as teleological and deontological, goal-based and right-based, maximizing and side-constraint; that utility and justice represent incommensurable considerations, aggregative and distributive in character; that political principles may be seen as being either want-regarding or ideal-regarding, where these categories are supposed to be mutually exclusive and jointly exhaustive. It trades upon a conventional picture of the intellectual history of England in the nineteenth century, in which John Stuart Mill is seen as breaking out of the traditions of thought of which Bentham and his father were important members, but as never fully admitting to himself the extent of his apostasy. His thought is naturally viewed, then, as an eclectic mixture of ill-assorted elements, which tends to disintegrate under any sustained critical pressure. When Mill speaks of "utility in the largest sense," for example, it is standardly supposed that he invokes values to do with self-development and originality that can have no real weight within the utilitarian tradition. The moral theory presupposed by such statements, it is thought, must be what Rawls has termed[10] a perfectionist theory in which human excellence is valued even where its promotion competes with want-satisfaction. Alternatively, Mill's talk of the individual's sovereignty over what concerns himself is thought to endorse a theory in which moral rights rather than any teleological principle must be fundamental. Taken together, these truisms of political theory and of intellectual history support the view of John Stuart Mill as above all an eclectic and transitional thinker whose writings cannot be expected to yield a coherent doctrine.

One of my purposes in this section is to challenge some of these conventional assumptions. In doing so, I will draw upon, and in some areas criticize, a number of recent interpretations of Mill on liberty and utility, of which the interpretations of Ryan, Rees, Ten, Wollheim, Honderich, Williams, Brown, Lyons, Copp, Halliday, Sartorius, Spitz, Dryer, Friedman, and Berger are the most noteworthy.[11] It is common ground among the exponents of a revisionary view of Mill's moral and political thought that much of the argument of *On Liberty* turns on a set of distinctions, adumbrated there and elsewhere in the body of Mill's writings, between questions of justice, of obligation, and of rightness. Making sense of Mill's doctrine of liberty presupposes an understanding of the account of Art of Life set out in the *System of Logic*, in which the principle of utility figures, not as a moral principle from which may be derived in any very direct way judgments about the rightness of actions, but as a standard of assessment for all branches of human conduct. The principle of liberty, on the other hand, is a principle of critical morality, which has important (though often misunderstood) implications for the rightness and the justice of acts and rules. These two principles are of such different logical types that the relations between them cannot perspicuously be characterized in terms of extensional equivalence or inequivalence. Further, if Mill's principle of utility, unlike some classical variants of that principle, imposes no duty of maximization of value on moral agents, then no necessary inconsistency will be involved in assenting to it while yet demanding an equal distribution of the minimum conditions of the good life. Finally, Mill's argument in *On Liberty* can be shown to be closely related to the theory of justice contained in the crucially relevant last chapter of *Utilitarianism*. The main result of my own argument will be to support an interpretation of *On Liberty* in which it contains a coherent liberal doctrine of human rights. But I will indicate an area of difficulty for Mill's argument, even when so interpreted, in virtue of which it must fail to yield that definite yardstick, that "one very simple principle," of which he speaks.

In sympathy with the dominant tendency of recent revisionist Mill scholarship, much of my interpretation will stress the unity of Mill's thought. Just as his doctrine of liberty must be seen in the context of his theory of morality, so the theory of morality itself is to be viewed against the background of his account of practical reasoning. For Mill, moral reasoning is a species of practical reasoning, in that, though there can be no question of proof as demonstration, yet "considerations may be presented capable of determining the intellect either to give or withhold its assent" to moral and (in general) practical judgments. Mill's arguments for freedom of expression about questions of "morals, religion, politics, social relations, and the business of life"[12] presuppose much that is argued in the *System of Logic*, in which it is recognized that different modes of criticism and justification are appropriate in different areas of thought and practice. My conclusion will be that, though it does not in the end always specify one right answer to questions about when liberty is to be restricted, Mill's liberalism composes a consistent doctrine.

Having followed the revisionary interpretation thus far, I will point to a range of as yet unresolved difficulties it generates in the reconstruction of Mill's doctrine of liberty, and I will consider the differing ways in which some of the most important recent scholars and critics of Mill have confronted them. As I shall try to show, all the difficulties in the many variants of the revisionary interpretation turn on the relationship between utility and the principle of liberty. If the two principles are of such different logical types, how can the liberty principle be *based* upon (or derived from, or implied by) the utility principle? If the two principles are so categorically distinct that they can never be in competition with one another, how can one of them *support* the other? Just what claim *does* the utility principle make on action? Such questions open up the whole problem of the structure of Mill's utilitarianism. What place have moral and legal rules in Mill's utilitarianism? Is the act-and-rule terminology infelicitous when used to characterize Mill's utilitarian theory of morality and practice? Can Mill's utilitarianism steer safely between rule worship and rule-of-thumb approach to social norms? My discussion of these questions concludes with the assertion that, whether or not Mill's doctrine of liberty is in the end true, the structure of moral reasoning that my exploration of it has disclosed is wholly self-consistent and in some measure plausible.

Assessing the truth of Mill's doctrine of liberty forces us to face the question of how far it is corrigible and defeasible by experience. A key aspect of my interpretation is the claim that a complicated web of internal relations, both conceptual and logical, holds between the notions of liberty and happiness in Mill's thought. His doctrine of liberty is deeply embedded in his conception of happiness, and in his theory of human nature, and may not even be fully intelligible when wrenched out of this context. Perhaps, it will be objected, Mill's thought is in a dilemma here. For, whereas his doctrine will be trivialized if happiness and liberty are treated as interdefinable terms, a complete conceptual disserveration of them will render the doctrine's truth precariously dependent on a range of empirical claims about the social consequences of liberal principles. We need an account of the relations of liberty with happiness, it seems, that is neither too logically tight nor yet straightforwardly causal. I shall contend that the argument that Mill's doctrine encapsulates a trivializing conflation of liberty with happiness, or else embodies empirical claims that are probably false, fails to address Mill's outlook. Such an argument involves imputing to Mill an impoverished notion of necessity that was not his, that has little to be said for it, and that obscures much of the plausibility of his doctrine. In my interpretation of his argument, liberty will indeed be partially constitutive of happiness; but the connection Mill argues for between liberty and happiness will retain an empirical aspect, in virtue of which his doctrine remains criticizable by appeal to experience.

III. MILL'S UTILITARIANISM

Drawing on the contributions of Ryan and Dryer, D. G. Brown in an important paper[13] has reminded us that Mill viewed the principle of utility as a very abstract principle, governing not just morality but the whole of the Art of Life. Brown's conclusion is that "whatever the subject matter or Mill's principle might be, it . . . [is] not the rightness and wrongness of actions." For Mill utility is the supreme principle of appraisal of all aspects of life — "the test of all conduct" — and the principle of utility specifies that happiness is the only thing desirable as an end. Since moral appraisal is only one sort of appraisal of conduct, and morality is only one area of practice or art, the principle of utility cannot be treated as if its place in Mill's moral theory is that of a moral principle. Mill's argument in support of the distinction between utility and morality has several layers. In part it proceeds by way of an analysis of the principal moral notions, and presupposes neither utilitarianism nor any other sugstantive moral theory. In *Utilitarianism* he also argues, more positively, that an act cannot be shown to be wrong unless the institution of some sanction against it can be justified utilitarianly. Inasmuch as any legal or social restraint may be presumed to incur some disutility, there is, after all, a standing utilitarian reason against restraint. (Note that this weak or presumptive principle against limitation of liberty — "all restraint, qua restraint, is an evil" — is an implication of the utility principle itself. But, inasmuch as it attaches a value to want-satisfaction that is independent of its contribution to protecting the agent's interests, it also supports an antipaternalist principle.) Given the connection between morality and enforcement, Mill may regret and deplore failures to maximize utility without condemning them as moral faults. In this his theory of moral obligation resembles Hume's account of the artificial virtues in that it contains a utilitarian rationale for the protection of an area of moral indifference. Mill's account of moral rights and of the obligation of justice contains a recognition that direct appeals to utility may even be self-defeating. His discussion in the last chapter of *Utilitarianism* echoes Hume and anticipates later writers[14] in suggesting that a concern for best conse-

quences may dictate support for legal institutions and moral practices that constrain its direct expression.

A number of questions need answering, however, before we can be
satisfied that we have here an interpretation of Mill's theory of morality that yields a coherent and defensible view. What exactly are the
demands made on action by the utility principle as it has here been
construed? Mill's own statements ar not luminously clear: in the
opening pages of *Utilitarianism,* for example, he says within a single
paragraph that the principle of utility "holds that actions are right in
proportion as they tend to produce happiness, wrong as they tend to
produce the reverse of happiness"; and he later clarifies the "theory
of life" on which this "theory of morality" is grounded as specifying
that "pleasure, and freedom from pain, are the only things desirable
as ends."[15] Here Mill seems to be acknowledging the utility principle
as primarily axiological in character, while yet insisting that conclusions about actions somehow flow from it. The combination of these
two claims has spawned an enormous interpretive literature on the
question of the structure of Mill's utilitarianism. Now, while the
issues involved are complex indeed, and any Mill scholar must tread
particularly carefully in this area, it is not too much to claim that a
fairly clear outline of Mill's conception of morality emerges from recent studies, in which the combination of these two claims can be
seen as presenting no special difficulties. It should be clear, in the
first place, that, whatever it may be, the utility principle cannot in
Mill's account of it range solely over actions. As a principle specifying
what is of value in the world; it will serve as a standard of assessment
of states of affairs, even where nothing can be done to affect them.
(It would enable us to judge a state of affairs in which a solitary wild
animal dies slowly of a painful disease a bad state of affairs, though it
is one that no one's actions have produced or could conceivably
alter.) But second, in specifying happiness as the only thing having
intrinsic value, does not the utility principle entail that all reasons for
or against any act, rule, policy, or practice (for example) must have
to do with its contribution to happiness? If so, then the utility principle will entail another principle, invoked by Mill but not named by
him, which (following Brown and Lyons) it may be convenient to call
the Principle of Expediency: an act, say, is expedient if it brings
about a net utility benefit, and it is maximally expedient if it brings
about greater utility than any available alternative. An avowed utilitarian, then, indeed fails to live according to his utilitarian commit-

ment if he acts inexpediently, but it is the burden of Mill's theory of morality that the man who acts inexpediently does not necessarily act wrongly.

At this point in the exposition of the revisionary interpretation, however, a number of awkward questions cannot be avoided. Is it really the case that the expediency principle issues inexorably from the principle of utility? If so, then the sharp contrast implied by Brown and others between utility as an axiological and metaethical principle and liberty as a practical (action-guiding) principle is blurred. For, whereas the principles of utility and of expediency might not be *equivalent,* the expediency principle does seem to embody a maximizing approach to utility. In such a case, endorsement of the utility principle would appear to entail adoption of a maximization strategy about utility, and the ancient competition between utility and liberty reemerges as a contest between expediency and liberty. Any utilitarianly defensible principle about the restriction of liberty must be an application of the principle of utility itself, if the rivalry between liberty and utility is to be circumvented within the framework of Mill's doctrine. What we have here is none other than the traditional objection to Mill's enterprise in *On Liberty,* powerfully restated by Honderich. Speaking of what he characterizes as "*the* Utilitarian principle about intervention," Honderich observes that "there is little to be said for it. What I mean is that it is no advance on something we have been entertaining throughout these reflections. What we have come to is patently the Principle of Utility as applied to the question of intervention."[16] What can be said in rebuttal of this charge?

Two remarks are in order. First, it is not at all self-evident that the principles of utility and of expediency are as intimately related as most of the revisionary interpreters have assumed. They are plainly distinct principles, and, whereas it would indeed be odd if a principle about intrinsic value had *no* bearing on action, it is at least not obvious that anyone who accepts such an axiological principle is *thereby* committed to maximizing whatever the principle tells him has value for its own sake. He might treat such an axiological principle as framing the boundaries of permissable action, forbidding him from action that tends to diminish the amount of utility already in the world, but not enjoining him to increase it, still less to maximize it. In any case, the notion of intrinsic value is itself so opaque that no one can with complete confidence elicit practical maxims from metaethical principles of the sort we are considering. Second, however, Mill's doctrine of utility and morality surely comprehends *both* a hedonist theory of value and a consequentialist view of the rationality of action; whereas these are distinct commitments, it seems beyond reasonable doubt that Mill made each of them. It will not do to attempt to evade the force of Honderich's criticism by denying that utility imposes any rational demand of value-maximization on agents. Rather, we must note that it is precisely the doctrine of the Art of Life that a morality which is minimalist in that it is maximally permissive with respect to liberty will be most productive of utility.

How, then, is the area of morality and of moral obligation to be determined? First of all, I think, by applying the Principle of Expediency to the question of enforcement and punishability. An act is morally right, not if it is maximally expedient that it be done, but only if it is maximally expedient that its performance be enforced by penalties for noncompliance. It is worth noting that revisionary interpreters differ here as to whether Mill's theory of morality is act- or rule-utilitarian. Some, including Lyons,[17] argue that it cannot be act-utilitarian since Mill's theory explicitly denies that an act's being maximally expedient generates any moral obligation to do it. Brown, on the other hand, argues for Mill's act-utilitarianism, while some like Copp have insisted that Mill's moral theory cannot be captured in traditional terminology. At the nub of this controversy is a disagreement as to how the theory of the Art of Life is to be assessed for truth values. Is it primarily intended by Mill as an elucidatory exercise, a piece of conceptual analysis, or is it a revisionary proposal about how the term "morality" is to be used? I have said that it is a mixture of both conceptual and revisionary claims, but I wish now to claim that it is the latter that are dominant in Mill's account. Further, Mill's revisionary suggestions about the nature of morality are supported decisively by appeal to utility itself. Nothing in Mill's account distinguishes it fundamentally from that of a Sidgwick or a Smart, in whose writings a distinction is marked between what it is utilitarianly a good thing to do and what it is utilitarianly a good thing to commend. If I am right that the differences apparent between Mill's theory of the Art of Life and other utilitarian accounts of the rationality of action and of approval for action are mainly semantical and not substantive, then Mill's theory of morality is not only consistent with act-utilitarianism but indistinguishable from sophisticated versions of it.

Mill may escape the accusation of rule worship: But does he avoid the other horn of Honderich's dilemma, that of treating his secondary maxims (such as the liberty principle) as mere rules of thumb? My reply begins by questioning the assumption that these are the only alternatives open to Mill. As I construe it, the liberty principle and the distinction between self-regarding and other-regarding actions that it embodies is a maxim specifying appropriate reasons for action and so excluding some considerations from this specification: it is a principle that aims to protect a domain of liberty and moral indifference by disqualifying as reasons for intervention an indeterminately large range of considerations. Mill's doctrine appears to resemble closely that of the sophisticated act-utilitarian in Rolf Sartorius' apt description of it:

"The act-utilitarian is therefore in fact able to give an account of social norms which bar direct appeals to utility as more than mere rules of thumb in a two-fold sense. Firstly, they perform the central function of directing human behaviour into channels that it would not otherwise take by restructuring the sets of considerations of consequences of which utilitarian moral agents must take account. Second, they provide reasons for action in that their conventional acceptance is tantamount to the existence of systems of warranted expectations the disappointment of which is a disutility according to standard or normal cases of their violation.[18]

Doesn't this account commit Mill to a sort of rule worship, after all? I think not. One way of characterizing the place of utility in Mill is to say that, whereas considerations of utility generate all good reasons for acting and abstaining, and whereas utility supplies a *criterion* for the expediency and indeed the rightness of actions, Mill recognizes[19] that an appeal to utility is not normally the proper procedure for deciding what to do. A man who governs his life by constant reference to utility may well do worse, utilitarianly speaking, than one whose conduct is regulated by more specific maxims. Whereas an appeal to utility is necessary for any appraisal of the expediency or of the morality of conduct, it is not normally necessary to settle the practical question of what to do. Of course, the self-defeating effect of direct appeals to utility is not imagined by Mill to be a necessary truth of any sort: it is an empirical matter, due to features of the predicament of man in society that may be unalterable and yet could conceivably have been otherwise. Given the contingent character of this aspect of Mill's argument, his account still allows an

area of autonomy to individual judgment in determining the circumstances in which secondary maxims may be overridden. Before
we can clarify the grounds and limits of Mill's most important secondary principle, the principle of liberty, we need to elucidate just what
Mill's principle of liberty enjoins, and how exactly it is related to
utility.

IV. MILL'S PRINCIPLE OF LIBERTY

Many of the references Mill makes to the liberal principles he is
concerned to defend suggest that he sees his task as that of providing
unequivocal guidance about the occasions in which a restriction of
liberty may be justified. Apart from the "one very simple principle"
passage in *On Liberty*, Mill refers to that essay in the *Autobiography*
as "a kind of philosophic textbook of a single truth." Such statements
have led many if not most interpreters to suppose that the "one very
simple principle" in question was a principle that singled out one
range of considerations exclusively as salient to the justification of
limits on liberty. Such a principle, sometimes taken to be Mill's is the
principle that a restriction on liberty is justifiable *if and only if* it will
prevent harm to others. Given that this is how Mill's principle has
been understood, and that the significance for it of his revision or enlargement of the notion of happiness or utility cannot be doubted, it
is not surprising that discussion has concentrated on problems generated by Mill's use of the concept of harm. One writer has gone so far
as to assert that the whole argument of *On Liberty* "is vitiated by the
ambiguity in Mill's use of the word 'harm'."[20] Certainly real problems
surround Mill's use of the term. Does he intend the reader to understand "harm" to refer only to physical harm, or must a class of moral
harms to character be included in any application of the liberty principle? Must the harm that the restriction on liberty prevents be done
directly to identifiable individuals, or may it also relevantly be done
to institutions, social practices, and forms of life? Can serious offense
to feelings count as harm so far as the restriction of liberty is concerned, or must the harm be done to interests, or to those interests
the protection of which is to be accorded the status of a right? Can a
failure to benefit someone, or to perform one's obligations to the
public, be construed as a case in which harm has been done? These
difficulties express a philosophical difficulty in the analysis of the
concept of harm — a difficulty emerging from the fact that judgments

about harm are often controversial as between exponents of different moral outlooks. Can a purely naturalistic account of the meaning of "harm" be accepted as adequate to the demands of ordinary thought and practice? Or, if writers such as Winch[21] are right in thinking that harm is not a concept judgments about which occupy some common ground of moral neutrality between differing ways of life, could Mill be warranted in working with a revisionary conception of harm? Though I do not doubt that these questions pose real questions for Mill, I will argue that the final inability of his theory of liberty to give definite answers to questions about the restriction of liberty does not derive from an indeterminancy in the concept of harm with which he operates. It derives, rather, from an area of evaluative disagreement, which can and does persist even when agreement has been reached about the coherence of the theory of liberty and about the criteria of the concept of harm it incorporates.

Those who think that the force of Mill's principle of liberty is ascertainable easily and uncontroversially cannot have noticed that, entirely characteristically, he formulates it in different ways in different places in *On Liberty,*[22] on one occasion[23] referring to *"two maxims"* as the book's prescriptive content. One implication of all the formulations of his principle, however, is that the whole range of human conduct may be divided into two domains: one where state and society are forbidden to intervene, and the other where they are under no such prohibition. One way of phrasing Mill's principle, common among his critics and interpreters, but not used by Mill himself, is to say that, whereas the state and society may properly act so as to limit liberty within the domain of "other-regarding" actions, it is never legitimate to restrict a man's liberty to perform "self-regarding" actions. It is commonplace of Mill criticism that the distinction between self-regarding and other-regarding actions is a difficult one, and I shall have much to say about how Mill's intentions in this matter are to be understood. At this point I want to ask a related question about the force of the liberty principle. As I interpret Mill's several statements of the principle, they specify as a *necessary condition* of rightful limitation of liberty that the action restricted be other-regarding and harmful. (I am ignoring here, though not because I think they are unimportant, complications about whether a good probability of harm to others might justify a limit on liberty and about how the relative success of a harm prevention policy bears on its justifiability, and I neglect for the moment the no less important question whether the liberty principle stipulates that a man's liberty may be restricted only if *his* actions harm or threaten harm to others.) Some scholars have taken the liberty principle as specifying, not a necessary condition of justified interference, but a necessary and sufficient condition for there being *a good reason for interference* with liberty. D. G. Brown, for instance, basing his interpretation mainly on the quasi-canonical "one very simple principle" passage, treats the liberty principle as equivalent, or nearly equivalent, to the principle that the fact that a limit on liberty will prevent harm to others is always a good reason for it, and nothing else is a good reason for it. Indeed, Mill in the "one very simple principle" passage does speak of coercion as being licensed for only one end or purpose, and it is a natural interpretation of what he says there that a nearly equivalent principle would specify a necessary and sufficient condition of there being a good reason to restrict liberty. Wollheim seems to endorse the same reading[24] of the principle. Honderich, however, states the principle as stipulating that "punishment may be justified when a man harms others by his actions and can never be justified on the grounds merely that his actions are taken to be immoral or to be harmful to himself."[25] The two formulations are certainly not equivalent. That preventing harm to others is a necessary condition of any justified restriction of liberty doesn't mean that preventing harm to others is *the only* necessary condition (i.e., a necessary and sufficient condition) thereof. Nor does Brown imagine this to be so: his reading of the principle makes it specify, not a necessary and sufficient condition for a restriction being *justified* — a principle Mill explicitly disavows, as Brown notes — but a necessary and sufficient condition for a restriction being at all *justifiable*. Brown does think, however, that it follows from or is presupposed by the claim that, in the absence of harm to others, there is no reason for limiting liberty, that in the absence of harm to others there is reason against it. As he makes clear, this latter principle follows, not from the liberty principle, but from the principle of utility.

What turns on this difference of interpretation? Brown notes that the liberty principle tells us less than it appears to do about just when intervention is justified: "The principle needs to be supplemented," he says, "by an account of the possible reasons against restriction and of the principles, if any, on which we are to weigh the reasons for and the reasons against." He goes on to claim that "On the negative side, the principle says all that we could ask of it. By giving this necessary condition of the existence of a reason for restriction, it rules out as irrelevant absolutely everything but the prevention of harm to others."[26] Brown is, I think, right in his interpretation of Mill as unequivocally intending his readers to understand that, unless "harm to others" can be prevented, there is *no reason at all* for any limit on liberty. But this interpretation raises in an acute form the problem that I have identified as Mill's: If he is a utilitarian committed to one supreme principle as yielding all reasons for or against any action, how can Mill at the same time endorse a principle — his principle of liberty — according to which the fact that an act promotes utility is no reason at all in its favor, if the act happens to be one that violates the liberty principle? This question, which opens up again the whole question of the structure of Mill's utilitarianism, might be answered if we attribute to Mill a kind of lexicographical ordering of the principles of liberty and of utility. On this view, the liberty principle, in Mill's doctrine, enjoys absolute lexical priority over the utility principle, whenever certain background conditions exist; and the liberty principle, understood here as forbidding restriction of liberty in all cases save those where harm prevention is in issue, must itself be seen as a further iteration of the principle of utility. Mill's doctrine of liberty, then, embodies the paradox that an iteration of the utility principle is on utilitarian grounds accorded priority over the utility principle itself. As Williams has observed,[27] it is a feature of all moral theories in which a single principle is dominant that all other principles within the morality are instantiations of the supreme principle. The peculiarity of Mill's doctrine is that one of utility's iterations is accorded priority over the sovereign principle itself.

In the form in which it has so far been formulated, however, this interpretation raises problems. First, on the view Brown shares with most of the revisionists, the lexical ordering must strictly be of liberty over expediency, since the liberty principle cannot really conflict with the principle of utility. Again, whereas the text generally supports Brown's view of the liberty principle as ruling out absolutely an indefinitely large range of considerations as irrelevant to the justification of restrictions on liberty, it is still not clear in the revisionary view whether these considerations may reappear as salient to the question of justifying limits on liberty once the barrier presented by the liberty principle has been crossed. Two positions are possible here. According to the first, whereas the liberty principle does entail an antipaternalist principle and an antimoralist principle stipulating that is can never be a good reason for restricting a man's liberty that he will otherwise harm himself, or violate positive or popular morality, paternalist and moralist considerations may enter into the justification of a limit on liberty once the liberty principle has been satisfied. Mill can even consistently allow moralist considerations, for example, a weight *independent* of their contribution to utility, provided always that they are never allowed to *override* utility, but function only as tie breakers. Mill is not *bound* to allow this: as a utilitarian, he might judge that, where two states of affairs are alike with respect to utility except that in one popular morality is observed, there is nothing to choose between them. It is only that nothing in the structure of Mill's moral theory *debars* him from drawing on considerations other than those contained in the sovereign principle and its many iterations. In such a case, while Mill cannot permit other considerations to constrain the operations of the various iterations of utility, he can give independent weight to other considerations, thus acknowledging that justifications for limiting liberty may be over-determined. His doctrine of liberty, then, specifies two principles as severally necessary to justify any limit on liberty: they are the principles of liberty and of utility; and, within the doctrine, these principles are lexically ordered, with the liberty principle being dominant. On the second view—which, like Brown, I take to be Mill's—his doctrine specifies the two principles, not merely as severally necessary, but as jointly sufficient to justify limiting liberty. In this case, considerations apart from those of utility are excluded once the liberty principle is satisfied; paternalist and moralist policies, for example, are justifiable *if and only if* they are dictated by utility. True, Mill's doctrine does permit such policies to be implemented once the barrier of the liberty principle has been crossed— but it accords specifically paternalist and moralist considerations no weight independent of that which they might borrow from their contribution to utility.

Now, the liberty principle tells us that it can never be right to limit liberty when "harm to others" cannot thereby be prevented; but, as it stands, this formulation is ambiguous. For, as Brown acknowledges and Lyons has reaffirmed,[28] Mill's liberty principle can be construed, either as a principle licensing restriction of liberty only *to prevent harmful conduct,* or else as a principle licensing liberty-limitation *for the sake of general harm-prevention.* Much turns on differences of interpretation as to which is Mill's principle, and each interpretation has costs and benefits. An advantage of the construal of the liberty principle as a general harm prevention principle is that it allows Mill to sanction interferences with liberty for the purpose of alleviating harms no one may have caused; and this more permissive reading of the liberty principle undoubtedly diminishes its counterintuitive aspects, while yet blunting the sharp libertarian cutting edge of *On Liberty*. A major disadvantage of this construal of Mill's liberty principle as a general harm prevention principle is that it allows a rivalry to reemerge between aggregative considerations of general utility and distributive considerations of equity. Negative utilitarian strategies such as that involved in a harm minimization program are no more congenial to equity than the more conventional utility-maximization strategies. An advantage of the stringent interpretation of the liberty principle as a harmful conduct principle is that, in forbidding restriction of liberty save where an action *causes harm* to another, it *presupposes* equality of liberty for all. How is this? The liberty principle viewed as a stringent principle of this sort allows restriction only when there has been a *departure* from nonaggression; it forbids social control by the use of coercion except when the conduct of the agent whose liberty is to be restricted is invasive of the moral rights of others. Mill's liberty principle, then, is a side-constraint principle about the prevention of harmful conduct and not a teleogical principle about harm prevention: in itself it is not obviously aggregative or distributive in character, but, supposing the derivation of the liberty principle from utility to have been achieved, no competition between utility and justice remains in the sphere of the distribution of liberty. I will return to this point later.

Further, however, the strict interpretation of the liberty principle has another advantage. If we adopt the more permissive reading of Mill's principle as a general harm preventation principle, are we to say that the principle thus understood licenses interference with purely self-regarding actions, or are we to say that any action interference that can prevent harm cannot be purely self-regarding? If we go along with the latter view, then indeed it seems to be true that the self-regarding area is an empty one, and the protection afforded to liberty by Mill's principle spurious. Even if we adopt the former view, we seem bound to acknowledge that any act may have both self-regarding and other-regarding aspects; but if we do not treat the distinction between the self-regarding and the other-regarding areas as framing a contrast between two mutually exclusive domains, the application of the liberty principle will become almost unmanageably complex. Are these difficulties avoided if, as I suggest, we adopt the strict reading of the liberty principle? Let us see.

V. THE SELF-REGARDING AREA:
A NECESSARY DIGRESSION

It seems indisputable that, if it is to be at all useful, the liberty principle must be taken as presupposing a domain of human action where what a man does, though it may benefit or harm him, is not beneficial or harmful to others. Ever since *On Liberty* was published, the commonest line of criticism of his argument has been that it presupposes what does not exist — a domain of purely self-regarding actions that affect only the agent and his agreeing partners and no one else. If this is so, then Mill's principle cannot do the job he had in mind for it — that of securing a determinate and important area of human life from liberty-limiting invasion.

One attempt to answer this traditional criticism is made by John Rees in a seminal paper.[29] Rees distinguishes between actions that affect others and actions that affect others' interests, and he claims that Mill's working conception of harm is that of *harm to interests.* Now, according to Rees, "when a person can be thought to have interests he is *thereby* possessed of a right," if only the right to have his interests taken into account. Rees emphasizes that interests "depend for their existence on social recognition and are closely connected with prevailing standards about the sort of behaviour a man can legitimately expect from others."[30] Two points are relevant to Ree's interpretation. First, though he emphasizes that neither he nor Mill is saying that rights and interests are synonymous terms, but only that they are very closely related to each other, rights and interests are importantly different in several ways, some of which Mill gives evidence of seeing as relevant to his argument. It is not, perhaps, an entirely trivial point that, whereas a man's interests may be damaged or obstructed by an impersonal process such as a natural catastrophe, his rights can be affected only by the actions of other human beings.[31] True enough, Mill is concerned in *On Liberty* not with all cases where a man's interests are damaged but only with those where his interests are invaded, that is, damaged by other men. But the fact that these cases can be distinguished shows that there are cases where what we say about a man's interests need have no implications for

what we think about his rights. Second, it should be noted that, when
in a passage Rees quotes Mill tries to demarcate the area of life in
which he may be held accountable to society, he speaks not of determining what are a man's interests, but of ascertaining his rights.
"This conduct," he says, "consists in not injuring the interests of one
another; or rather *certain* interests which, either by express legal provision or by tacit understanding, *ought to be considered as rights.*"
Here the test is not whether a man's interests have been damaged by
other men but whether his interests ought to be protected as rights.

Mill does not think, then, that, if a man has an interest, he
"thereby" has any kind of right. His reference to "certain interests"
suggests that only *some* interests can give rise to rights, but which? In
order to distinguish interests from "arbitrary wishes, fleeting fancies,
or capricious demands,"[32] Rees stresses their dependence on norms
and values that enjoy social recognition. But this is open to the objection (made by Wollheim) that the liberty principle in Ree's interpretation becomes relativistic and conservative in character. The
boundaries of the self-regarding domain will be determined by the
currently dominant conception of interests, and the liberty principle
will expand freedom only insofar as legal limitations on liberty lag
behind changing conceptions of human interests. Wollheim's objection to Rees is forceful, if Rees' account may be interpreted as making human interests subordinate to their social recognition; and so
thoroughly relativistic a conception of interests clearly cannot accord
with Mill's intentions. Such relativism can be avoided, however,
without making interests wholly invariant socially and historically.
Men's interests might be, and indeed must be shaped by the standards and circumstances of their time and culture, but to say this is
not to say that men's interests wholly depend upon, or are entirely
constituted by, recognition by society. The liberty principle need not
itself be relativistic in character, even if (as must surely be the case)
its application is relativistic in some degree. Mill needs a conception
of interests that is universalistic inasmuch as it specifies an area essential to human well-being, but which has also developmental or historical aspect. To affirm that this is what Mill needs — and to argue,
as I will go on to do, that this is what his writings contain — is not to
lose sight of the vital insight contained in Rees's interpretations,
namely, that for Mill an intimate connection did hold between moral
rights and "certain interests." Such a connection is recognized in
Williams's interpretation that, while it does not claim that these vital

interests are definable by reference to conventional social norms, aims to develop further some of the most valuable aspects of Rees's contribution. On this issue, at any rate, the interpretations of Rees and Williams seem compatible with the claims I am myself urging, according to which Mill's theory of moral rights grounds them or explicates them by reference to certain essential human interests. Part of the rationale of my contention derives from the conviction that such an interpretation allows us to see the younger Mill's thought in these areas as less abruptly discontinuous with that of his utilitarian ancestry than is conventionally supposed. It needs to be demonstrated, on my account of his theory, that Mill could and did build up his theory of justice and the moral rights, not by invoking some independent principle or intuition of equity, but by elucidating some of the implications of the utility principle itself. What in Mill's work supports my claim?

It will be recalled that in *Utilitarianism* Mill declares: "The moral rules which forbid mankind to hurt one another (in which we must never forget to include wrongful interference with each other's freedom) are more vital to human well-being than any maxims, however important, which only point out the best mode of managing some department of human affairs." He goes on to assert that "the moralities which protect every individual from being harmed by others, either directly or by being hindered in his freedom of pursuing his own good, are at once those which he himself has most at heart, and those which he has the strongest interest in publishing and enforcing by word and deed . . . it is these moralities primarily which compose the obligations of justice." Mill continues by affirming that "The most marked cases of injustice . . . are acts of wrongful aggression, or wrongful exercise of power over some one; the next are those which consist in wrongfully withholding from him something which is his due; in both cases, inflicting on him a positive hurt, either in the form of direct suffering, or of the privation of some good which he had reasonable ground, either of a physical or of a social kind, for counting upon." He concludes by observing summarily that "justice is a name for certain moral requirements, which, regarded collectively, stand higher in the scale of social utility, and are therefore of more paramount obligation, than any others . . ."[33]

Mill here identifies as man's most vital interests his interests in autonomy and in security. The significance of this claim for the argument of *On Liberty* can scarcely be exaggerated. These are the

"certain interests" that Mill there specifies are to be protected *as
rights*. Except in certain contractual circumstances where special
rights exist, and in circumstances of emergency when there is a
natural duty,[34] these interests are satisfied when men refrain from invading one another's autonomy and from undermining one another's
security. Unless these vital interests are endangered, no policy that
aims at preventing men from harming themselves, or at compelling
them to benefit others, can ever be justified. It is to these interests
that Mill refers in the introductory chapter of *On Liberty* when he
makes the appeal to "the permanent interests of a man as a progressive being" and that function in Mill's theory of liberty in a fashion
analogous to that of the primary goods in Rawls's theory of justice.
These vital interests are to be protected before any others a man may
have; and they are not to be invaded or damaged simply because it
seems that a greater satisfaction of overall preferences might thereby
be achieved. These are the interests that define the self-regarding
area, and that ground the moral rights. Mill argues to this effect in
his *Auguste Comte and Positivism,* asserting that "It is incumbent on
everyone to restrain the pursuit of his personal objects within the
limits consistent with the essential interests of others."[35] That Mill
does work with a theory of essential interests or primary goods cannot, I think, reasonably be doubted, but it might still be objected
that nothing has yet been said that supports the contention that these
are the interests in security and in autonomy. Still less has it been
shown that there are good arguments in Mill for ascribing a priority
to the vital interest in autonomy where this conflicts with the
demands of security. Until we know Mill's account of the scope and
importance of these vital interests, we have not captured the structure of his argument from utility to the principle of liberty. It is in
order to show how such a ranking or weighting of interests can be
given a utilitarian rationale that I turn now to consider Mill's theory
of happiness.

VI. MILL'S CONCEPTION OF HAPPINESS

Mill's doctrine of liberty is supported by a conception of happiness
that is embedded in his theory of human nature. Much in the *Liberty*
is suggestive of a view of human nature in which its openness to self-
transformation and its consequent partial indefinability are central

features. A major part of his argument turns on this view. For, if human nature is thus liable to self-alteration, then apart from man's vital interests no fixed order of wants or needs can ever be established, and no single thing will be more important to man than a social framework in which autonomy and security are protected and in which experiments in living may be made. As both *Utilitarianism* and *On Liberty* make clear, Mill cannot conceive the happiness that is distinctively human except against a background of autonomy and security; the happiness made possible by the framework of moral rights is, further, that specified in Mill's account of the higher pleasures. These are forms of life and activity whose content is distinctive and peculiar in each individual case but that necessarily involve the exercise of generically human powers of autonomous thought and choice. Since the domain of the higher pleasures is bounded by the exercise of these powers, its contents are not absolutely indeterminate; but a list of the higher pleasures can never be drawn up, given the openness of human nature to self-alteration. How, precisely, does this view of human nature support the doctrine of liberty?

We can begin to sort out this problem if we acknowledge the *abstractness* and *complexity* of Mill's conception of happiness. For all his references to pleasure and the absence of pain, Mill never endorsed the primitive view that pleasure is a sort of sensation that accompanies our actions, and he did not identify happiness with pleasurable states of mind. Mill's departures from Benthamite utilitarianism in the direction of modern preference utilitarianism were in part motivated by an awareness of the inadequacies of the moral psychology of classical utilitarianism. While he continues to adhere to a belief in the *uniformity* of human nature (in that he never abandons the belief that the way to render human actions intelligible and to explain them is to subsume them under some lawlike principles), he breaks with the Enlightenment belief in the *constancy* of human nature. Though he affirms that a science of ethology will one day ascertain the laws of mind, he goes further than Hume, who acknowledged that variable customs and institutions alter men's motives, in ascribing to human nature a potentiality for progressive alterations and unpredictable mutation. His conception of human nature and thus his view of happiness accordingly have an ineradicable developmental and historical dimension.

Mill's departures from the classical utilitarian view of human nature, which he criticizes so sharply in his *Bentham* and *Coleridge,* support the doctrine of liberty in at least four ways. First, in abandoning the passive conception of the mind that he ascribed to Bentham and his father, Mill embraced a conception of happiness that was Aristotelian in that it was inseparably connected with *activity.* No longer could a happy human life be conceived as one containing a number of goods supposed to be enjoyable independently of man's energetic pursuit of them. Second, it was Mill's belief that, once a certain level of social development has been reached, men will find their happiness in activities of which choice or "individuality" is a necessary ingredient. Whereas Mill does not, I think, attach to choice-making itself an intrinsic value, he does claim that men are creatures of such a kind that once they have known them, they will not lightly give up the forms of happiness into which choice-making enters as a necessary ingredient. Third, Mill's conception of happiness was avowedly individualist and pluralist. When he makes his appeal to utility, he specifies that "it must be utility in the largest sense grounded on the permanent interests of man as a progressive being."[36] Fourth, Mill thought of the pursuit of happiness as issuing, not in a Rawls-type rational plan of life, but rather in a series of "experiments in living,"[37] each of which was to be altered successively in view of what had been learned from the others. For the individual as for the species, this must be conceived as an open-ended venture. Even where particular experiments are irreversible and disastrous, the liberty to undertake them is necessary if contemporaries and future generations are to be able to benefit from the knowledge they yield.

Mill's conception of happiness is abstract and pluralistic in that it is decomposed into the projects, attachments, and ideals expressed in an indefinitely large set of happy human lives. If we treat Mill's distinction between the higher and the lower pleasures as being between different kinds of activity or forms of life rather than between different states of mind, we can see that, though he is far from supposing that the higher pleasures will be the same for all men, he does think they have the common feature of being available only to men who have developed their distinctively human capacity for autonomous thought and action. Mill's view is not, indeed, that highly autonomous men are bound to be happy, but rather that autonomous thought and action is a necessary feature of the life of a man who enjoys the higher pleasures. The priority of liberty in Mill's utilitarian account of the moral rights derives from its conceptual and empirical connections with autonomy. Autonomy designates the capacities and opportunities involved in self-critical and imaginative choice-making, and the classical liberal freedoms listed in the introductory chapter of the *Liberty* can all be seen as indispensable to the exercise of powers of autonomous thought and action. Because of its links with autonomy, liberty in Mill's doctrine becomes a necessary ingredient of happiness and not just a causally efficacious means to it. Mill clearly assumes for the purposes of his argument a philosophical psychology akin to that which Rawls has epitomized in his Aristotelian principle.[38]

We may now be able to discern part of the complex structure of Mill's utilitarianism. It has at least three distinct tiers. First we have the utility principle in its role as an axiological principle specifying happiness alone as of intrinsic value. The happiness here is that of any sentient creature — jellyfish, lower mammal, or human being — with states of mind or feeling or preferences determinate enough for the utility principle to operate upon. Next we have utility in its applications to human beings, whose generic powers allow for happy and wretched lives whose qualities are (so far as we know) peculiar to our species. Third, there are the applications of the utility principle to reflective and civilized men in whom the capacities for an autonomous life have been developed and to whom the higher pleasures are accessible. In according a special weight to the higher pleasures, the utility principle in Mill may seem to have an ideal-regarding aspect and to express a sort of procedural perfectionism in which choice-making itself rather than the style of life chosen has intrinsic value. Once the three-tiered structure of Mill's utilitarianism is appreciated, the attribution to his utility principle of a perfectionist aspect only in its application to men who have attained a certain stage of cultural development; for it remains throughout want-regarding in the third tier of Mill's utilitarianism reposes on the wager that civilized men will *in fact* prefer the life of free men *because* it is in such a life that they find their happiness. The importance of the hierarchical structure of Mill's utilitarianism is revealed, again, in the fact that at the second level autonomy will not enjoy the centrality and priority among man's vital interests that it possesses at the third. It is a criticism of Mill's doctrine of liberty, in fact, that in virtue of the necessary conditions that he specifies in the *Logic*[39] as being indispensable to any stable social order, the third level is never to be reached in human life. I will not comment on this criticism here, for I think it can be shown that none of the arguments for a *Liberty* versus *Logic* competition in this area seems to me to be fully persuasive. More serious are a number of questions about the structure of Mill's argument that are raised by the role of security and autonomy in promoting utility, and it is to these that I turn.

VII. THE LOGIC OF MILL'S ARGUMENT FOR MORAL RIGHTS

A central difficulty in explicating Mill's theory of the moral rights, and so of identifying the force of the liberty principle, is that of determining what is comprehended within men's vital interests in security and in autonomy. For, unless the domains of these interests can be clearly demarcated from other human interests, the liberty principle will not be able to guide action in the way Mill hoped for it. It might be thought that difficulties about Mill's conception of harm, which I have acknowledged to be real but which I have denied are fundamental to the weakness of Mill's doctrine, here reemerge. More radically, when discussing the nature of the demands upon action imposed by the principle of utility, I adopted the strategy of assuming for the purposes of my interpretation that Mill's utilitarianism does entail a maximizing commitment about utility's promotion. In this I forswore the alternative strategy of denying that maximization is either a rational or a moral requirement of a plausible theory of value. We are now able to point to the two central obscurities in the logic of Mill's argument for moral rights as I have presented it so far. First, what justifies the weighting of men's vital interests over all men's other interests? How can any theory appealing finally to general welfare resist a trade-off between some interests, however vital, and others, when protecting the latter will yield a net utility benefit? Second, it is not at all clear that we have yet demarcated the vital interests satisfactorily from the others — that is to say, we have not yet framed the self-regarding area in any acceptable way.

The first of these problems is posed clearly in a passage in chapter of *Utilitarianism:* "To have a right, then, is I conceive, to have something which society ought to defend me in the possession of. If the objector goes on to ask, why it ought? I can give him no other reason than general utility."[40] How can a strong commitment to moral rights coexist with affirmation of the overriding value of the general welfare? It is clear that, if the liberty principle is construed as forbidding restriction of liberty except when damage to vital interests (and so violation of moral rights) is threatened, then by the same token intervention to benefit some at the expense of others is forbidden. On this reading, nothing is *added* to the liberty principle by the requirement that moral rights to security and autonomy by distributed equally, since the liberty principle (unlike that of utility) actually *presupposes* such a requirement. If the liberty principle is (as I have earlier contended) to be construed in this way as a side-constraint principle forbidding trade-offs between the vital interests or moral rights, how can it be shown to flow from a utility principle whose maximizing implication I have not contested? Mill's own view of this question should not be in doubt. In *Thornton on Labour and Its Claims* he asserts:

> Mr. Thornton seems to admit the general happiness as the criterion of social virtue, but not of positive duty — not of justice and injustice in the strict ideas that his doctrine differs from that of utilitarian moralists. But this is not the case. Utilitarian morality fully recognises the distinction between the province of positive duty and that of virtue, but maintains that the standard and rule of both is the general interest. From the utilitarian point of view, the distinction then is the following: — There are many acts, and a still greater number of forbearances, the perpetual practice of which by all is so necessary to the general well-being, that people must be held to it compulsively, either by law, or by social pressure. These acts and forbearances constitute duty. Outside these bounds there is the innumerable variety of modes in which the acts of human beings are either a cause, or a hindrance, of good to their fellow-creatures, but to which it is, on the whole, for the general interest that they should be left free; being merely encouraged, by praise and honour, to the performance of such beneficial actions as are not sufficiently stimulated by benefits flowing from them to the agent himself. This larger sphere is that of Merit or Virtue.[41]

Again, in a passage in *Auguste Comte and Positivism,* part of which I have already quoted, Mill says:

> It is incumbent on every one to restrain the pursuit of his personal objects within the limits consistent with the essential interests of others. What these limits are, it is the province of ethical

science to determine; and to keep all individuals within them, is
the proper office of punishment and of moral blame . . . The
proper office of those sanctions is to enforce upon everyone, the
conduct necessary to give all other persons their fair chance:
conduct which chiefly consists in not doing them harm, and not
impeding them in anything which without harming others does
good to themselves.[42]

Finally, in his review of George Cornewall Lewis's book, *The Use
and Abuse of Political Terms,* Mill observes:

Whatever obligation any man would lie under in a state of nature, not to inflict evil upon another for the sake of good to himself, the same obligation lies upon society towards every one of
its members. If he injure or molest any one of his fellow- citizens, the consequences of whatever they may be obliged to do in
self-defence, must fall upon himself; but otherwise the government fails in its duty, if on any plea of doing good to the community in the aggregate, it reduces him to such a state, that he is
on the whole a loser by living in a state of government, and
would have been better off if it did not exist. This is the truth
which was dimly shadowed forth, in howsoever rude and unskil-
ful a manner, in the theories of the social compact and of the
rights of man.[43]

It is important to be clear what is *not* claimed in this and similar
passages. Mill does not say that coercion is never justified unless it
claims to defeat coercion. He does not espouse here a policy governed
by the principle of limiting liberty only for the sake of liberty; he recognizes implicitly, as he elsewhere acknowledges explicitly, that individual liberty may rightly be limited for the sake of important benefits such as the prevention of harm and suffering. (Admittedly, in the
Liberty Mill seems to recognize only emergency situations as circumstances in which the liberty principle may be abridged. As I will suggest in the last section of this chapter, it may reasonably be supposed
that this is too limited a range of cases in which the avoidance of
harm and suffering licenses the principle's abridgment.) Again,
though he repudiates policies as a result of which a man may be
worse off on balance than he would be in an anarchical state of nature, and does so even where they might be thought likely to yield

maximum aggregate welfare, Mill does not hold that any man's moral rights are inviolable. Even Nozick wavers at the point where refusing to violate a moral right would bring about a moral catastrophe,[44] and Rawls's doctrine explicitly allows for such violations. No less than Rawls, then, does Mill emerge as a partisan of justice and moral rights. But this is not a contractarian argument intended by Mill to supply independent reasonings for a principle of liberty. If it were, it would be open to the sort of criticisms of Rawls's method, which have shown that there is no uniquely determinate distribution of liberties and advantages that a rational man in a circumstance of ignorance and uncertainty is *bound* to choose. Rather, it invokes Mill's overall utilitarian theory of moral rights, which rests on a conjecture about what practical maxims ought to be adopted if utility is to be promoted.

It is evident that nothing in Mill's argument can support a principle according each man's moral rights an infinite weight and consequently forbidding any trade-off between them and other values. Again, as we have seen to be true even of Nozick, who conceives the system of moral rights as a structure of compossible side constraints each of which has an infinite weight, no one is really happy with such a stringent principle. Mill's argument does, however, allow him to support the institution of moral rights, and it supports a demand for their equal distribution. Why is this? The force of the priority attaching to protection of the vital interests and so of the moral rights held by individuals is that *these* interests may never (once the background conditions Mill specifies exist) be traded off against any other interests men may have. Mill holds that these moral rights may not be traded off against each other — he is not, in other words, a negative utilitarian regarding moral rights. Mill's position, I think, is nowhere explicitly stated on this problem, but it would be consistent with his overall view if he were to argue that, whereas no violation of a man's moral rights can reasonably be ascribed an infinite disutility, trading off between moral rights is unjustified except to forestall a catastrophic drop in general welfare. Thus, avoiding even a lower average level of rights protection will not justify violating anyone's rights, if this is not *also* necessary to prevent general moral catastrophe.

The second problem — that of determining just what is encompassed within the vital human interests in security and autonomy — cannot be adequately treated here, but the main outlines of its solution can perhaps be sketched. Mill's enlargement of the notion of utility in its applications to human beings affects his conception of "harm to interests" (which, following Rees, I take to be the sense of "harm" central in *On Liberty*), first, by according a primary importance to the damage that may be done to a man's powers as a reflective and choice-making creature, and, second, by designating the vital interest a man has in security of person and property. The structure of Mill's argument here is that as far as human beings are concerned, utility must always include these primary goods: this is what I have called the second level of his three-tiered utilitarianism. At the third level, the interest in autonomy is always given priority over that in security. In its applications to the affairs of civilized men — at which I have called its third tier — utility *contains* liberty inasmuch as liberty enters into autonomy. The connection between liberty and utility at this level is not merely stipulative, however; it is a necessary connection, to be sure, but a conjectural one in virtue of certain truths about human nature in its developed condition. (The conception of necessary connection at work here is akin to the Quinean one operative in Rawls's account of the Aristotelian principle.) Again, liberty and utility are nowhere simply identified, since even at the third level there is more to utility than liberty (which must itself be regarded as constituting only one of the necessary conditions of autonomy). There are massive and complex problems contained in this argument-sketch, but it is not obvious that any of them is intractable.

The structure of Mill's argument for moral rights depends on three empirical claims. First, a claim about the self-defeating effect of direct appeals to utility: it is in virtue of certain contingent (but perhaps unalterable) features of man and society, mainly to do with limited information and partial altruism and with the conditions necessary to social cooperation, that Mill recommends the adoption of a side-constraint principle about liberty as a self-denying ordinance with respect to the promotion of utility. Second, a historical claim in developmental human psychology: with the unfolding of powers of autonomous thought and action, Mill believes, men will come to derive satisfaction increasingly from activities involving the exercise of these powers. Third, he claims that it is in a liberal social environment that the powers of men as autonomous agents, having once reached the level necessary to take them out of barbarism, are further developed and refined. These are all empirical claims, revisable and defeasible by experience, but, once they are granted, there is nothing inadvertent or inconsistent in Mill's argument for moral rights and for the priority of the right to liberty. Even if his doctrine is false, it is not unacceptable on grounds of incoherence or self-contradiction.

VIII. THE TRUTH OF MILL'S THEORY OF MORAL RIGHTS

If my interpretation has shown anything, it is that Mill's doctrine of liberty must be assessed in the context of his theory of human nature. It is no accident, accordingly, that the most perspicacious criticisms of Mill's doctrine are those that attack his theory of human nature. Thus, it has been argued that it exaggerates the importance that "individuality" has or could ever have in the lives even of highly civilized human beings. We can certainly envisage pictures of human life—such as that suggested in the fable of the Grand Inquisitor, as recounted in Dostoevski's *Brothers Karamazov*—which, in their emphatic statement of the role of moral and intellectual perversity and longing for authority in human life, tear apart happiness and freedom from the intimate union they enjoy in Mill's conception of human nature. It is such a disserveration that James Fitzjames Stephen is concerned to achieve in his well-known *Liberty, Equality, Fraternity,* which must still be ranked as the most formidable criticism of Mill's liberalism. If the view of human nature propounded by liberalism's conservative critics is true, then surely Mill's liberalism is fatally undermined. Utilitarians would then be forced back to the doctrines of Bentham and Austin, in which a utilitarian theory of moral rights may perhaps be found, but one in which security rather than liberty enjoys primacy. In this case, a breach will have been opened up between the author of *On Liberty* and his predecessors and (contrary to the revisionary view incorporated in this paper) the continuity of the utilitarian tradition broken. Mill would again be seen as a thinker who seeks refuge from the authoritarian implication of utilitarian ethics by invoking a largely aprioristic and implausible view of human nature. In response to this criticism, which I have acknowledged to be the most forceful of those advanced by Mill's traditional critics, two observations may be made. First, since we are in an area of considerable and perhaps unavoidable uncertainty when we compare rival conceptions of human nature, Mill's own conception must be shown to be actually unreasonable in the context of much available evidence if we are to abandon it. Second, even if the dispositions and capacities specified in his conception of human nature are far rarer than Mill imagined, this would not overthrow his principle of liberty, so far as I can see, but only restrict its application more drastically than Mill himself would have allowed.

Another important range of objections are addressed to the moral acceptability and the action-guiding force of the liberty principle. Let us take the latter first. The liberty principle forbids interventions restrictive of liberty except where they aim to prevent damage to the vital interests of another—to his interests in autonomy and security. Now, it is incontestable that reasonable men may disagree as to the weight they attach to the prevention of insecurity in comparison with the protection of autonomy, and, for this reason, it is plain that not all reasonable men will accept that the right to autonomy enjoys an absolute priority over the other considerations comprehended in the right to security. If I am right in construing the liberty principle as a side-constraint principle licensing intervention only to prevent harmful conduct, it seems that these are powerful moral reasons against its adoption. The first difficulty in the application of the liberty principle is compounded by a deeper one. This concerns the autonomy Mill's principle aims to protect. I do not mean here any difficulty in determining the "concept of liberty" with which Mill worked in *On Liberty*. By liberty I take it that Mill intends here the absence of moral and legal obligation. Mill *argues* for such liberty partly by pointing to its role as a necessary ingredient of autonomy, individuality, and well-being, and he might want to refuse the title of a free society to a society of men whose minds are bound to the yoke of custom; but still, the subject matter of essay is the limits of moral and legal obligation. The difficulty I have in mind is that of moving from judgments about autonomy in toto to judgments about the various liberties insofar as they affect autonomy. I have said already that reasonable men may reasonably differ about the proper trade-offs between autonomy and security. Such disagreements may be no less intractable when we must make a choice of liberties. This is to say that, even for those who unreservedly endorse the liberty principle, areas of intractable controversy are likely always to remain in virtue of the controversial character of on-balance judgments about autonomy. Having said this, however, we must not suppose that the liberty principle is therefore practically empty. For, in specifying the kinds of reason that may sanction restriction of liberty, the principle does supply an admittedly open-textured notion of the self-regarding area whose salience to questions of law and policy in a liberal society it is impossible to deny.

It may be thought that, if the liberty principle is morally objectionable when its implications for action are clear, and if there are in addition large areas in which its implications for action are unclear, then Mill's enterprise in *On Liberty* founders. That this may be so I have not denied. But, whatever the ultimate fate of the enterprise of *On Liberty,* the difficulties I have just canvased do not suggest that Mill's enterprise there was a misconceived one. And I hope that, if the argument of the paper has been at all persuasive, it has shown that many of the central objections of the traditional interpretation — objections in which the incoherence of a utilitarian theory of moral rights is taken for granted — are unfounded.

NOTES

This essay emerged from an ongoing study of liberalism that I began under the supervision of the late John Plamenatz. For their comments on previous versions of this paper, I wish to thank Fred Berger, Donald Brown, David Copp, Jonathan Glover, Ted Honderich, D. G. Long, David Lyons, Joseph Raz, Rolf Sartorius, G. W. Smith, C. L. Ten, W. L. Weinstein, G. L. Williams, and Richard Wollheim. For their long-standing and continuing interest in my work on Mill's *Liberty,* I wish to thank Sir Isaiah Berlin, H. L. A. Hart, Alan Ryan, Steven Lukes, and especially J. C. Rees. Without the help I have received from others, this would be a far worse paper than it is; but it ought to go without saying that responsibility for everything in it, including its remaining defects, is mine alone.

1. J. S. Mill, *On Liberty* (London: Everyman, 1972), p. 72.
2. Ibid., p. 73.
3. Ibid., p. 74.
4. J. S. Mill, Ethics (New York: Oxford University Press, 1966), p. 121.
5. See J. Glover's *Causing Death and Saving Lives* (London Penguin, 1977), pp. 62 ff., and John Mackie's *Ethics: Inventing Right and Wrong* (London Penguin, 1978), pp. 143 ff., for the distinction between mental state and preference versions of utilitarianism.
6. Barry's arguments about the self-defeating effect of liberal principles, which draw on the distinction between want-regarding and ideal-regarding considerations that he made in *Political Argument* (London: Routledge and Kegan Paul, 1965), pp. 41–42, may be found summarized on pp. 126–27 of his *The Liberal Theory of Justice* (Oxford: Clarendon Press, 1973).
7. That liberalism is neutral with respect to competing views of the good life is claimed by Dworkin, most explicitly in his "Liberalism," in *Public and Private Morality* ed. S. Hampshire. (Cambridge: Cam-

bridge University Press, 1978),, Dworkin reiterates the claim in the revised edition of his *Taking Rights Seriously* in the "Reply to his Critics" (London: Duckworth, 1978).

8. The view of Mill as a moral totalitarian is developed in Maurice Cowling, *Mill and Liberalism* (Cambridge: Cambridge University Press, 1963), and in S. R. Letwin, *The Pursuit of Certainty* (Cambridge: Cambridge University Press, 1965). The view that, if Mill endorses a specific ideal of human excellence, then he is necessarily implicated in a kind of moral totalitarianism, is very ably criticized by C. L. Ten in his "Mill and Liberty," *Journal of the History of Ideas*, 30 (1969): 47-68.

9. J. C. Rees, "The Two Mills—Again," unpublished paper, March 1977, p. 1.

10. "Perfectionism" is explicated by Rawls in his *A Theory of Justice* (Oxford: Oxford University Press, 1972), p. 325.

11. By "traditional" and "revisionary" interpretations, I do not intend to refer to two groups of writers, each of which shares a common view on all important points in the interpretation and criticism of Mill on liberty. But important recent statements of a traditional view of Mill on liberty may be found in H. J. McCloskey, *John Stuart Mill: A Critical Study* (New York: Macmillan, 1971); in the writings of Ted Honderich, especially his *Punishment: The Supposed Justifications* (London: Hutchinson, 1969), pp. 175 ff. See also Honderich's "Mill on Liberty," *Inquiry*, (1967), and his "The Worth of J. S. Mill on Liberty," *Political Studies*, 22, no. 4, pp. 463-70; and in Isaiah Berlin "John Stuart Mill and the Ends of Life," in *Four Essays on Liberty*, (Oxford: Oxford University Press, 1969), pp. 173 ff. The revisionary view designates that wave of reinterpretation of Mill begun by Alan Ryan and J. C. Rees in the 1960s. Alan Ryan's main contributions are to be found in "Mr. McCloskey on Mill's Liberalism," *Philosophical Quarterly* (1946); "John Stuart Mill's Art of Living," *The Listener*, October 21, 1965; *The Philosophy of John Stuart Mill* (New York: Macmillan, 1970); *John Stuart Mill* (London: Routledge and Kegan Paul, 1974); "John Stuart Mill and the Open Society," *The Listener*, May 17, 1973. For Rees's contributions, see "A Re-reading of Mill on Liberty," *Political Studies* (1960); reprinted with an important postscript (1965) in Peter Radcliff, ed., *Limits of Liberty* (Belmond, Calif.: Wadsworth, 1966) Rees's articles, "A Phase in the Development of Mill's Ideas on Liberty," *Political Studies* (1958, "Was Mill for Liberty," *Political Studies* (1966); "The Reaction to Cowling on Mill," *Mill News Letter*, no. 2,; and "The Thesis of the 'Two Mills,' " *Political Studies* (1977) should also be consulted, as should his *Mill and His Early Critics*, (Leicester: Leicester University College, 1965). Among other revisionary interpretations, the most notable are those of D. G. Brown and C. L. Ten. See D. G. Brown, "Mill on Liberty and Morality," *Philosophical Review*, 81 (1972): 133-58. I am indebted also to Brown's papers on "What Is Mill's Principle of Utility?" *Canadian Journal of Philosophy*, 3 (1973): 1-12; "Mill's Act-

Utilitarianism," *Philosophical Quarterly* (1974): 67-68; "John Rawls: John Mill," *Dialogue,* 12, no. 3 (1973). I have profited also from Brown's "Mill on Harm to Others' Interests," *Political Studies* (1978), and from his (forthcoming) "Mill's Criterion of Wrong Conduct." For Ten's contributions, see C. L. Ten, "The Liberal Theory of the Open Society," in Dante Germino and Klaus von Beyme, ed., *The Open Society in Theory and Practice* (The Hague: Martins Nijhoff, 1974), p. 160. Ten's important "Mill on Self-Regarding Actions," *Philosophy* (1978), should also be consulted, as should his "Paternalism and Morality," *Ratio,* 13 (1971): 56-66; "Enforcing a Shared Morality," *Ethics,* 82 (1972): 321-29; "Crime and Immorality," *Modern Law Review* (1969): 648-63; "Self-Regarding Conduct and Utilitarianism," *Australasian Journal of Philosophy* (1977): 105-13. Ten's "Mill and Liberty" and his review of G. Himmelfarb's *On Liberty and Liberalism* (New York: Knopf, 1974), in *Political Theory* (1975): 337-40, should also be consulted. Other important revisionary interpretations are as follows: R. Wollheim, "John Stuart Mill and the Limits of State Action," *Social Research* (Spring 1973). See also Wollheim's important Introduction to the World Classics Edition of *On Liberty, Representative Government and the Subjection of Women* (1975). Wollheim's "Crime, Sin and Mr. Justice Devlin," *Encounter* (November 1959), deserves also to be consulted for its indirect relevance to Mill. G. L. Williams: "Mill's Principle of Liberty," *Political Studies* (1976); see also his introduction to his *J. S. Mill on Politics and Society,* London: Fontana, 1976 pp. 41-42. For David Lyon's contributions, see his "Mill's Theory of Morality," *Nous,* 10, no. 2 (May 1976); "Human Rights and the General Welfare," *Philosophy and Public Affairs,* 6, no. 2 Winter 1977; his books, *Forms and Limits of Utilitarianism,* and especially his *In the Interest of the Governed,* a revisionary interpretation of Bentham's legal and political thought, are relevant to the interpretation of *On Liberty.* His recent essay, "Mill's Theory of Justice," in A. I. Goldman and J. Kim, eds. *Values and Morals* (Dordrecht, Holland: D. Reidel, 1978), pp. 1-20, and the unpublished 1978 drafts of his "Benevolence and Justice in Mill' and "Mill on Liberty and Harm to Others" are also important sources for the revisionary interpretation. I have also benefited from: David Copp, "The Iterated-Utilitarianism of John Stuart Mill," *Canadian Journal of Philosophy* (1979); R. J. Halliday, "Some Recent Interpretations of J. S. Mill," *Philosophy* (1968), and "John Stuart Mill's Idea of Politics," *Political Studies* (1979), together with Halliday's book, *John Stuart Mill* (London: Allen and Unwin, 1976); Rolf Sartorius, *Individual Conduct and Social Norms* (Encino, Calif.: Dickenson, 1975); J. P. Dryer, "Mill's Utilitarianism," may be found in J. M. Robson, ed., *Essays on Ethics, Religion and Society; Collected Works of John Stuart Mill* (Toronto: Toronto University Press, 1969) vol. X. Richard B. Friedman, "A New Exploration of Mill's Essay on Liberty," *Political Studies,* 14 (1966): 281-304; and Fred Berger, "John Stuart Mill on Justice and Fairness," forthcoming in *Canadian Journal of Philosophy,* Supplementary Volume V, (Summer 1979) and "Mill's Concept of Happiness," forthcoming in *Interpretation.* Vol. VII, No. 3, 1979 D. G. Long's *Bentham on Liberty,* (Toronto: University of Toronto Press, 1977), is an important study of utilitarian thought, whose appendix on Bentham and J. S. Mill on liberty should especially be consulted (pp.. 115-18).

12. J. S. Mill, *Utilitarianism,* p. 4; *On Liberty,* p. 96.
13. Brown, "Mill on Liberty and Morality." The quotation immediately following the beginning of this section of my argument is from page 1 of Brown's "What Is Mill's Principle of Utility?"
14. The writers I have in mind are D. H. Hodgson, *Consequences of Utilitarianism* (Oxford: Oxford University Press, 1967), and G. J. Warnock, who offers a somewhat different version of the argument that many or most, perhaps all, forms of utilitarianism are self-defeating in The *Object of Morality* (London: Mehtuen, 1971), pp. 31-34.
15. Mill, *Utilitarianism,* p. 106.
16. Honderich, "The Worth of J. S. Mill on Liberty," p. 467.
17. See Lyons, "Mill's Theory of Morality."
18. Sartorius, *Individual Conduct and Social Norms,* pp. 70-71.
19. See Mill's *Collected Works,* vol. X, p. 111, for an example of this.
20. J. R. Lucas, *Principles of Politics* (Oxford: Clarendon Press, 1966), p. 174.
21. See Peter Winch, "Can a Good Man be Harmed," in his *Ethics and Action* (London: Routledge and Kegan Paul, 1976), for an exposition of this view.
22. For example, on pp. 72-73, 135, and 149-50 of *On Liberty.*
23. The "two maxims" passage occurs on pp. 149-50 of *On Liberty.*
24. See R. Wollheim, "John Stuart Mill and the Limits of State Action," *Social Research* (Spring 1973): 2.
25. See Honderich, *Punishment: The Supposed Justifications,* p. 175.
26. Brown, "Mill on Liberty and Morality," p. 136.
27. Williams, "Mill's Principle of Liberty," p. 137.
28. Lyons acknowledges this in his draft paper, "Benevolence and Justice in Mill." Brown gives his reason for adopting the stringent interpretation of the liberty principle in his "Mill on Liberty and Morality," p. 135. The crucial passage in *On Liberty* occurs on p. 74 of the Everyman Edition.
29. J. C. Rees, "A Re-reading of Mill on Liberty."
30. Rees, in Radcliff, *Limits of Liberty,* p. 119.
31. I owe this point to Joel Feinberg's "Harm and Self-Interest," in *Law, Morality and Society: Essays in Honour of H. L. A. Hart* (Oxford: Clarendon Press, 1977), p. 285. Feinberg's *Social Philosophy* (Englewood Cliffs, N.J.: Prentice-Hall, 1973), contains much that is germane to this subject, especially in chap. 3.
32.. Rees, in Radcliff, *Limits of Liberty,* pp. 101-2.
33. Mill, *Utilitarianism,* p. 59.
34. Mill recognizes natural duties as providing reasons that may justify

restricting liberty in certain cases in *Utilitarianism*, pp. 59–60.

35. See "Auguste Comte and Positivism," in the Everyman Edition of *Utilitarianism*, p. 406.
36. Mill, *On Liberty*, p. 74.
37. I owe this point to J. L. Mackie's "Can There Be a Right-Based Moral Theory," *Midwest Studies in Philosophy*, 3 (1978), in which the discussion on p. 355 is especially useful. T. M. Scanlon's "Rights, Goals and Fairness," in *Public and Private Morality* (Cambridge: Cambridge University Press, 1978), also contains much that is germane to this theme.
38. See Rawls, *A Theory of Justice*.
39. Mill, *System of Logic*, book VI, chap. 10, p. 5.
40. Mill, *Utilitarianism*, p. 50.
41. This passage is reproduced in G. L. Williams, *John Stuart Mill on Politics and Society*, p. 309.
42. See the Everyman Edition of *Utilitarianism*, p. 406.
43. Quoted by Brown, *Dialogue*, pp. 478–79.
44. Robert Nozick, *Anarchy, State and Utopia*, (New York: Basic Books, 1974), p.30, fn.

THE JUSTIFICATION OF
HUMAN RIGHTS

6

THE BASIS AND CONTENT OF
HUMAN RIGHTS

ALAN GEWIRTH

Despite the great practical importance of the idea of human rights, some of the most basic questions about them have not yet received adequate answers. We may assume, as true by definition, that human rights are rights that all persons have simply insofar as they are human. But are there any such rights? How, if at all, do we know that there are? What is their scope or content, and how are they related to one another? Are any of them absolute, or may each of them be overridden in certain circumstances?

I

These questions are primarily substantive or criterial rather than logical or conceptual. Recent moral philosophers, following on the work of legal thinkers,[1] have done much to clarify the concept of a right, but they have devoted considerably less attention to substantive arguments that try to prove or justify that persons have rights other than those grounded in positive law. Such arguments would indicate the criteria for there being human rights, including their scope or content, and would undertake to show why these criteria are correct or justified.

The conceptual and the substantive questions are, of course, related, but still they are distinct. If, for example, we know that for one person A to have a right to something X is for A to be entitled to X and also for some other person or persons to have a correlative duty to provide X for A as his due or to assist A's having X or at least to refrain from interfering with A's having X, still this does not tell us whether or why A is entitled to X and hence whether or why the other person or persons have such a correlative duty to A. Appeal to positive recognition is obviously insufficient for answering these substantive questions. The answer is not given, for example, by pointing out that many governments have signed the United Nations Universal Declaration of Human Rights of 1948 as well as later covenants. For if the existence or having of human rights depended on such recognition, it would follow that prior to, or independent of, these positive enactments no human rights existed.

The questions, "Are there any human rights?" or "Do persons have any human rights?" may indeed be interpreted as asking whether the rights receive positive recognition and legal enforcement. But in the sense in which it is held that humans have rights (so that such rights exist) even if they are not enforced, the existence in question is normative: it refers to what entitlements legal enactments and social regulations ought to recognize, not or not only to what they in fact recognize. Thus, the criterion for answering the question must not be legal or conventional but moral. For human rights to exist there must be valid moral criteria or principles that justify that all humans, qua humans, have the rights and hence also the correlative duties. Human rights are rights or entitlements that belong to every person; thus, they are universal moral rights. There may of course be other moral rights as well, but only those that morally ought to be universally distributed among all humans are human rights.

This answer, however, seems to get us into more rather than less difficulty. In order to ascertain whether there are legal rights we need only look to the statute books; these, for present purposes, may be held to supply the criteria for the existence of such rights. But if for a moral or human right to exist is for it to satisfy valid moral criteria which justify or ground the right, where do we look for such criteria? What is the moral analogue of the statute books? If there were a single set of universally accepted moral criteria, our task might be somewhat easier, although even in this case we should still have to take account of the distinction indicated above between positive social recognition and moral validity.

In fact, however, the field of moral criteria is full of controversy: consider the competing substantive views epitomized by such thinkers as Kant, Kierkegaard, Nietzsche, Mill, and Marx, who hold, respectively, that the criteria for having rights consist in or are determined by reason, religion, power, utility, and economic class or history. The disagreements among these thinkers do not respresent merely different "second-order" analyses of a commonly accepted body of "first-order" moral judgments, in the way philosophers may differ about the analysis of knowledge while recognizing (except for some borderline cases) a commonly accepted body of knowledge. In contrast to these, the divergences among moral philosophers are disagreements of basic substantive first-order moral principle about what rights persons have, about how persons ought to regard and act toward one another, about what interests of which persons are worth pursuing and supporting, and the like. Considerable evidence also indicates that many contemporaries, both philosophers and nonphilosophers, would share (although perhaps less systematically) one or another of such divergent moral principles.

Nor does the difficulty end there. For in many fields of empirical science and of practice where the "authorities" or ordinary persons disagree, we have some common conception at least of the context or subject matter to which one must look as a kind of independent variable for testing their divergent assertions. Examples of these subject matters are natural or experimental phenomena in the case of natural science, physical health in the case of medicine, rates of inflation or unemployment in the case of economics. But it seems that the very context or subject matter to which one should look to resolve the disagreements of moral principle is itself involved in such disagreements. Obviously, we should already be taking sides on this issue of moral principle if we were to urge that religion or economic history or social utility or aesthetic sensibility be appealed to as the independent variable for this purpose. Although Thomas Jefferson, following a long tradition, wrote that "all men . . . are endowed by their Creator with certain unalienable rights," it does not seem true to say that persons are born having rights in the sense in which they are born having legs. At least their having legs is empirically confirmable, but this is not the case with their having rights. And whereas it is indeed possible to confirm empirically, although in a more complex way, that most persons are born having certain *legal* rights, this, as we have seen, is not sufficient to establish that they have *moral* or *human* rights.

These general difficulties about moral criteria are reinforced when we look at recent attempts of moral philosophers to answer the substantive questions of what are the specific criteria for having moral rights and how it can be known that humans have such rights. For even where the philosophers agree at least in part on the scope or content of the rights, they disagree as to how the existence of these rights can be established or justified. We may distinguish five different recent answers. The intuitionist answer that humans' possession of certain inalienable rights is self-evident, most famously expressed in the Declaration of Independence, is reiterated in Nozick's peremptory assertion that "Individuals have rights, and there are things no person or group may do to them (without violating their rights)."[2] Like other intuitionist positions, this one is impotent in the face of conflicting intuitions. The institutionalist answer that rights arise from transactions grounded in formal or informal rules of institutions, such as promising,[3] incurs the difficulty that some institutions may be morally wrong, so that an independent moral justification must still be given for the institutional or transactional rules that are held to ground the rights. A third answer is that persons have rights because they have interests.[4] This, however, indicates at most a necessary condition for having rights, since there would be an enormous and indeed unmanageable proliferation of rights if the having any interest X were sufficient to generate a right to X. Even if "interests" are restricted to basic or primary interests or needs, there still remain both the logical question of how a normative conclusion about rights can be derived from factual premises about empirically ascertainable characteristics such as having interests, and also the substantive question of why moral rights are generated by characteristics that all humans have in common rather than by more restrictive, inegalitarian characteristics that pertain only to some persons, or to persons in varying degrees, such as expert knowledge or will to power or productive ability.

The fourth answer, that persons have moral rights because they have intrinsic worth or dignity or are ends in themselves or children of God,[5] may be held simply to reduplicate the doctrine to be justified. Such characterizations are directly or ultimately normative, and if one is doubtful about whether persons have moral rights one will be equally doubtful about the characterizations that were invoked to justify it. The fifth answer is Rawls's doctrine that if persons were to choose the constitutional structure of their society from behind a veil of ignorance of all their particular qualities, they would provide that each person must have certain basic rights.[6] Insofar, however, as this doctrine is viewed as giving a justificatory answer to the question whether humans have equal moral rights, it may be convicted of circularity. For the argument attains its egalitarian conclusion only by putting into its premises the egalitarianism of persons' universal equal ignorance of all their particular qualities. This ignorance has no independent rational justification, since humans are not in fact ignorant of all their particular qualities. Hence, apart from an initial egalitarian moral outlook, why should any actual rational informed persons accept the principle about equal moral rights that stems from such ignorance?

It may be objected that all the above difficulties about moral or human rights arise because I have taken too "cognitive" or "ontological" a view of them. Thus, it may be held that moral rights are not something known or existent; the correct analysis of a rights-judgment is not "descriptive" but rather "prescriptive" or of some other noncognitivist sort. Rights-judgments are claims or demands made on other persons; they do not state that certain knowable facts exist; rather, they advocate, urge, or exhort that certain facts be brought into existence. Hence, questions of justification or validity are logically irrelevant to such judgments.

Now the prescriptivist interpretation of rights-judgments is partly true, but this does not remove the point of the justificatory questions I have asked. For one thing, as we have seen, different persons may make conflicting right-claims, so that the question still remains which of these claims is correct. Moreover, ascriptions of correctness or justification are intrinsic to rights-judgments: these consist not only in certain claims or demands but also in the implicit view, on the part of the persons who make them, that the claims have sound reasons in their support. If this were not so, discussion or debate about rights would consist only in vocal ejaculations or attempts at propagandistic manipulation; it would not have even potentially the aspects of rational argument or reflective appraisal of evidence that it in fact can and does display. In addition, the logical connections that hold among rights-judgments would be obscured or even left unexplained if the ejaculatory or manipulative interpretation were the sole or the main correct analysis of such judgments.

II

Let us now begin to develop answers to these questions about human rights. First, since these rights derive from a valid moral criterion or principle, we must consider what I have referred to as the context or subject matter of morality. We saw that although in many other fields their subject matters serve as independent variables for testing the correctness of conflicting judgments made within them, it was difficult to find such a non-question-begging subject matter for morality. Nevertheless, it does exist and can be found. To see what it is, we must consider the general concept of a morality. I have so far been using the words "moral" and "morality" without defining them. Amid the various divergent moralities with their conflicting substantive and distributive criteria, a certain core meaning may be elicited. According to this, a morality is a set of categorically obligatory requirements for actions that are addressed at least in part to every actual or prospective agent, and that are intended to further the interests, especially the most important interests, of persons or recipients other than or in addition to the agent or the speaker.

As we have seen, moralities differ with regard to what interests of which persons they view as important and deserving of support. But amid these differences, all moralities have it in common that they are concerned with actions. For all moral judgments, including right-claims, consist directly or indirectly in precepts about how persons ought to act toward one another. The specific contents of these judgments, of course, vary widely and often conflict with one another. But despite these variations and conflicts, they have in common the context of the human actions that they variously prescribe or prohibit and hence view as right or wrong. It is thus this context which constitutes the general subject matter of all morality.

How does the consideration of human action serve to ground or justify the ascription and content of human rights? To answer this question, let us return to the connection indicated above between rights and claims. Rights may be had even when they are not claimed, and claims are also not in general sufficient to establish or justify that their objects are rights. As against such an assertoric approach to the connection between claims and rights, I shall follow a dialectically necessary approach. Even if persons' having rights cannot be logically inferred in general from the fact that they make certain claims, it is possible and indeed logically necessary to infer, from the fact that certain objects are the proximate necessary conditions of human action, that all rational agents logically must hold or claim, at least implicitly, that they have rights to such objects. Although what is thus directly inferred is a statement not about persons' rights but about their claiming to have them, this provides a sufficient criterion for the existence of human rights, because the claim must be made or accepted by every rational human agent on his own behalf, so that it holds universally within the context of action, which is the context within which all moral rights ultimately have application. The argument is dialectically necessary in that it proceeds from what all agents logically must claim or accept, on pain of contradiction. To see how this is so, we must briefly consider certain central aspects of action. Since I have presented the argument in some detail elsewhere,[7] I shall here confine myself to outlining the main points.

As we have seen, all moral precepts, regardless of their varying specific contents, are concerned directly or indirectly with how persons ought to act. This is also true of most if not all other practical precepts. Insofar as actions are the possible objects of any such precepts, they are performed by purposive agents. Now, every agent regards his purposes as good according to whatever criteria (not necessarily moral ones) are involved in his acting to fulfill them. This is shown, for example, by the endeavor or at least intention with which each agent approaches the achieving of his purposes. Hence, *a fortiori,* he also, as rational, regards as necessary goods the proximate general necessary conditions of his acting to achieve his purposes. For without these conditions he either would not be able to act for any purposes or goods at all or at least would not be able to act with any chance of succeeding in his purposes. These necessary conditions of his action and successful action are freedom and well-being, where freedom consists in controlling one's behavior by one's unforced choice while having knowledge of relevant circumstances, and well-being consists in having the other general abilities and conditions required for agency. The components of such well-being fall into a hierarchy of three kinds of goods: basic, nonsubtractive, and additive. These will be analyzed more fully below.

In saying that every rational agent regards his freedom and well-being as necessary goods, I am primarily making not a phenomenological descriptive point about the conscious thought processes of agents but rather a dialectically necessary point about what is logically involved in the structure of action. Since agents act for purposes they regard as worth pursuing — for otherwise they would not control their behavior by their unforced choice with a view to achieving their purposes — they must, insofar as they are rational, also regard the necessary conditions of such pursuit as necessary goods. Just

as the basic goods are generically the same for all agents, so too are
the nonsubtractive and additive goods. I shall call freedom and well-
being the *generic features* of action, since they characterize all action
or at least all successful action in the respect in which action has been
delimited above.

It is from the consideration of freedom and well-being as the necessary goods of action that the ascription and contents of human
rights follow. The main point is that with certain qualifications to be
indicated below, there is a logical connection between necessary
goods and rights. Just as we saw before that from "X is an interest of
some person A" it cannot be logically inferred that "A has a right to
X," so too this cannot be logically inferred from "X is a good of A" or
from "X seems good to A." In all these cases the antecedent is too
contingent and variable to ground an ascription of rights. The reason for this is that rights involve *normative necessity*. One way to see
this is through the correlativity of rights and strict "oughts" or duties.
The judgment "A has a right to X" both entails and is entailed by,
"All other persons ought at least to refrain from interfering with A's
having (or doing) X," where this "ought" includes the idea of something due or owed to A. Under certain circumstances, including
those where the subject or right-holder A is unable to have X by his
own efforts, the rights-judgment also entails and is entailed by,
"Other persons ought to assist A to have X," where again the "ought"
includes the idea of something due or owed to A. Now, these strict
"oughts" involve normative necessity; they state what, as of right,
other persons *must* do. Such necessity is also involved in the frequently
noted use of "due" and "entitlement" as synonyms or at least as components of the substantive use of "right." A person's rights are what
belong to him as his due, what he is entitled to, hence what he can
rightly demand of others. In all these expressions the idea of normative necessity is central.

This necessity is an essential component in the ascription of rights,
but it is not sufficient to logically ground this ascription. Let us recur
to freedom and well-being as the necessary goods of action. From "X
is a necessary good for A" does it logically follow that "A has a right
to X"? To understand this question correctly, we must keep in mind
that "necessary good" is here used in a rational and invariant sense.
It does not refer to the possibly idiosyncratic and unfounded desires
of different protagonists, as when someone asserts, "I must have a
Florida vacation (or a ten-speed bicycle); it is a necessary good for

me." Rather, a "necessary good" is here confined to the truly grounded requirements of agency; hence, it correctly characterizes the indispensable conditions that all agents must accept as needed for their actions.

Now, it might be argued that when "necessary good" is understood in this universal and rational way, from "X is a necessary good for A" it does follow that "A has a right to X." For since the idea of a right involves normative necessity, "A has a right to X" is entailed by "It is normatively necessary that A have X," and this seems equivalent to "X is a necessary good for A." There are three interrelated considerations, however, that show that "X is a necessary good for A" is not sufficient to provide the logical ground for "A has a right X" as a matter of logical necessity. First, as we have seen, "A has a right to X" entails that other persons, B, C, and so forth, have correlative duties toward A. But how can these duties of other persons be logically derived from "X is a necessary good for A," which refers only to A, not to other persons?

Second, it must be kept in mind that rights involve not only "oughts" or normative necessity but also the idea of entitlement, of something due to the right-holder. There is logical correlativity between "A has a right to X," on the one hand, and "Other persons ought to refrain from interfering with A's having X and ought also, under certain circumstances, to assist A to have X," on the other, only when these "oughts" are viewed as indicating what A is entitled to or ought to have as his due. But in "X is a necessary good for A" this idea of A's entitlement to X, of its being due or owed to him, is not found. Hence, it cannot serve to generate logically the conclusion, "A has a right to X."

A third consideration that shows this is that, as we saw above, a rights-judgment is prescriptive: it advocates or endorses that the subject or right-holder A have the X that is the object of the right. But such advocacy need not be present in "X is a necessary good for A." For this statement, as such, does not necessarily carry with it any advocacy or endorsement on A's behalf by the person who makes the statement, even while he recognizes its truth. Hence, again, "X is a necessary good for A" is not sufficient to logically generate or entail "A has a right to X."

What these considerations indicate is that for the concept of necessary goods logically to generate the concept of rights, both concepts must figure in judgments made by the agent or right-holder himself

in accordance with the dialectically necessary method. It will be recalled that this method begins from statements or judgments that are
necessarily made or accepted by protagonists or agents, and the
method then traces what these statements or judgments logically imply. Thus, in the present context of action, the method requires that
the judgments about necessary goods and rights be viewed as being
made by the agent himself from within his own internal, conative
standpoint in purposive agency.

When this internal, conative view is taken, the logical gaps indicated above between judgments about necessary goods and ascriptions of rights are closed. The agent is now envisaged as saying, "My
freedom and well-being are necessary goods." From this there does
logically follow his further judgment, "I have rights to freedom and
well-being." For the assertion about necessary goods is now not a
mere factual means-end statement; on the contrary, because it is
made by the agent himself from within his own conative standpoint
in purposive agency, it carries his advocacy or endorsement. In effect, he is saying, "I must have freedom and well-being in order to
pursue by my actions any of the purposes I want and intend to pursue." Thus his statement is prescriptive.

By the same token, his statement carries the idea of something that
is his due, to which he is entitled. It must be kept in mind that these
concepts do not have only moral or legal criteria; they may be used
with many different kinds of criteria, including intellectual, aesthetic, and prudential ones. In the present context the agent's criterion is prudential: the entitlement he claims to freedom and well-being is grounded in his own needs as an agent who wants to pursue his
purposes. He is saying that he has rights to freedom and well-being
because these goods are due to him from within his own standpoint as
a prospective purposive agent, since he needs these goods in order to
act either at all or with the general possibility of success.

This consideration also shows how, from the agent's judgment "My
freedom and well-being are necessary goods," there also logically follows a claim on his part against other persons. For he is saying that
because he must have freedom and well-being in order to act, he
must have whatever further conditions are required for his fulfilling
these needs; and these further conditions include especially that
other persons at least refrain from interfering with his having freedom and well-being. Thus, the agent's assertion of his necessary
needs of agency entails a claim on his part to the noninterference of

other persons and also, in certain circumstances, to their help.

There may be further objections against the derivation of the agent's right-claims from his judgment about necessary goods; I have dealt with these elsewhere.[8] What I have tried to show is that every agent must claim or accept, at least implicitly, that he has rights to freedom and well-being, because of the logical connection between rights and necessary goods as involving normative necessity, prescriptiveness, and entitlements when these are viewed from the internal, conative standpoint of the agent himself who makes or accepts the respective judgments. The argument may be summed up by saying that if any agent denies that he has rights to freedom and well-being, he can be shown to contradict himself. For, as we have seen, he must accept (1) "My freedom and well-being are necessary goods." Hence, the agent must also accept (2) "I, as an actual or prospective agent, must have freedom and well-being," and hence also (3) "All other persons must at least refrain from removing or interfering with my freedom and well-being." For if other persons remove or interfere with these, then he will not have what he has said he must have. Now suppose the agent denies (4) "I have rights to freedom and well-being." Then he must also deny (5) "All other persons ought at least to refrain from removing or interfering with my freedom and well-being." By denying (5) he must accept (6) "It is not the case that all other persons ought at least to refrain from removing or interfering with my freedom and well-being," and hence he must also accept (7) "Other persons may (are permitted to) remove or interfere with my freedom and well-being." But (7) contradicts (3). Since, as we have seen, every agent must accept (3), he cannot consistently accept (7). Since (7) is entailed by the denial of (4), "I have rights to freedom and well-being," it follows that any agent who denies that he has rights to freedom and well-being contradicts himself.

III

Thus far I have shown that rights and right-claims are necessarily connected with action, in that every agent, on pain of self-contradiction, must hold or accept that he has rights to the necessary conditions of action. I shall henceforth call these *generic rights,* since freedom and well-being are the generic features of action. As so far presented, however, they are only prudential rights but not yet moral ones, since their criterion, as we have seen, is the agent's own pursuit of his purposes. In order to establish that they are also moral and human rights, we must show that each agent must admit that all other humans also have these rights. For in this way the agent will be committed to take favorable account of the purposes or interests of other persons besides himself. Let us see why he must take this further step.

This involves the question of the ground or sufficient reason or sufficient condition on the basis of which any agent must hold that he has the generic rights. Now, this ground is not subject to his optional or variable decisions. There is one, and only one, ground that every agent logically must accept as the sufficient justifying condition for his having the generic rights, namely, that he is a prospective agent who has purposes he wants to fulfill. Suppose some agent A were to hold that he has these rights only for some more restrictive necessary and sufficient reason R. This would entail that in lacking R he would lack the generic rights. But if A were to accept this conclusion, that he may not have the generic rights, he would contradict himself. For we saw above that it is necessarily true of every agent that he must hold or accept at least implicitly that he has rights to freedom and well-being. Hence, A would be in the position of both affirming and denying that he has the generic rights: affirming it because he is an agent, denying it because he lacks R. To avoid this contradiction, every agent must hold that being a prospective purposive agent is a sufficient reason or condition for having the generic rights.

Because of this sufficient reason, every agent, on pain of self-contradiction, must also accept the generalization that all prospective purposive agents have the generic rights. This generalization is an application of the logical principle of universalizability: if some predicate P belongs to some subject S because S has the quality Q (where the 'because' is that of sufficient reason or condition), then it logically follows that every subject that has Q has P. If any agent A were to deny or refuse to accept this generalization in the case of any other prospective purposive agent, A would contradict himself. For he would be in the position of saying that being a prospective purposive agent both is and is not a sufficient justifying condition for having the generic rights. Hence, on pain of self-contradiction, every agent must accept the generalization that all prospective purposive agents have the generic rights.

Thus, we have now arrived at the basis of human rights. For the generic rights to freedom and well-being are moral rights, since they require of every agent that he take favorable account of the most important interests of all other prospective agents, namely, the interests grounded in their needs for the necessary conditions of agency. And these generic rights are also human rights, since every human being is an actual, prospective, or potential agent. I shall discuss the distribution of these rights among humans more fully below. But first I must also establish that the generic rights are human rights in the further respect indicated above, namely, that they are grounded in or justified by a valid moral criterion or principle.

The above argument for the generic rights as moral rights has already provided the full basis for deriving a supreme moral principle. We have seen that every agent, on pain of self-contradiction, must accept the generalization that all prospective purposive agents have the generic rights to freedom and well-being. From this generalization, because of the correlativity of rights and strict "oughts," it logically follows that every person ought to refrain from interfering with the freedom and well-being of all other persons insofar as they are prospective purposive agents. It also follows that under certain circumstances every person ought to assist other persons to have freedom and well-being, when they cannot have these by their own efforts and he can give them such assistance without comparable cost to himself, although more usually such assistance must operate through appropriate institutions. Since to refrain and to assist in these ways is to act in such a way that one's actions are in accord with the generic rights of one's recipients, every agent is logically committed, on pain of self-contradiction, to accept the following precept: *Act in accord with the generic rights of your recipients as well as of yourself.* I shall call this the *Principle of Generic Consistency (PGC),* since it combines the formal consideration of consistency with the material consideration of the generic features and rights of agency. To act in accord with someone's right to freedom is, in part, to refrain from coercing him; to act in accord with someone's right to well-being is, in part, to refrain from harming him by adversely affecting his basic, nonsubtractive, or additive goods. In addition, to act in accord with these rights may also require positive assistance. These rights, as thus upheld, are now moral ones because they are concerned to further the interests or goods of persons other than or in addition to the agent. The *PGC*'s central moral requirement is the *equality of generic rights,* since it requires of every agent that he accord to his recipients the same rights to freedom and well-being that he necessarily claims for himself.

The above argument has provided the outline of a rational justification of the Principle of Generic Consistency as the supreme principle of morality, both for the formal reason that if any agent denies or violates the principle he contradicts himself and for the material reason that its content, the generic features of action, necessarily imposes itself on every agent. For it is necessarily true of every agent that he at least implicitly attributes to himself the generic rights and that he acts in accord with his own generic rights; hence, he cannot rationally evade the extension of these rights to his recipients. This material necessity stands in contrast to principles centered in the purposes, inclinations, or ideals for which some agent may contingently act and whose requirements he may hence evade by shifting his desires or opinions. The *PGC* is the supreme principle of morality because its interpersonal requirements, derived from the generic features of action, cannot rationally be evaded by any agent. (It must be kept in mind that action is the universal context of morality.) The main point may be put succinctly as follows: What for any agent are necessarily goods of action, namely, freedom and well-being, are equally necessary goods for his recipients, and he logically must admit that they have as much right to these goods as he does, since the ground or reason for which he rationally claims them for himself also pertains to his recipients.

We have now seen that every agent must hold, on pain of self-contradiction, that all other persons as well as himself have moral rights grounded in the *PGC* as the principle of morality. It follows from the argument to the *PGC* that the primary criterion for having moral rights is that all persons have certain needs relative to their being actual or prospective agents, namely, needs for freedom and well-being as the necessary conditions of action. Simply by virtue of being actual or prospective agents who have certain needs of agency, persons have moral rights to freedom and well-being. Since all humans are such agents having such needs, the generic moral rights to freedom and well-being are human rights.

This argument for human rights has avoided the problem of how rights can be logically derived from facts. For, in proceeding by the dialectically necessary method, it has remained throughout within the facts of agents' necessary judgments about goods and rights. The argument has established not that persons have rights *tout court* but rather that all agents logically must claim or at least accept that they have certain rights. This relativity to agents and their claims does not, however, remove the absoluteness of rights or the categoricalness of the *PGC*. For since agency is the proximate general context of all morality and indeed of all practice, whatever is necessarily justified within the context of agency is also necessary for morality, and what logically must be accepted by every agent is necessarily justified within the context of agency. Thus, the argument has established that since every agent logically must accept that he has rights to freedom and well-being, the having of these rights is morally necessary. Hence, the requirement indicated above is fulfilled: the rights to freedom and well-being exist as human rights because there is a valid moral criterion, the *PGC,* which justifies that all humans have these rights.

Questions may be raised about the extent to which the generic rights as I have defined them are indeed human rights. To be human rights they must be had by every human being simply as such. The generic rights, however, are rights to the necessary conditions of agency. But may not some humans lack these rights because they are incapable of agency in one degree or another? Examples of such humans include children, mentally deficient persons, paraplegics, persons with brain damage, fetuses, and so forth. From these examples it might seem to follow that the generic rights to the necessary conditions of action are not truly human rights in the sense in which such rights were initially defined.

This question rests in part on a variant of the dictum that "ought" implies "can," for it assumes that for some person A to have a right to something *X,* A must be capable of having or doing *X.* Now this assumption is correct, but only if the capability in question is correctly interpreted. All normal adult humans are fully capable of action as this has been interpreted here, as voluntary and purposive behavior, for all such persons have the proximate ability to control their behavior by their unforced choice with a view to attaining their goals while having knowledge of relevant circumstances. This description applies even to paraplegics, despite the lesser range of the control of which they are proximately capable, for they can think, choose (although within narrower limits), and plan.

In the other cases mentioned, the capabilities for action are less, and hence their rights too are proportionately less. Children are potential agents in that, with normal maturation, they will develop the full abilities of agency. In their case, as well as in that of mentally deficient persons and persons with brain damage, their possession of the generic rights must be proportional to the degree to which they have the abilities of agency, and this must be with a view to taking on the fullest degree of the generic rights of which they are capable so long as this does not result in harm to themselves or others. All other adult humans have the generic rights in full. In the case of the human fetus, this raises problems of the justification of abortion because of possible conflicts with the rights of the mother; I have considered this elsewhere.[9]

The equation of the generic rights with human rights thus does not derogate from the universality of the latter. It enables us to understand the varying degrees to which the rights are had by certain humans, as well as the connection of human rights with action and practice. The derivation of these rights from the argument for the *PGC* also enables us to understand the traditional view that human rights are grounded in reason so that they have a normative necessity or categorical obligatoriness that goes beyond the variable contents of social customs or positive laws.

IV

There remain two broad questions about human rights as so far delineated. First, the rights to freedom and well-being are very general. What more specific contents do they have, and how are these contents related to one another? Second, human rights are often thought of in terms of political effectuation and legal enforcement. How does this relation operate in the case of the generic rights? Should all of them be legally enforced or only some, and how is this to be determined?

To answer the first question we must analyze the components of well-being and of freedom. It was noted above that well-being, viewed as the abilities and conditions required for agency, comprises three kinds of goods: basic, nonsubtractive, and additive. Basic goods are the essential preconditions of action, such as life, physical integrity, and mental equilibrium. Thus, a person's basic rights — his rights to basic goods — are violated when he is killed, starved, physically incapacitated, terrorized, or subjected to mentally deranging drugs. The basic rights are also violated in such cases as where a person is drowning or starving and another person who, at no comparable cost to himself, could rescue him or give him food knowingly fails to do so.

Nonsubtractive goods are the abilities and conditions required for maintaining undiminished one's level of purpose-fulfillment and one's capabilities for particular actions. A person's nonsubtractive rights are violated when he is adversely affected in his abilities to plan for the future, to have knowledge of facts relevant to his projected actions, to utilize his resources to fulfill his wants, and so forth. Ways of undergoing such adversities include being lied to, cheated, stolen from, or defamed; suffering broken promises; or being subjected to dangerous, degrading, or excessively debilitating conditions of physical labor or housing or other strategic situations of life when resources are available for improvement.

Additive goods are the abilities and conditions required for increasing one's level of purpose-fulfillment and one's capabilities for particular actions. A person's additive rights are violated when his self-esteem is attacked, when he is denied education to the limits of his capacities, or when he is discriminated against on grounds of race, religion, or nationality. This right is also violated when a person's development of the self-regarding virtues of courage, temperance, and prudence is hindered by actions that promote a climate of fear and oppression, or that encourage the spread of physically or mentally harmful practices such as excessive use of drugs, or that contribute to misinformation, ignorance, and superstition, especially as these bear on persons' ability to act effectively in pursuit of their purposes. When a person's right to basic well-being is violated, I shall say that he undergoes basic harm; when his rights to nonsubtractive or additive well-being are violated, I shall say that he undergoes specific harm.

Besides these three components of the right to well-being, the human rights also include the right to freedom. This consists in a person's controlling his actions and his participation in transactions by his own unforced choice or consent and with knowledge of relevant circumstances, so that his behavior is neither compelled nor prevented by the actions of other persons. Hence, a person's right to freedom is violated if he is subjected to violence, coercion, deception, or any other procedures that attack or remove his informed control of his behavior by his own unforced choice. This right includes having a sphere of personal autonomy and privacy whereby one is let alone by others unless and until he unforcedly consents to undergo their action.

In general, whenever a person violates any of these rights to well-being or freedom, his action is morally wrong and he contradicts himself. For he is in the position of saying or holding that a right he necessarily claims for himself insofar as he is a prospective purposive agent is not had by some other person, even though the latter, too, is a prospective purposive agent. Hence, all such morally wrong actions are rationally unjustifiable.

It must also be noted, however, that these rights to freedom and well-being may conflict with one another. For example, the right to freedom of one person A may conflict with the right to well-being of another person B when A uses his freedom to kill, rob, or insult B. Here the duty of other persons to refrain from interfering with A's control of his behavior by his unforced choice may conflict with their duty to prevent B from suffering basic or specific harm when they can do so at no comparable cost to themselves. In addition, different persons' rights to well-being may conflict with one another, as when C must lie to D in order to prevent E from being murdered, or when F must break his promise to G in order to save H from drowning. Moreover, a person's right to freedom may conflict with his own right to well-being, as when he commits suicide or ingests harmful drugs. Here the duty of other persons not to interfere with his control of his behavior by his unforced choice may conflict with their duty to prevent his losing basic goods when they can do so at no comparable cost to themselves.

These conflicts show that human rights are only *prima facie*, not absolute, in that under certain circumstances they may justifiably be overridden. Nothing is gained by saying that what is justifiably overridden is not the right but only its exercise. For since a person's having some right has a justificatory basis, when this basis is removed he no longer has the right. In such a case it is his right itself and not only its exercise that is justifiably removed or overridden.

Another argument for the absoluteness of human rights is that their alleged *prima facie* character stems from their being incompletely described. Thus, it is held that the right to life or the right not to be killed, for example, must be specified more fully as the right not to be killed unless one has committed a murder, or as the right of innocent persons not to be killed. Such devices, however, either include in the description of the right the very overriding conditions that are in question, or else they restrict the distribution of the right so that it is not a right of all humans.

But although human rights may be overridden, this still leaves the Principle of Generic Consistency as an absolute or categorically obligatory moral principle. For the *PGC* sets the criteria for the justifiable overriding of one moral right by another and hence for the resolution of conflicts among rights. The basis of these criteria is that the *PGC* is both a formal and a material principle concerned with transactional consistency regarding the possession and use of the necessary conditions of action. The criteria stem from the *PGC*'s central requirement that there must be mutual respect for freedom and wellbeing among all prospective purposive agents. Departures from this mutual respect are justified only where they are required either to prevent or rectify antecedent departures, or to avoid greater departures, or to comply with social rules that themselves reflect such respect in the ways indicated in the procedural and instrumental applications of the *PGC*. Thus the criteria for resolving conflicts of rights or duties fall under three headings of progressively lesser importance.

The first criterion for resolving the conflicts of rights is the prevention or removal of transactional inconsistency. If one person or group violates or is about to violate the generic rights of another and thereby incurs transactional inconsistency, action to prevent or remove the inconsistency may be justified. Whether the action should always be undertaken depends on such circumstances as the feasibility and importance for subsequent action of removing the inconsistency: this may be very slight in the case of some lies and very great in the case of basic harms. Thus, although the *PGC* in general prohibits coercion and basic harm, it authorizes and even requires these as punishment and for prevention and correction of antecedent basic harm.

This criterion of the prevention of transactional inconsistency sets a limitation on the right to freedom. This right is overridden when a person intends to use his freedom in order to infringe the freedom or well-being of other persons. Such overriding stems from the *PGC*'s general requirement that each person must act in accord with the generic rights of his recipients, since this requirement sets limits on each person's freedom of action. The prohibition against coercion or harm is itself overridden, however, by two considerations, each of which also stems from the *PGC*. First, one person A may coerce or harm another person B in order to prevent B from coercing or harming either A himself or some other person C. Thus if B physically assaults A or C, A may physically assault B in order to resist or prevent the assault. Second, coercion or harm may be justified if it is inflicted in accordance with social rules or institutions that are themselves justified by the *PGC*. I shall discuss this latter justification below.

A second criterion for resolving conflicts of rights is the degree of their necessity for action. Since every person has rights to the necessary conditions of action, one right takes precedence over another if the good that is the object of the former right is more necessary for the possibility of action, and if that right cannot be protected without violating the latter right. For example, A's right not to be lied to is overridden by B's right not to be murdered or enslaved, where B or C has to lie to A in order to prevent him from committing these crimes against B. A person's right to freedom is also overridden in such ways. It will have been noted that whereas the first criterion for resolving conflicts among rights deals mainly with rights to goods of the same degree of importance, the second criterion deals with goods of different degrees, but within the same general context of preventing transactional inconsistency.

This criterion of degrees of necessity for action also applies to such limiting cases as where a person intends to use his freedom in order to attack his own well-being. As we have seen, there are levels of well-being, such that basic well-being is more necessary for action than nonsubtractive well-being, while the latter in turn is usually more necessary for action than additive well-being. Hence, in general, force may be used at least temporarily to prevent a person from killing or maiming himself, especially so long as there is doubt whether he fulfills the emotional and cognitive conditions of freedom or voluntariness. But such interference with someone's freedom is not justified to prevent him from diminishing his nonsubtractive or additive well-being, because his freedom is itself more necessary for his actions than are these levels of his well-being. The remaining complexities of this issue cannot be dealt with here.[10]

V

The conflicts among rights require further criteria besides the two given so far. To deal with these, we must move from the individual, transactional applications of the *PGC* so far considered to its institutional applications. The latter applications will also bring us to the second general question presented above, concerning the legal enforcement and political effectuation of human rights.

Although this legal, institutional context is perhaps the most familiar area of discussion of human rights, it must be emphasized that these rights also figure centrally in individual interpersonal transactions. A person's human rights to freedom and well-being are violated just as surely, although perhaps less powerfully and irrevocably, if he is kidnapped and held for ransom as if he is subjected to unjust imprisonment; and torture by a private person is just as much an infringement of one's human rights as torture by an agent of the state. So, too, although in lesser degrees, a person's human rights are violated when he is lied to, discriminated against, or made to work for starvation wages when better conditions could be made available. Moreover, a large part, although not the whole, of the human rights that should be legally enforced consist in the legal protection of individuals from suffering violations of their most important human rights to just treatment on the part of individuals or groups other than those representing the state.

To deal with the legal context of the protection of human rights, we must turn to another kind of application of the *PGC* besides the one so far considered. The *PGC* has two different kinds of applications: direct and indirect. In the direct applications, the *PGC*'s requirements are imposed on the actions of individual agents; the actions are morally right and the agents fulfill their moral duties when they act in accord with the generic rights of their recipients as well as of themselves. In the indirect applications, on the other hand, the *PGC*'s requirements are imposed in the first instance on social rules and institutions. These are morally right, and persons acting in accordance with them fulfill their moral duties, when the rules and institutions express or serve to protect or foster the equal freedom and well-being of the persons subject to them. Thus, by the indirect applications recipients may even be coerced or harmed, yet this does not violate their human rights to freedom and well-being, because the rules or institutions that require such coercion or harm are themselves justified by the *PGC*. For example, when the umpire in a baseball game calls three strikes, the batter is out and must leave the batter's box even if he does not consent to this. This calling him out operates to coerce the batter so that he is forced to leave the batter's box. Nevertheless, the umpire's action is morally justified and the batter's right to freedom is not violated insofar as he has freely accepted the rules of the game. Or again, a judge who sentences a criminal to prison operates to coerce and harm him, yet this is morally justified and the criminal's rights to freedom and well-being are not violated insofar as the rules of the criminal law serve to protect and restore the mutuality of occurrent nonharm prescribed by the *PGC*.

As these examples may suggest, the indirect, institutional applications of the *PGC* are of two kinds. The *procedural* applications derive from the *PGC*'s freedom component: they provide that social rules and institutions are morally right insofar as the persons subject to them have freely consented to accept them or have certain consensual procedures freely available to them. The *instrumental* applications derive from the *PGC*'s well-being component: they provide that social rules and institutions are morally right insofar as they operate to protect and support the well-being of all persons.

Each of these applications, in turn, is of two sorts. The procedural applications may be either *optional* or *necessary*. They are optional according as persons consent to form or to participate in voluntary associations. The procedural applications are necessary according as the consent they require operates as a general decision procedure using the civil liberties to provide the authoritative basis, through elections and other consensual methods, of specific laws or governmental officials.

The *PGC*'s instrumental applications may be either *static* or *dynamic*. The static applications, embodied in the minimal state with its criminal law, serve to protect persons from occurrent violations of their rights to basic and other important goods and to punish such violations. The dynamic applications, embodied in the supportive state, serve to provide longer-range protections of basic and other rights where these cannot be obtained by persons through their own efforts.

In the remainder of this chapter I want to indicate how these distinctions of the *PGC*'s indirect applications help to clarify the question of the legal enforcement of human rights. As we have noted, the institutions of law and government are instrumentally justified by the *PGC* as means for enforcing its most important requirements. Not all the human rights upheld by the *PGC* should receive legal enforcement. The specific harms done by violations of a person's nonsubtractive rights, such as when he is lied to or when a promise made to him is broken, are ordinarily less important in their impact on their recipient's well-being than are the harms done by violations of basic rights, and hence do not justify the state's coercive legal resources to combat or correct them.

The human rights that should receive legal enforcement are those comprised in the last three of the indirect applications of the *PGC* distinguished above. Each of these applications reflects a certain justification of social rules that set requirements for persons and for the state. First, there is what I have called the static-instrumental justification of social rules, consisting in the criminal law. This serves to protect basic and other important rights from occurrent attack by other persons, including the rights to life, physical integrity, and reputation. But the *PGC* also sets standards or limits as to how this protection is to operate: only persons who have violated these rights of others are to be punished; all persons must be equal before the law; trials must be fair; *habeas corpus* must be guaranteed; punishment must not be cruel, vindictive, or inhuman.

Second, there is the dynamic-instrumental justification of social rules. This recognizes that persons are dispositionally unequal in their actual ability to attain and protect their generic rights, especially their rights to basic well-being, and it provides for social rules that serve to remove this inequality. Thus, where the static phase (the criminal law) tries to restore an occurrent antecedent status quo of mutual nonharm, the dynamic phase tries to move toward a new situation in which a previously nonexistent dispositional equality is attained or more closely approximated. Social rules supporting the various components of well-being, but especially basic well-being, are justified in this dynamic way.

These supportive rules must have several kinds of contents. First, they must provide for supplying basic goods, such as food and housing, to those persons who cannot obtain them by their own efforts. Second, they must try to rectify inequalities of additive well-being by improving the capabilities for productive work of persons who are deficient in this respect. Education is a prime means of such improvement, but also important is whatever strengthens family life and enables parents to give constructive, intelligent, loving nurture to their children. The wider diffusion of such means is a prime component of increasing equality of opportunity. Third, the rules must provide for various public goods that, while helping all the members of the society, serve to increase the opportunities for productive employment. Fourth, the rules must regulate certain important conditions of well-being by removing dangerous or degrading conditions of work and housing.

A third area of legal enforcement of human rights is found in what I have called the necessary-procedural justification of social rules. This justification is an application of the *PGC*'s freedom component to the constitutional structure of the state. It provides that laws and state officials must be designated by procedures that use the *method of consent*. This method consists in the availability and use of the civil liberties in the political process. The objects of these liberties include the actions of speaking, publishing, and associating with others, so that, as a matter of constitutional requirement, each person is able, if he chooses, to discuss, criticize, and vote for or against the government and to work actively with other persons or groups of various sizes to further his political objectives, including the redress of his socially based grievances. In this way each person has the right to participate actively in the political process.

The civil liberties also extend to contexts of individual and social activity other than the political process. The *PGC*'s protection of the right to freedom requires that each person be left to engage in any action or transaction according to his unforced choice so long as he does not coerce or harm other persons. This requirement sets an important limit on the legitimate powers of the state: it must not interfere with the freedom of the individual except to prevent his coercing or harming others in ways that adversely affect their basic or other important well-being. The criteria of this importance are found in what affects persons' having the abilities and conditions required for purposive action. Thus, an immense array of kinds of action must be exempted from governmental control, while at the same time the freedom to perform these actions must be protected by the state.

These freedoms are hence called "civil liberties" for three interconnected reasons, bearing on three different relations the freedoms must have to the state. First, they are passive and negative in that they must not be restricted or interfered with by the state. Second, they are passive and positive in that they must be protected by the state as rights of persons. Third, they are active in that the actions that are their objects function in the political process to help determine who shall govern in the state. In all relations, the *PGC* requires that the civil liberties pertain equally to each prospective purposive agent (except criminals): each person has an equal right to use his freedom noncoercively and nonharmfully (according to the criteria of harm specified above), to participate freely and actively in the political process, and to be protected by the state in that participation and in his other actions using his freedom in the way just indicated. Insofar as there are diverse states, this equal right pertains to each citizen, and each person has a right to be a citizen of a state having the civil liberties.

We have now seen that the *PGC*'s indirect applications require that three kinds of rights receive legal enforcement and protection: the personal-security rights protected by the criminal law, the social and economic rights protected by the supportive state, and the political and civil rights and liberties protected by the Constitution with its method of consent.

The second of these kinds comprises important phases of the right to well-being, the third encompasses a large part of the right to freedom. I wish to conclude by considering two opposite extreme views about how the social and economic rights figure in the legal enforcement and protection of human rights.

One view is that these rights, including the right to be given food and the other goods needed for alleviating severe economic handicaps and insecurities, cannot be "human" rights because they do not meet two tests: universality and practicability. [11] According to the test of universality, for a moral right to be a human one it must be a right of all persons against all persons: all persons must have the strict duty of acting in accord with the right, and all persons must have the strict right to be treated in the appropriate way. Thus, all persons must be both the agents and the recipients of the modes of action required by the right. This test is passed by the rights to life and to freedom of movement: everyone has the duty to refrain from killing other persons and from interfering with their movements, and everyone has the right to have his life and his freedom of movement respected by other persons. But in the case of the right to be relieved from starvation or severe economic deprivation, it is objected that only some persons have the right: those who are threatened by starvation or deprivation; and only some persons have the duty: those who are able to prevent or relieve this starvation by giving aid.

The answer to this objection need not concede that this right, like other economic and social rights, is universal only in a "weaker" sense in that whereas all persons have the right to be rescued from starvation or deprivation, only some persons have the correlative duty. Within the limits of practicability, all persons have the right and all have the duty. For all persons come under the protection and the requirements of the *PGC* insofar as they are prospective purposive agents. Hence, all the generic rights upheld by the *PGC* have the universality required for being human rights.

It is, indeed, logically impossible that each person be at the same time both the rescuer and the rescued, both the affluent provider and the deprived pauper. Nevertheless, the fact that some prospective purposive agent may not at some time need to be rescued from deprivation or be able to rescue others from deprivation does not remove the facts that he has the right to be rescued when he has the need and that he has the duty to rescue when he has the ability and when other relevant conditions are met. This duty stems, in the way indicated earlier, from the claim he necessarily makes or accepts that he has the generic rights by virtue of being a prospective purposive agent. The universality of a right is not a matter of everyone's actually having the related need, nor is it a matter of everyone's actually fulfilling the correlative duty, let alone of his doing so at all times. Nor is it even a matter of everyone's always being able to fulfill the duty. It is rather a matter of everyone's always having, as a matter of principle, the right to be treated in the appropriate way when he has the need, and the duty to act in accord with the right when the circumstances arise that require such action and when he then has the ability to do so, this ability including consideration of cost to himself.

When it is said that the right to be relieved from economic deprivation and the correlative duty pertain to all persons insofar as they are prospective purposive agents, this does not violate the condition that for human rights to be had one must only be human, as against fulfilling some more restrictive description. As was indicated earlier, all normal humans are prospective purposive agents; the point of introducing this description is only to call attention to the aspect of being human that most directly generates the rights to freedom and well-being. In this regard, the right in question differs from rights that pertain to persons not simply by virtue of being prospective purposive agents but only in some more restricted capacity, such as being teachers as against students, umpires as against batters, or judges as against defendants. The universality of human rights derives from their direct connection with the necessary conditions of action, as against the more restrictive objects with which nongeneric rights are connected. And since both the affluent and the economically deprived are prospective purposive agents, the latter's right to be helped by the former is a human right.

These considerations also apply to the contention that the social and economic rights are not human rights because they do not pass the test of practicability, in that many nations lack the economic means to fulfill these rights. Now, it is indeed the case that whereas the political and civil rights may require nonaction or noninterference rather than positive action on the part of governments, the economic rights require the positive use of economic resources for their effective implementation. This does not, however, militate against governments' taking steps to provide support, to the extent of their available resources, to persons who cannot attain basic economic goods by their own efforts. There is a considerable distance between the position that the same high levels of economic well-being are not attainable in all countries and the position that a more equitable distribution of goods and of means of producing goods is not feasible for countries at the lower end of the scale.

This point is also relevant to a view that stands at the opposite extreme from the one just considered: that for most persons in many parts of the world the social and economic rights are the only human rights that should be legally implemented. According to this view, the political and civil rights, by contrast, are of little importance for persons in the Third World with its predominant illiteracy, traditionalism, poverty, nonindividualist ethos, and lack of regard for the rule of law. This position is epitomized in the dictum, "Food first, freedom later," where the "freedom" in question consists especially in the political and civil liberties. The contention is that until the economic rights to subsistence, housing, and employment are effectively implemented, persons who lack these have little interest or opportunity or need for the political and civil rights and that fulfillment of the former rights is a necessary prerequisite for fulfilling the latter.

A distinction may be drawn between such personal-security rights as *habeas corpus* and noninfliction of torture or cruel punishment, and the political rights of the method of consent with its civil liberties of speech, press, and association. Nevertheless, the latter provide important safeguards for the former. Both these kinds of rights, in turn, are far from being antithetical to, or needless for, the economic and social rights. Indeed, the order of priority may be the reverse of that upheld in the view under consideration. The effective distribution of the civil liberties, far from being a passive effect of the proper distribution of food, housing, and health care, can strongly facilitate the latter distribution. When governments are not subject to the political process of the method of consent, there is to that extent less assurance that the authorities will be responsive to the material needs of all their citizens. As is shown by sad experience in many of the underdeveloped countries, the lack of effective political participation by the masses of the poor permits a drastic unconcern with their needs for food even when it is locally available.[12]

What I have tried to show in this essay is that all the human rights have a rational foundation in the necessary conditions or needs of human action, so that no human agent can deny or violate them except on pain of self-contradiction. Thus, the demands the human rights make on persons are justified by the *PGC* as the supreme principle of morality. It is also through the moral requirements set by this principle that the political and legal order receives its central justification as providing for the protection of human rights. In addition to this instrumental function, possession of the civil liberties together with the effective capacity for participating in the method of consent is required for the dignity and rational autonomy of every prospective purposive agent. Thus, the rationally grounded requirements of human action provide the basis and content of all human rights, both those that apply in individual transactions and those that must be protected by social rules and institutions.

NOTES

1. See W. N. Hohfeld, *Fundamental Legal Conceptions* (New Haven: Yale University Press, 1919); John Salmond, *Jurisprudence*, 10th ed. (London: Sweet and Maxwell, 1947), pp. 229 ff.

2. Robert Nozick, *Anarchy, State and Utopia* (New York: Basic Books, 1974), p. ix.

3. See H. L. A. Hart, "Are There Any Natural Rights?" *Philosophical Review*, 64 (1955): 175 ff.

4. See H. J. McCloskey, "Rights," *Philosophical Quarterly*, 15 (1965): 124. Elsewhere, McCloskey holds that persons have a *prima facie* right to the satisfaction of needs: "Human Needs, Rights and Political Values," *American Philosophical Quarterly*, 13 (1976): 9-10.

5. See Jacques Maritain, *The Rights of Man and Natural Law* (London: Geoffrey Bles, 1944).

6. John Rawls, *A Theory of Justice* (Cambridge, Mass.: Harvard University Press, 1971), chaps. 2, 3.

7. See Alan Gewirth, *Reason and Morality* (Chicago: The University of Chicago Press, 1978), chap. 2.

8. Ibid., pp. 82-103.

9. Ibid., pp. 142-144.

10. See ibid., pp. 259-267.

11. See Maurice Cranston, *What Are Human Rights?* (London: Bodley Head, 1963), pp. 66 ff. See also his contribution to D. D. Raphael, ed., *Political Theory and the Rights of Man* (London: Macmillan, 1967), pp. 96 ff. For the "weaker" sense of the universality of rights referred to below, see Raphael in *Political Theory and the Rights of Man*, pp. 65 ff., 112.

12. See Thomas T. Poleman, "World Food: A Perspective," *Science*, 188 (1975): 515; Pierre R. Crosson, "Institutional Obstacles to World

Food Production," ibid., pp. 522, 523; Harry Walters, "Difficult Issues Underlying Food Problems," ibid., p. 530; Gunnar Myrdal, *Asian Drama: An Inquiry in the Poverty of Nations* (New York: Twentieth Century Fund, 1969), vol. II, pp. 895–899; S. Reutlinger and M. Selowsky, *Malnutrition and Poverty* (Baltimore: The Johns Hopkins University Press, 1976).

7

THE BASIS OF HUMAN RIGHTS:
A CRITICISM OF GEWIRTH'S THEORY
RICHARD B. FRIEDMAN

Among the many issues raised by Alan Gewirth's theory of human rights in the preceding chapter, I propose to concentrate on one in particular. This has to do with the distinctive method of argument Gewirth has developed to "prove or justify that persons have [human] rights" (p. 119). Gewirth is firmly convinced that he has discovered and articulated the method of argument appropriate to this formidable task, and it is this belief that I wish to question. Much else in Gewirth's treatment of human rights is worth considering, especially his contention that the distinction between civil rights and economic rights has no theoretical significance bearing on his main enterprise, the enterprise of establishing the "basis" of human rights (pp. 140–46). But it is first necessary to examine what he takes to be that "basis."

I. MAIN CHARACTERISTICS OF
GEWIRTH'S THEORY

Gewirth's treatment of human rights seems to me to possess four main characteristics that may be delineated for purposes of the ensuing discussion as follows:

1. Character and Purpose of Human Rights.
Gewirth understands a human right to be a right to which every human being is morally entitled, and accordingly he conceives the problem facing a "theory" of human rights to be the problem of

identifying some property, feature, or "fact" (as he puts it), characteristic of human beings, that can be shown to warrant the imputation of such rights to all humans. This "fact" is found by Gewirth in man's capacity for "agency" or action, and he goes on to argue that, since action is possible for a human being only if he commands certain "conditions" — "The necessary conditions of action," "freedom," and "well-being" — the purpose of human rights in human affairs is properly to be construed as that of securing or supplying every human being qua agent with these "necessary conditions." From this standpoint, Gewirth pictures a society in which human rights are given the fullest possible recognition as a society in which the requirements of action are "distributed" (pp. 130-32) to every member of the society as rights to which he is recognized as being entitled as a matter of principle. The legal order and political institutions are, in turn, understood to receive the justification appropriate to them in seeing to it that this "distribution" does effectively take place. The "state" is thus said to be "instrumentally justified" (p. 140); it exists to secure the antecedently defined human rights and is limited in the exercise of its authority to the "enforcement" and "administration" of these rights. Conversely, a society that denies human rights comes across, by implication, not as a society in which the possibility of action is destroyed for every human (this presumably is a logical impossibility in any society that can be said to exist), but rather as a society in which the possibility of action for each person is left (or made) to depend on a morally unacceptable distribution of the requirements of action. The theory of human rights thus becomes coterminus with the theory of social or distributive justice, and is certainly not confined to the concern of traditional natural rights theory with limitations on political authority.

2. Starting Point of the Argument.

Gewirth thus presents a moral theory that is recognizably individualistic in the sense that he starts with the "most important interests" (pp. 130-31) or "requirements" of the individual human defined in abstraction from political or social context and stripped of all religious or metaphysical (substantive teleological) considerations, and then proceeds to derive the principles that are to govern all laws, political institutions, and basic social relations from these antecedently determined requirements of the individual. However, on Gewirth's theory, in contrast to the more usual versions of individualistic theory, this individual is not defined in terms of universal psychological propensities or desires of so-called human nature (including, it should be noted, the desire to be an agent), but instead in terms of the capacity for agency, so that the "most important interests" of the individual human are in turn construed not as the arrangements needed to satisfy basic desires, but as the conditions required for human beings to have and to act on their own purposes. It may be observed, however, that this key notion of "the necessary conditions of agency" is ambiguously specified as the conditions necessary for choosing and pursuing one's purpose and as the conditions necessary for purpose-fulfillment (pp. 129–30); or as Gewirth puts it elsewhere, "the necessary conditions of the existence and the success of all his actions."[1]

3. Method of Argument.

The crux of Gewirth's theory is, then, the method of argument he employs to pass from the "fact" of "necessary conditions of action" to his chief normative conclusion, the "Supreme Moral Principle," that every human, in virtue of being an agent, has a right to these conditions. The most well-known program of argument used by individualistic theories to get from individual requirements to social norms is the application of rational choice theory to a previously constructed condition in which the individuals are hypothetically situated: that condition is so structured that the only way in which any individual can rationally expect to secure the human requirements for himself is to join together with others in a society in which those requirements are secured to all. Now, Gewirth, in setting out his own special argument, also explicitly posits a rational agent (p. 125),[2] but he eschews rational choice theory in favor of a mode of argument he calls the "dialectically necessary approach" (p. 124), a mode of argument marked by a rather conspicuous indifference to the context in which his rational prudential agent is situated. Thus, starting from his analysis of the necessary conditions of action, Gewirth argues that a "rational agent," whose "criterion is prudential" (p. 128), must necessarily claim a right to these requisites of action. To refuse to do so would be self-contradictory: it would be to deny his character as an agent. A rational prudential agent must then assert his right to these conditions, but this right-claim is not based on the alleged desirability of the particular purposes that the possession of the conditions of action will enable him to pursue, but rather on the ground that in lieu of such conditions he will be unable to pursue any purposes whatever. "Freedom and well-being are necessary goods to the agent"; they are "basic goods such as is required for his pursuit of any other goods";[3] and a rational prudential agent will thus claim them as rights on the ground that he cannot do without them and be (or remain) an agent. But since the agent claims a right to them on the ground of their necessity to him as an agent, it follows that he must acknowledge that all other agents have an equally good right-claim to these same conditions. But such a generalized right-claim, extended to all agents, imposes a correlative duty on all agents, namely the "Supreme Moral Principle." Thus, Gewirth concludes that he has derived a categorical moral principle from the concept of action as such, and consequently has succeeded in resolving the so-called is-ought problem.

4. Content and Priority of Human Rights

The criterion Gewirth employs for determining the content of human rights is drawn from the theoretical "basis" for human rights established by his argument. Human rights are thus understood to consist of both civil rights and economic rights, since both are conceived as requisites of action. And here Gewirth's buxom version of "the necessary conditions of action" comes in handy. Interpreting "the necessary conditions of action" as embracing both the "conditions of the existence and the success of actions," Gewirth is able to include within the category of human rights both positive enablements required to insure "success" or "purpose-fulfillment" as well as negative liberties required for a person to pursue his own choices without interference. Further, when he comes to the question of conflict between the different basic rights, Gewirth employs a priority scheme for settling the conflict that is also drawn from the "basis" of human rights. Thus, those rights that are "more necessary for the possibility of action" are given priority (p. 138); and in this regard Gewirth asserts that the right to freedom has priority over economic rights because freedom is "more necessary" to action than "well-being" (p. 138). Here, then, a narrower interpretation of "the necessary conditions of action" would seem to be operative, appealing to the common belief that a person can properly be said to be engaged in action if he is not subject to coercion by others. The ambiguity in his basic concept can thus be recognized as playing a functional role in the prescriptive portion of his theory.

II. GEWIRTH'S ARGUMENT CRITICIZED

All four of these features of Gewirth's theory merit discussion, but I will concentrate on his method of argument, touching on the other three features when this proves illuminating. With regard, then, to the method of "dialectical necessity," it seems to me that Gewirth's line of reasoning contains a logical gap and that this gap is filled by an assumption that goes unrecognized by Gewirth. Moreover, this assumption is normative, thus undercutting Gewirth's contention that the "dialectical" method of argument he has devised has succeeded in resolving "the 'is-ought' problem." However, the real importance of identifying this hidden assumption lies elsewhere, for it seems to me that the peculiar enterprise of trying to bridge "the 'is-ought' gulf" is much overrated; and my main reason for calling attention to the normative assumption secreted in the structure of Gewirth's argument is that it places his entire way of treating the problem of human rights in a different perspective from the one his formal argument suggests.

The heart of Gewirth's argument for human rights is that since certain things are necessary conditions of action, a prudential agent must claim a right to them for himself; and since he claims a right to them on the ground that he cannot do without them as an agent, he must in turn logically extend the same right-claim to all other agents. Now, it is certainly the case that if the agent does stake his claim to the requirements of action on the ground that they are necessary to him as an agent, he is appealing to a title to rights that logicaly commits him to recognize the rights of all other agents to the same conditions. He cannot deny other agents the basic rights to freedom and well-being without contradicting his own claim to these rights. But it is not at all evident why a "rational agent," whose "criterion is prudential," *must* stake his claim to rights to freedom and well-being on the ground of their necessity. Strictly speaking, all that Gewirth's argument shows (starting from the inescapable features of action) is that it would be self-contradictory (irrational) for a rational agent, whose criterion is prudential, to refrain from claiming a right to the necessary conditions of action, but not that it would be self-contradictory (irrational) to claim these same rights *on some other ground.* For although it is true, given Gewirth's starting point, that a human being would be abdicating his character as an agent were he to refuse to assert a right to the necessary conditions of agency, he would not be denying his character as an agent were he to stake his claim on some title other than necessity, on some title involving individual merit or desert. But no such argument is forthcoming from Gewirth. It is not that he advances a bad or weak or inconsequential argument to this effect but that he shows no sign of recognizing that the structure of his own theory calls for an argument of this kind at this point.

Gewirth's argument, does, then, exhibit a logical gap, and the reason for this gap has now become visible. Gewirth's program of argument is composed of two logically separate stages. First, starting from the indispensable conditions of action, Gewirth has to establish that a rational prudential agent must claim these as rights. Second, he has to show that this same agent must stake his claim on the ground of necessity. The agent, is, then, as it were, confronted with two choices, and the trouble with Gewirth's formal argument is that only the first of these two choices is logically constrained by the starting point. For whereas the "fact" that certain things are necessary to action does entail that a rational agent, operating on a prudential criterion, must claim these things as rights, it does not entail that he must claim them on any particular ground. It entails only the rather sweeping consideration, that the ground on which he does choose to base his right-claim must be consistent with the prudential perspective he is postulated as adopting; and, in lieu of some additional assumptions or arguments that impose some further constraints on the prudential agent's deliberations, this sweeping consideration is compatible with the agent's basing his claim on a wide variety of possible and indeed well-known grounds for rights.[4] The logic of "dialetical necessity" eventuates in a determinant right-claim, but not in a determinant title on which the claim is based. But this won't do. In order for Gewirth's theory to work, the second choice must also be constrained in a particular direction: the agent has got to be made to claim basic rights on the ground of their necessity. Thus, another argument is required, showing that the only prudentially eligible choice open to the agent seeking to command the requisites of action is to base his claim on necessity, an argument foreclosing as imprudent all other possible titles to rights. But no such argument is advanced by Gewirth, and his silence on this key point invites us to go on to inquire into the identity of the intervening assumption that is implicitly being relied on to fill the gap in the argument.

As I see it, there are two possible candidates for the required assumption. The first I will call the "moral" interpretation, and I mention it here in order to help clear the air, even though I think that it is at odds with the theoretical intentions informing Gewirth's attempt to develop a theory of human rights. The first candidate for the assumption underlying Gewirth's key contention (that a rational agent *must* base his right-claim to the necessary conditions of action on the ground of their necessity) is the assumption that the necessity of a thing to a distinctively human life constitutes an independent moral title to that thing. The "must" in Gewirth's argument has become a "moral must," and the agent's "criterion" has thus shifted from a prudential to a moral criterion. Now, it scarcely needs to be added that such a substantive moral theory of human rights has frequently received expression.[5] But whether or not this doctrine is sound or compelling, it clearly introduces an independent normative principle into the premises of the argument, so that the contention that "the is-ought gulf" has been bridged proves to be illusory. Indeed, to construe Gewirth's theory of human rights in this fashion reduces that theory to nothing more than the utterly familiar argument: (i) major premise — human beings are morally entitled to rights to what is necessary to a distinctively human life; (ii) minor premise — freedom and well-being are such necessary goods; (iii) conclusion — all humans are morally entitled to rights to freedom and well-being. In effect, the result of this interpretation is to presuppose what Gewirth sets out to prove; the entire argument from "dialectical necessity" becomes excess verbal baggage; and this interpretation thus turns out to be at odds with Gewirth's expressed intention to "prove," not assume, that human beings are morally entitled to rights to the necessary conditions of action.

The second interpretation is, then, "prudential" throughout. It takes seriously Gewirth's often repeated declaration that "the agents' criterion is prudential," that "a strict 'practical ought' in the view of the agent"[6] is the perspective being adopted from within the "dialectical" framework, and the like. Here not only the first stage of the argument (that the agent must claim rights to the requisites of action), but the second stage (that he must base his claim on necessity) is subject to prudential determination. From this standpoint, what is required to make Gewirth's theory work is an argument showing not only that a rational prudential agent would contradict himself (self-destruct) were he to refuse to claim rights to the conditions of action, but a further argument showing that he would contradict himself (self-destruct) were he to stake his claim on any ground other than necessity. However, the agent would contradict himself were he to base his claim on some conception of individual merit, desert, achievement only on the supposition that he could not rationally count on the latter, that is, only if so staking his right-claim would constitute an arbitrary gamble, too grave a risk for the agent to bear given what is at stake, not any things at all, but the necessary conditions of action. Thus, the assumption required on the "prudential" interpretation is an assumption whereby all other grounds-for-rights are foreclosed as unavoidably imprudent.

To put the point a bit differently, dropping the language of rights for a moment and adopting a vocabulary that surfaces occasionally in Gewirth's presentation: the assumption required to make Gewirth's theory work is an assumption that would make it irrational for a prudential agent to stake his claim to the "distribution" of "basic goods" on criteria of individual achievement in contrast to an allocative scheme guaranteeing to every agent a distributive share of the "basic goods" independently of considerations of individual merit, and so forth, and hence of variations therein. But what sort of assumption is this? From what standpoint would it be cogent for a rational prudential agent to reach the conclusion that reliance on criteria of individual merit or desert for the "distribution" of "basic goods" is unavoidably an imprudent gamble not to be risked? (From what standpoint would it be unavoidably imprudent, for example, to allow getting and keeping "property" to depend on the Lockian "labor" title?) In the present state of political theory, the general form the answer must take has been canvased repeatedly: it is some version of the state of nature or Rawlsian "original position." Only if it is presupposed that the rational prudential agent is situated in (hypothetical) circumstances in which he is notionally debarred from relying on, or in taking into account, any particular "facts" about himself or the society in which he lives, only if he is stripped of all individuating characteristics, does it become cogent for him to forgo criteria of individual achievement as the basis of the (subsequent) "distribution" of "basic goods." In other words, if a prudential agent is to be persuaded to stake his claim to the "basic goods" on their necessity to him as an agent, it is essential to increase as far as is notionally possible the uncertainty and riskiness of appealing to any distributive criteria that do not guarantee a requisite distributive share to him, quite apart from any and all variations in (what turn out to be) his individuating characteristics. It is therefore necessary to postulate that Gewirth's agent is abstracted from "ordinary" circumstances and located in a situation in which that uncertainty and risk is maximized; in short, located in the theoretical equivalent of Rawls' version of "The State of Nature." So the theoretical terrain we have now entered is familiar enough: the constraints imposed on the deliberations of a rational prudential agent by this hypothetical device presuppose a moral outlook according to which variations in individual abilities are seen as morally arbitrary and thus not allowed to enter into the determination of the principles governing the allocation of the basic goods. It would thus seem that, on the "prudential" interpretation of Gewirth's method of argument, as well as on the "moral" interpretation, a fundamental moral idea is entrenched in the premises of the argument.

The particular conception of man introduced into the basis of a theory of human rights is of crucial significance. Given the appropriate view, it becomes possible to guarantee inference to just about any conclusion about the purpose and content of human rights. At the very outset of his argument, in an attempt to dissociate his theory of rights from Rawls's theory of distributive justice, Gewirth remarks that Rawls's theory rests on "an initial egalitarian moral outlook" and is therefore "convicted of circularity" (pp. 122–23). My contention is that Gewirth's theory rests on and requires precisely the same "initial moral outlook"[7]: Gewirth reads back into his model of man as agent the assumption required for the existence of the social arrangements it is the purpose of his theory to justify.

In conclusion, it may also be observed that even the initial step in Gewirth's chain of argument — that an agent must claim the necessary conditions of actions as rights — requires a special assumption. A rational agent will indeed desire to secure the necessary conditions of action for himself, but were he able to get and keep these things by his own "natural" wit and power, it would be superfluous for him to claim that he is entitled to them, that is, that others are duty-bound to acknowledge his claim. It would appear again that an assumption must be made about the context in which this agent is located vis-a-vis the other agents, namely, that a relative equality of power exists between them, so that no one can count on securing the requisites of action by his own efforts. With respect to this assumption, the reader may again be referred to Rawls's account of "the circumstances of justice," not to mention Hobbes's ferocious discussion of equality in the state of nature. Gewirth's theory is implicitly contractarian, and it would be better for this to be openly acknowledged so that the egalitarian assumptions of his version of human rights theory could be debated directly.

NOTES

1. "The 'Is-Ought' Problem Resolved," *Proceedings and Addresses of the American Philosophical Association,* 47 (1973-74): 34-61; p. 52. The reference to "conditions necessary for choosing and pursuing one's purpose" is based upon Gewirth's paper as read at the meetings of the Society. (Ed.)
2. This is stressed by Alan Gewirth; see especially his reply to his critics in the symposium that *Ethics* devoted to his theory of rights: "Action and Rights: A Reply," *Ethics,* 86 (July 1976): 288-93, p. 291.
3. "The 'Is-Ought' Problem Resolved," p. 53. Cf. now Alan Gewirth, *Reason and Morality* (Chicago: The University of Chicago Press, 1978), p. 48.
4. It is perhaps arguable that this sweeping consideration does impose some significant limitation on the notional universe of grounds for rights eligible to be chosen by a prudential agent seeking to secure the requisites of action for himself. For it is perhaps arguable that a human being would "contradict" his character as an agent were he to claim rights to the requisites of action on the basis of, say, his race or nationality, since to take these things as the distinguishing feature of a human being, which warrants the attribution of rights, might be shown to involve a conception of a human being at odds with the idea of agency as a distinguishing feature of "human nature." This is a complicated business, and it points in a direction requiring intellectual resources Gewirth's theory does not supply. But in any case this line of thought cannot be used to rule out the agent's basing his right-claim on criteria of individual achievement, criteria that are surely compatible with agency as the distinguishing feature of "human nature."
5. For example, D. D. Raphael, "Human Rights, Old and New," in *Political Theory and the Rights of Man,* ed. Raphael (Bloomington Ind., and London: Indiana University Press, 1967).
6. Gewirth, "Action and Rights: A Reply," p. 291.
7. Cf. also Alan Gewirth, "The Justification of Egalitarian Justice," *American Philosophical Quarterly, 8 (October 1971): 331-41.*
   The first of the two remarks are from Gewirth's paper as presented at the meetings of the Society. See above pages 122-23 for Gewirth's amended statement. (Ed.)

8

A DIFFERENTIAL THEORY OF
HUMAN RIGHTS

ARVAL A. MORRIS

"Human rights," or "generic rights," as Alan Gewirth calls them, "are rights which all persons have simply insofar as they are human." "But," he pointedly asks, "are there any such rights?" Gewirth answers in the affirmative, and devotes his paper "to substantive arguments," which to his satisfaction, "prove or justify that persons have rights other than those grounded in positive law." The question is whether Gewirth's substantive arguments are satisfactory. Do they, as he himself requires of such arguments, "indicate the criteria for there being human rights, including their scope or content, and [do they] undertake to show why these criteria are correct or justified"?

I. UNIVERSALIZATION:
EQUAL HUMAN RIGHTS FOR ALL HUMANS?

Midway through his remarks Alan Gewirth tells us that the "equation of generic rights with human rights does not derogate from the universality of the latter." Earlier, in his first paragraph, he asserts that "human rights [i.e., Gewirth's generic rights] are rights that all *persons* have simply insofar as they are human [italics mine]." But this formulation of "generic" or "human" rights introduces an ambiguity that is crucial to Gewirth's claim of universalization.

Does Gewirth's thesis assert that human beings have rights simply because they are human beings and nothing more, or does his thesis assert that human beings have rights only insofar as they *also are persons;* that is, have human agency?

If the first formulation is actually Gewirth's thesis, that is, human beings qua human beings have certain rights, then another consideration becomes critical. The set of criteria defining "humanness" must be identified. This set of criteria is necessary in order to set human beings and their unique human rights apart from all other beings and their rights. Gewirth does not argue for any such set of mutually exclusive criteria separating human beings and their human rights from all other beings and their rights. Consequently, assuming his thesis pertains to human beings qua human beings, and not to human beings as uniquely distinct persons, one cannot be confident that the rights Gewirth identifies are solely and truly human rights. Without a set of defining criteria, the rights he identifies could be rights humans hold in common with other beings. I shall not pursue this point further. Instead I return to the distinction between human beings and persons, and their rights.

The distinction between humans and persons is important for Gewirth's claim to universality of generic or human rights. A consideration of Karen Anne Quinlan's condition will serve to bring out the nature of the importance I have in mind. Karen Anne Quinlan is not dead. On empirical grounds, we have good reason to believe her brain stem is alive and her heart functions normally. But, on equally excellent grounds, we can say that she is in a condition of irreversible coma and that it is extremely unlikely she will ever again be restored to a condition of human agency; that is, return to being a person in the sense in which Gewirth uses that term. I think it is clearly proper to hold that, today, Karen Anne Quinlan is a human being who is in a condition of irreversible coma and who does not need a respirator, nor uses any. It is also clear, I believe, that her condition cannot be analogized in any principled way to a respirated human corpse that no longer is a living human being but rather has become a receptacle for maintaining the life of certain organs such as kidneys, eyes, and heart. Clearly, we would not say that a respirated human corpse has human rights in the same sense that we say a normal, living person has human rights. Nor would we say that Karen Anne Quinlan is a human corpse.

If Gewirth's argument is sound and if his thesis asserts that human beings have rights solely because they are existing human beings, and for no other reason, then Karen Anne Quinlan has, or should have, all of the human rights he identifies. If, on the other hand, Gewirth's argument is sound but his thesis is that human beings have certain rights solely in virtue of the fact that they also are persons having the characteristics of human agency, then Karen Anne Quinlan has no human rights in Gewirth's sense because she is not a person in Gewirth's required sense; that is, she currently lacks the capacity to think, to choose, to plan, and to act on the basis of her plans. Moreover, it is extremely unlikely she ever again will be a "person" with any capacity of human agency.

Gewirth does not deny that he relies heavily on the notion of human agency when deriving his generic or human rights. His move is to generalize from persons having full human agency to other human beings with some impairment of agency. The question is whether this move to universalization of human rights succeeds.

Gewirth does deal with certain categories of human beings about whom, on empirical grounds, it correctly can be claimed that they lack varying degrees of human agency. He does not deal with human beings who completely lack one or all of the elements necessary for human agency. For example, he seeks to escape the problem posed by a lack of human agency in normal infants by relying on a view of the infant's human "potentiality." (But what about highly defective infants born with severe brain damage or Trisomy 21?) He states that normal children "are potential agents in that, with normal maturation, they will develop the full abilities of agency." Even if that view be granted, it is clear that it can have no application to Karen Anne Quinlan. She lacks "potentiality" in the required sense, and consequently she cannot be expected, in the normal course of affairs, naturally to develop the abilities of human agency in the same way in which a normal infant becomes a person. Gewirth also deals with other human beings who lack human agency; for example, "mentally deficient *persons*" and "*persons* with brain damage [italics mine]." He recognizes that these human beings are *persons*. He states that they more or less have capacities of human agency and for "action as this has been interpreted here, as voluntary and purposive behavior." He continues, saying that since their "capabilities for action are less," then "their rights too are proportionately less"; that is, "to the degree to which they have the abilities of agency."

Gewirth apparently holds that the degree of human agency present in a human being at any given instant of time determines the number and character of human rights that the human being has at that time. Thus, he really constructs a sliding scale of human rights which ranges from one to N and is calibrated in the varying degrees in which human agency exists in human beings. He then awards his "generic" or "human" rights accordingly, with human beings having the greatest degree of human agency being awarded the greatest amount of human rights. It appears, therefore, if his arguments are sound, that Gewirth is fully committed to an elitist conception of human rights. Gewirth's scale ranges from fully complete persons having full human agency and all human rights to persons with impaired human agency and only a few human rights. Moreover, a human could have differing human rights at different times in his life. For, presumably, as normal persons age, suffering impairment of their human agency as they drift into senility, they would lose human rights that they once had, but normal infants, as they age and mature, developing human agency, would acquire additional new human rights.

Gewirth's view, then, leaves us with this question: What are the human rights held by a human being who fully lacks all human agency and the potentiality for its development? In what Gewirthian sense can this human being be said to have human rights? Yet, this being is human. Karen Anne Quinlan does not appear to have human "agency" to any degree, in the sense in which Gewirth uses that term, and therefore she cannot be considered a "person" in his sense of the term. Thus, she completely escapes the sliding scale of human agency he has constructed for awarding human rights. She would have none of Gewirth's human rights. I also suspect that full-blown and complete psychopaths or sociopaths, and others, would also fully escape Gewirth's sliding-scale analysis. By definition, full-blown, 100 percent complete psychopaths fully lack at least one element crucially necessary for human "agency" in Gewirth's sense. They are incapable of responding to the demands of a moral environment. Complete psychopaths cannot meet one of Gewirth's tests of human agency because they are incapable of engaging in action responsibly so as not to "result in harm to themselves or others."

On this analysis, Gewirth's equation of generic rights with human rights does derogate from the universality of the latter. Gewirth's generic rights are relativistic and are awarded to human beings in accordance with their degree of human agency. As I have argued, some human beings exist who are completely lacking in one or more, or all, of the necessary elements for human agency in Gewirth's sense of that term. Accordingly, they would receive none of Gewirth's "generic" or "human" rights. If so, then assuming the soundness of his argument, we do not have a demonstration showing that human beings have rights simply because they are human beings. But, assuming the soundness of the main argument, we have a demonstration showing that "persons" having varying amounts of "generic" or "human" rights because they are persons having varying degrees of human agency. If a human being does not qualify as a "person," he has no "human" rights. Thus, a not inconsiderable part of Gewirth's theory turns on the adequacy of the set of criteria defining who is to be counted as a "person" and to what "degree"? But Gewirth neither argues for a set of criteria nor offers one. Nevertheless, assuming the soundness of his arguments and that a satisfactory set of "person" criteria could be formulated, Gewirth's view, I believe, appropriately can be termed an elitist theory of human rights. Some human beings are considered to be more fully "persons of human agency" than others, and they constitute the elite having a greater amount of human rights.

II. GEWIRTH'S METHOD OF DIALECTICAL NECESSITY

The prior section assumed Gewirth's arguments were sound. This section tests that assumption.[1]

Gewirth seeks to defend a supreme categorical moral principle: The Principle of Generic Consistency *(PGC)*, which is a foundation for his generic or human rights. Ultimately, invoking this principle requires every fully human agent, on the pain of self-contradiction, to recognize the rights of all other fully human agents, which Gewirth then identifies as "human" rights. His defense of this principle stands or falls on the adequacy of a method which Gewirth conceives as dialectically necessary.

Using this method, Gewirth says, "it is possible and indeed logically necessary to infer, from the fact that certain objects are the proximate necessary conditions of human action, that all rational agents logically must hold or claim, at least implicitly, that they have rights to such objects," and although "what is thus directly inferred is a statement not about persons' rights but about their claiming to have them, this provides a sufficient criterion for the existence of human rights, because the claim must be made or accepted by every rational human agent on his own behalf, so that it holds universally within the context of action, which is the context within which all moral rights ultimately have application." Gewirth's method "is dialectically necessary in that it proceeds from what all agents logically must claim or accept, on pain of contradiction." The two requirements of this method are that a fully human agent assent to the logically necessary implications of his prior statements, but only to them and to no others.

Gewirth's dialectically necessary argument can be stated in four major steps. The word "good" in the following steps cannot mean intrinsic or "morally good" because that, ultimately, is what Gewirth's dialectically necessary argument seeks to establish as its final conclusion:

(1) "I, as a fully human agent, on self-serving, prudential grounds, claim freedom to do X in order to achieve my purpose Y." This statement requires the agent to agree that he considers act X as instrumentally[2] good for achieving Y and Y as a good to be achieved.

(2) "I consider X and Y as good" commits the agent to "my freedom and basic well-being are goods for me serving as necessary conditions of all my actions."

(3) "My freedom to act and basic well-being are goods for me and are necessary conditions of all my actions" commits the agent to "I have rights to my freedom of action and basic well-being."

(4) By universalizability: "I, as a fully human agent, must recognize the rights of every other fully human agent to his freedom of action and basic well-being."

If the word "good" in step one should not be taken to mean "intrinsic" or the "morally good" in Gewirth's argument, then that leaves only some meaning like instrumentally good. On this view, an agent can be seen as correctly[3] regarding X as a necessary condition for bringing about Y, which itself can be regarded as a necessary condition for bringing about Z, and so forth. To remain faithful to Gewirth's purpose of justifying human rights as moral rights, step one should carry an instrumentally good interpretation. But this interpretation requires an agent to value his freedom and well-being only instrumentally—as necessary conditions for his actions. Moreover, his actions are instrumental to his purposes. Thus, the conclusion of step two should reflect two instrumentalities instead of only one: (1) "My freedom and basic well-being are instrumental goods serving as necessary conditions of my action *(X)*," and (2) "My actions are the necessary conditions for my achieving my purpose *(Y)*."

This required reformulation of step two is, I believe, fatal to Gewirth's argument. The reason is that step three does not follow from it, and therefore, step four cannot universalize the necessary statement. Considering the reformulated step two, it can be seen that the right claims an agent will make will depend entirely upon the purposes he wishes to achieve. He values his freedom and his well-being only instrumentally as necessary conditions for achieving his purposes. On this analysis, it seems clear that an agent can morally justify his claims to freedom and well-being, as against others, only if he can morally justify his purposes. But Gewirth's third step requires an agent to believe that he has a right to his freedom and well-being without considering whether his purposes are morally justified. Thus, Gewirth's third step is defective in light of steps one and especially in light of reformulated step two. Moreover, on this analysis, and without an agent's purpose first having been moraly justified, no valid ground exists for precluding others from interfering with the actions of an agent; that is, there is no valid basis on which an agent might claim freedom to act as a human right. Furthermore, in the absence of a morally justified purpose, an agent is not dialectically required to claim a right to freedom and well-being, as required in step three of Gewirth's argument, which in turn means there is no right that can be universalized to other fully human agents in step four.

NOTES

1. I rely, in part, on Grunebaum, "Gewirth and a Reluctant Protagonist," *Ethics*, 86 (1976): 274.

2. Contrary to Grunebaum, I do not claim that doing X or achieving Y are only instrumentally good. It is possible, of course, that an agent might consider doing X or achieving Y as being intrinsically good, and they may be. But I have no interest in this intrinsically good version, since Gewirth should not and does not rest his case on it. Indeed, the point of Gewirth's argument is, after all, to provide an unassailable foundation for the morally good and not to assume it.

3. It is possible, of course, as Professor Margolis has pointed out, that an agent initially could be mistaken; i.e., he mistakenly could believe that doing X is necessary to achieve Y when, really, he must do A. Or he could be mistaken that Y is good. According to Gewirth's dialectically necessary method, this mistaken judgment could cause some confusion. If the mistaken judgment were worked through Gewirth's method, would it result in all fully human agents having human rights to do X in order to achieve Y when they really need rights to do A? Gewirth does not discuss mistaken judgments by agents, and, I assume, his paper is predicated on the belief that agents are always correct in their judgments.

9

FROM PRUDENCE TO RIGHTS:
A CRITIQUE

MARTIN P. GOLDING

In his essay, "The Basis and Content of Human Rights," Professor
Gewirth employs a strategy of argument that might be called the
ideal philosophical procedure. This strategy involves the derivation
of powerful or rich conclusions from weak or minimal premises, and
it is quite understandable why someone should wish to adopt it. Contrary to popular belief, philosophers sometimes do reach the same
conclusions on some issue, but they usually do so by means of arguments that employ substantive premises over which disagreement is
sharp. More often, perhaps, there is little or no unanimity on premises and conclusions. In either case, the soundness of the arguments
is thrown into question and the conclusions cannot be said to be firmly
established. So it is tempting to seek premises that are very weak in
terms of philosophical commitment, which in consequence are likely
to be acceptable to a wider range of thinkers and are likely to result
in more generally accepted conclusions. The risk in employing this
strategy is obvious: the weaker premises often will be inadequate to
sustain the particular conclusions that one wants to reach. In philosophy one can't always get to there from here.

It seems to me that Gewirth takes this risk and loses. He begins by
pointing out that there are a variety of moralities and theories of ethics, and therefore much controversy on the existence, basis, and content of human rights. He seeks to bypass this circumstance by adopting
the strategy mentioned above. All moralities and theories of ethics are
concerned with action, and all of us, presumably, are rational agents.
Starting from the morally neutral stance of the self-interested rational

agent, Gewirth attempts, by use of the dialectical method, to derive important and powerful conclusions. I do not think he succeeds.

Gewirth's argument moves in three stages. In the first, he tries to establish that a rational agent is committed to making certain claims, in particular claims of rights to freedom and well-being, which are conditions of action. The rights so claimed are characterized as "prudential rights." In the second stage, these prudential rights are transformed into moral or human rights by appeal to the principle of universalization. Finally, in the third stage of the argument, the scope, content, and limits of these rights are spelled out. I am sympathetic toward much of what Gewirth has to say about the content of human rights, and though I would quibble here and there, I agree with a good deal of his technical discussion of moral rights. My major difficulties come at the first stage of the argument. This is developed in great detail and with exemplary subtlety in the second chapter of his book, *Reason and Morality*. Professor Gewirth there considers and replies to objections that are similar to some of the objections I have to offer. I shall confine myself to the presentation in Gewirth's work in this volume, which contains all the essentials. In this way it will be possible to throw into relief fatal difficulties that in my opinion still remain in his argument, given the self-denying strategy that he employs.

The crux of the matter can be quickly formulated: To what kinds of claims is a rational agent committed? Are rational agents committed to claiming that they have *rights* to certain things?

Let me begin by conceding, for the sake of discussion, that freedom and well-being are generic features of action and that they are necessary goods for any individual agent. I also concede that *if* any agent claims a right to have his freedom and well-being respected on the grounds that they are necessary conditions of action, he is committed to recognizing a similar *(prima facie)* right for others for whom these are also necessary goods. But I do not think that a rational self-interested agent is required to make any such claim of right. Professor Gewirth, himself, admits that a statement of the form "X is a necessary good for A" is not sufficient to ground a statement of the form "A has a right to X" as a matter of logical necessity. That is to say, simply as a matter of bare meaning, a statement of the first form does not entail a statement of the second. "I need X" no more logically implies "I have a right to X" than does "I want X" imply it. How, then, can we construe the agent's judgment of what is his necessary good (or his demand for anything whatsoever) as a rights-claim?

It is essential to grasp the full import of this question within the structure of Professor Gewirth's argument and the strategy that he is using. The question arises not merely because the first form of statement does not, as a matter of meaning, logically imply the second. It arises, rather and primarily, because of the specified situation with which we have begun: utter moral neutrality. This is the situation of the prudent, self-interested agent who is a rational amoralist. Such an individual does, of course, recognize certain objects as goods, and even as necessary goods, for himself. He may also acknowledge certain objects as goods, and even as necessary goods, for others. The term "good," however, is never used by him in an unqualified way: nothing is good *simpliciter.* In the prudent amoralist's language statements of the form "X is good" are incomplete; they must be construed as statements asserting that X is good for someone. Strictly speaking, however, the term is eliminable from his language. Those objects that he takes to be good for himself (or others) are the objects that fulfill his desires (or the desires of other agents). Some objects are designated by him as necessary goods because of the vital role they play in the fulfillment of desire over the long run. This, in fact, is part of what we mean by "prudence." A prudent agent, one who is genuinely self-interested in Bishop Butler's sense, is one who recognizes that all of his desires are not equal in status. He not only recognizes that the fulfillment of certain desires is a materially necessary condition for the fulfillment of his wider set of desires, and their objects are thus necessary goods for him; but he also recognizes, at the other extreme, that the fulfillment of certain other desires can be a source of ultimate frustration. Nevertheless, though desires and their objects are distinguished in these ways, the term "good" functions as no more than a shorthand expression in the language of the prudent amoralist.

But more important than the status and function of the term "good" is the question of the status and function of such terms as "right," "duty," and "obligation." (By "right" here I am referring to rights in the personal, subjective sense — my rights, your rights, his rights, what one has a right to — as distinguished from what is right — right in the objective sense. I have discussed the development of this distinction elsewhere.)[1] I think it crucial for an understanding of the situation of the prudent amoralist to see that, except for a special kind of circumstance I shall describe shortly, he does not use these terms at all. He neither claims something as his right, nor does he deny someone else's claim of a right. He does neither of these things, and he can do neither of them, because the term "a right" does not occur in his basic language. The amoralist, so to speak, does not play in the moral ballpark.

All this, of course, is denied in effect by Professor Gewirth. In summarizing the main point in the second stage of his argument, he writes: "what for any agent are necessarily goods of action, namely, freedom and well-being, are equally necessary goods for his recipients, and he logically must admit that they have as much right to these goods as he does, since the ground or reason for which he rationally claims them for himself also pertains to his recipients" (p. 132). I am at the first stage of Gewirth's argument, however, and I maintain that the prudent amoralist admits nothing of the kind, for he never claims anything as his right. Whether he *logically* must admit anything of this sort, I shall discuss later. Before I do so I want to spend a few more sentences on describing the situation of the amoralist.

The prudent amoralist does, of course, demand things from other agents, but it can be seriously misleading to describe him as claiming anything from them or as asserting a claim. For the terminology of "claiming" easily suggests that the amoralist is saying that he *has* a claim against others. If we wish to retain the terminology of "claiming" in describing the situation of the amoralist, we must be careful to use it in the sense of *acts* of claiming or, if one likes, claimings. The amoralist can make demands, he can express what it is he wants others to do or give him; and we may call these "claims" only if we do not construe him as asserting that he has a claim to what he wants. I do believe that the notion of claiming is important for the development of a theory of rights, as I have argued elsewhere, but I hold that other factors must be present in the situation in order to pass from making claims to having claims.[2]

Now, there is a special kind of circumstance in which the prudent amoralist might use the language of "rights." For instance, suppose a group of prudent amoralists want to accomplish a task that requires their mutual cooperation. Let us suppose further that they get together to deliberate on how they are going to do this. It might quickly be seen that they are going to have to introduce some rules of discussion, lest the whole affair degenerate into a shambles that would be counterproductive for each. So they agree to allot the floor in a specific order and that no one may speak for more than five minutes, say. After the first amoralist has spoken his piece for five minutes, the second amoralist may now claim the floor; in fact, he may say that he has a claim to the floor, and even that he has right to it that others have an obligation to respect. This right might be characterized as a "prudential right," for it is a right that derives from prudent self-interest, and the obligation that corresponds to it has the same origin. When the term "prudential right" is tied to circumstances of this kind, I think I understand what the term means. Gewirth, I suspect, means something else, which I must confess I haven't grasped.

It should be noticed that the circumstance just described is not simply one in which the solitary amoralist has judged some object to be a good or a necessary good. Other factors have been introduced: mutual cooperation and mutual undertakings. We have, so to speak, strengthened or enriched the premises from which the prudential rights are derived. I leave it as an open question whether such rights should be regarded as moral rights. I tend to think that a further strengthening will be needed. At any rate, it is some such addition that is required before the prudent amoralist can begin to speak the language of rights at all. Otherwise, the term does not occur in his basic, neutral language: as I have described his situation, the amoralist neither claims something as his right nor denies someone else's claim of right.

Professor Gewirth disagrees. He advances two arguments: the first offers a description of the situation of the amoralist that is different from the one I have presented; the second is an application of the dialectically necessary method. Let us examine each in turn.

As stated earlier, Gewirth concedes that "X is a necessary good for A" is not sufficient to ground "A has a right to X" as a matter of logical necessity. Three conceptual difficulties are mentioned as obstacles to the implication: (1) Since "X is a necessary good for A" does not refer to others, duties of others do not seem to be derivable from it; (2) the idea of A's entitlement to X is not found in "X is a necessary good for A"; (3) "X is a necessary good for A" does not carry advocacy, so it is not prescriptive. Now, according to Gewirth, the logical gap between the two statements in question exists only because we have viewed the agent's judgment from the outside. Once an internal, conative view is taken, the logical gap will be closed because the concept of rights will be seen to have already figured in the agent's own judgment that X is a necessary good for him. Gewirth proceeds next to an account of the agent's judgment as perceived from this point of view. The agent under consideration, it should be remembered, is our prudent amoralist friend. If my description of his situation is correct, something is radically wrong in Gewirth's account; not that I think it completely wrong, for I do grant two minor points.

Taking the three conceptual difficulties in reverse order, Gewirth resolves them as follows: Regarding (3), the agent's assertion about necessary goods is not a mere means-ends statement (as contrasted with a statement such as "Wrenches are necessary for fixing kitchen sinks"). Since it is made from his conative standpoint it carries his endorsement. Regarding (2), the agent conceives of necessary goods as due to him from within his own (prudential) standpoint. And finally regarding (1), the agent is making a claim on others because these others must not interfere with his having freedom and well-being, which are generic features of action. I do not think any of this works.

Let me begin with a point that I grant. I agree, regarding difficulty (3), that the assertion about his necessary goods does carry the agent's endorsement. But then so does any statement that he wants something. I do not see, however, how either of these statements prescribes anything for someone else: Does the agent have a "moral gun" in his recipient's back? Of course, there are very special kinds of (enriched) circumstances when an expresison of a want might be construed as prescriptive. For example, if I am a patron in a restaurant my statement to a waiter that I want a cup of coffee may, I suppose, be construed as prescriptive for him. Absent special circumstances (which are equivalent to the strengthening of the premises of the argument), however, neither a statement of one's wants nor an assertion of one's necessary goods is prescriptive for anyone else. It is possible that what Gewirth means when he says that "X is a necessary good for A" is prescriptive is that it is prescriptive *for A*. That is to say, that A, being a rational, self-interested agent, will recognize that he should seek those objects that are necessary goods for him. This may be so, but it is quite irrelevant to the question at issue.

I also grant, regarding difficulty (1), that a rational, self-interested agent will demand of others that they not interfere with his freedom and well-being and that the impulse for making such a demand stems from his judgment that these objects are necessarily good for him. But it is precisely here that the term "claim," which Gewirth uses, can be misleading. Gewirth speaks of the agent who judges some object to be a necessary good as, in effect, making a claim *on* other persons, and this suggests that the agent is asserting, in effect, that he *has* a claim against others. But this would be incorrect. A rational, self-interested agent is, of course, not indifferent to how the behavior of others might affect his own freedom and well-being. Nevertheless, the lack of indifference should not be construed as an abandonment of moral neutrality by the amoralist. So even if it be conceded that the agent's judgment "*X* is a necessary good for me" does contain the demand that others not interfere with his freedom or well-being, this demand is not a claim being made as a matter of right. Absent other special circumstances, the terminology of "rights" is not part of the amoralist's vocabulary.

Finally, regarding difficulty (2), Gewirth states that the prudent, self-interested agent is, in effect, asserting that necessary goods are "due to" him from his own standpoint. I frankly am at a loss to understand what "due to" could possibly mean here. I cannot see how any entitlement enters into the picture, even on — and perhaps especially on — a prudential criterion. The only sense that might be made of the agent's claim, on a prudential criterion, that a necessary good is due to him is that he has uttered the tautology that his necessary goods are necessary for him. If he means something more, I don't know what it is.

In sum, then, I conclude that Professor Gewirth has failed to show that the concept of rights figures in the self-interested agent's judgment "*X* is a necessary good." Gewirth's description of the situation of the prudent amoralist is radically incorrect.

Gewirth is, of course, not finished with his attempt to establish that a claim of rights is present in the situation. He deploys the dialectical method to demonstrate that a rational, self-interested agent is *logically* committed to such claims. Gewirth's argument is clever and impressive, but, again, I don't think it succeeds.

This argument maintains that if a prudent agent denies he has rights, he can be shown to contradict himself. Very briefly stated (relettering the original), the argument is as follows. A prudent agent who asserts in respect of himself (a) "My freedom and well-being are necessary goods" is logically committed to the assertion (b) "All others must refrain from interfering with my freedom and well-being." But suppose he denies (c) "I have rights to freedom and well-being." He then is logically committed to the assertion (d) "Other persons may (are permitted to) interfere with my freedom and well-being." Since, says Gewirth, (d) contradicts (b), a prudent agent who acknowledges that freedom and well-being are necessary goods for him cannot logically deny that he has rights to them.

I have two criticisms to make of this argument. First of all, I think it is far from certain that (d) really does contradict (b). The term "must" in (b) is a nonnormative "must"; the term "may" in (d) is the normative "may" of moral license. (If there is any other kind of normative "may," e.g., a so-called deontic "may," it is irrelevant here.) It is true that (b) is asserted from the internal, conative point of view of the agent and that it perhaps implies some sort of prudential prescription for him (e.g., "See to it that others do not interfere . . ."). But it is hardly prescriptive for some other person. I see no contradiction in asserting both "I need X" and "You have a moral license to stop me from getting X, if you can," even if the objects needed are freedom and well-being, *unless* other considerations are added to the situation. This criticism, I think, is enough to refute Gewirth's argument.

Second, and more interesting, is the logical status of denials of statements of the form "I have a right to X." Earlier, I argued that the terminology of "rights" is not part of the prudent amoralist's vocabulary. Professor Gewirth's dialectical argument may be interpreted as holding that the prudent amoralist *is* committed to moral ("rights") language whether he likes it or not. The argument is similar to dialectical refutations of epistemological skepticism: the skeptic who denies that we know anything at all is refuted by his own words, for he is claiming, in effect, to know at least that. Without passing on the adequacy of the refutation of the skeptic, I do not think that the prudent amoralist is refuted by his own words. For there are two respects in which a rights-claim can be denied.

We should distinguish, I think, between the strong denial of a rights-claim, on the one hand, and its weak denial, on the other. This nomenclature is borrowed from some deontic logicians (e.g., von Wright), and I am not sure my use conforms completely to theirs. The field of deontic logic is unsettled enough, however, to allow me mine. The strong denial of rights-claim, as I use the term, is equivalent to the assertion of a counterclaim of rights or implies some other normative claim. Thus, if I deny (in the strong sense) that you have a right to X, I would be implying that I (or perhaps someone else) has a moral license to take X away from you (under appropriate conditions). The strong denial of a rights-claim entails the assertion that some other rights-claim or normative claim is true. This entailment does not necessarily hold for the weak denial of a rights-claim; such a denial says merely that the rights-claim in question is not true, from which it does not follow that some other rights-claim or normative statement is true. Thus, though the strong denial of rights-claim, *R*, might entail the truth of normative claim, *N*, it is not necessarily the case that the weak denial of *R* entails the truth of *N*. (Weak denial, here, seems similar to negation in intuitionist logic. The law of excluded middle or, perhaps more accurately, the principle of bivalence, does not seem to hold for weak denial. But I don't know enough about the technicalities to press the similarity.)

Turning back to Gewirth's dialectical argument, we can now say that in denying (c) our rational, self-interested agent is *not* committed to (d) in the sense in which (d) asserts a moral license to interfere with his freedom and well-being. *At most* the agent is weakly denying (c), which could, in fact, be compatible with a weak denial of the assertion that someone has a moral license to interfere with his freedom and well-being. In saying that (c) is not true, he is not saying that (d) is true in the full sense required by Gewirth's argument.

Indeed, I should go further than this. I should want to say that the prudent amoralist neither asserts nor denies any rights-claims, nor does he ever have to assert or deny them. He cannot assert or deny them, because the terminology of "rights" is not part of his vocabulary. Of course, the prudent amoralist makes conversation very difficult. When he refuses to assert his right to freedom and well-being, we are nonplussed and we push on by asking whether he means to deny that he has such rights. He should, of course, refuse to answer, but if he does go on to issue his denial we have to construe it as weak denial, at most. The prudent amoralist is not, therefore, caught in a contradiction. The weak denial of a rights-claim does not necessarily entail the acceptance of another normative assertion.

The heart of my disagreement with Professor Gewirth can now be simply restated. In accordance with the strategy of the ideal philosophical procedure, Gewirth starts with a philosophically minimal given, the situation of the rational, self-interested agent, and goes on to derive philosophically substantial conclusions. I have argued that careful attention to this situation, and to what such an agent is committed to, undercuts Gewirth's enterprise. An enriched starting point, stronger philosophical premises, is needed in order to demonstrate the existence of human rights.

It is not incumbent upon me to develop the kind of argument that I think is required; I have tried to suggest what it is elsewhere. In ending this essay, however, it might be useful to compare Gewirth's approach with an earlier similar attempt.

In terms of its structure and in terms of some of its content, the first stage of Gewirth's argument is very much like that of Thomas Hobbes. The problem of the *De Cive* and the *Leviathan* can be interpreted as follows: How can we get from the subjective value judgments of rational, self-interested agents (judgments of what is good or bad, according to Hobbes) to transsubjective value judgments (judgments of what is just or unjust, as Hobbes puts them in the introduction to the *De Cive*), since the latter presuppose common standards of judgment? Hobbes in particular wants to pass from the state of nature ("the natural condition of mankind") to civil society. In strategic terms, he wants to derive strong conclusions from minimal premises. What Hobbes in fact does is to enrich the original starting point by sneaking in rights via the so-called right of nature. More significantly, he enriches the situation when he appeals to peace as a necessary good that is also a common and noncompetitive good. Although I do not favor Hobbes's theory, I suggest that it is something like a common good or an unqualified good that is needed in order to establish the existence of human rights, and this is what is missing from the first stage of Gewirth's argument. Success is impossible if one faithfully adheres to the strict terms of the ideal philosophical procedure.

NOTES

1. Martin P. Golding, "The Concept of Rights: A Historical Sketch," in E. and B. Bandman, eds., *Bioethics and Human Rights* (Boston: Little, Brown, 1978), pp. 44–50.
2. M. P. Golding, "Towards a Theory of Human Rights," *The Monist*, 52 (1968): 521–49.

10

HUMAN RIGHTS:
WHICH, IF ANY, ARE THERE?

JAN NARVESON

Human rights are the rights one has by virtue of being human. Nothing else about the subject is so easy. What are these things called "rights," whose possession is in question here? Just what are to be accounted "humans" for this purpose? And anyway, most important of all, why should we suppose that humans have them? Where, so to speak, do these rights come from? And what do we say to any who might deny our claims about human rights? If we lack reasonably solid answers to these questions, we cannot plausibly claim to know which rights humans have, or even whether they have any.

In this essay I shall try to make some progress on these questions by exploring what I take to be the most powerful of the current theories on the subject. Limited though the exploration must be, I hope it leads to an understanding of which rights we could have by virtue merely of being human—if any. The qualification, unfortunately, expresses a real uncertainty, not a Cartesian doubt.

I. CONCEPTUAL MATTERS

Perhaps the one indisputable point about the concept of rights is that they entail duties, obligations, or "oughts": if A has a right against B, then there is something, x, that B ought to do. But it is not generally felt that if B ought to do x concerning A, it follows that A has a right against B that he do that. There are two questions, then. First, what sorts of duties are entailed by rights? Second, what is the difference between those duties that are related to rights and those that are not?

Taking these in reverse order, I suggest that the differentia in question is provided by the notion of enforceability: a right entails a duty that may, in principle, be enforced. It may be impractical, or other rights may conflict with a given right's enforcement, but qua right, enforcement is *prima facie* in order. Duties to which rights of others do not correspond are duties we may not enforce. Rights, then, concern enforceability.

Is A's right nothing more nor less than B's (enforceable) duty? Or must we suppose that B's duty is genuinely explained by A's possession of a right? Does the right give the *reason for* the obligation, or is it just another way of talking about the obligation? It is not clear whether this intriguing question really matters. For certainly the normative content — the moral "punch" — of statements about rights consists in the "oughts" entailed by them. Now, any normative statement requires that some reason be given or giveable. The reason will consist in specifying some property or facts that are thought to support that normative claim. In the case of rights, the property or fact will be one concerning the other party, the party whose alleged rights entail the "ought" statement. And does it make any difference whether we go directly from that property to that "ought," rather than supposing that the property gives rise to an intermediary thing, the "right," which in its turn gives rise to the duty, or whatever, being claimed? To say that there is this other entity seems both obscure and unnecessary, under the circumstances. And we will have no truck, surely, with the idea that rights might be merely interesting but toothless facts, ones with no particular bearing on what we ought to do. If rights can be cheerfully ignored, even by the conscientious, then something is really wrong.

I conclude that we had best regard rights talk as in principle dispensable; which is not to say that it is useless. It is often more compendious to talk of A's rights than of reasons pertaining to A why B has certain enforceable duties. Nor, of course, is it to say that rights are "unreal." In moral philosophy, something is real if it matters. And whether we may properly be coerced regarding some point decidedly is important if anything is.

Perhaps some will regard rights as purely legal matters: for A to have a right is for some government to *provide* it to A. The present understanding plainly denies that. The normative claims which are entailed by rights-claims may or may not be premised on the existence of certain legal rules and/or institutions. If it is insisted that laws underlie rights, then they will have to be unwritten and unlegislated laws at bottom.

The other question about the concept of rights is what the general form of the duties entailed by them is. And here we come to a crucial distinction, that between "negative" and "positive" rights. Suppose that A's right against B is the right that *p*. Then the difference in question is brought out by observing that B's duty may consist either in *avoiding bringing it about that not-*p, or in *helping to bring it about that* p. The difference, notice, is not the difference between rights to do and rights to have, between "liberty" and "possession" rights. Whether the state of affairs *p* is an action of A's or a thing or state, the difference between B's not interfering and B's positively assisting (if need be) remains. A's right to walk, for example, if negative, requires B to *do* nothing at all; it merely forbids him to do such things as breaking A's legs. But the positive version of that right would require B, for instance, to help provide A with crutches if needed, or with places to walk, and so on. Negative rights are generally only valuable to those whose rights they are if they are able to do or have that which the right involves, for example, to walk. If they cannot or do not, then a merely negative right could be useless. A positive right, on the other hand, will not normally be of much help to someone who already has what such a right would require others to help supply him with. A negative right, then, can be useless, and a positive one redundant. And if negative rights are all we grant, then we may expect the poor and unadvanced to be disgruntled, while if we insist on positive rights as well, the wealthy and powerful might similarly be unhappy. And if the question of human rights were a political one, then those facts would set the basic parameters of our problem. But perhaps it is not, and so perhaps they don't.

II. THE TERMS OF REFERENCE

Since the question of what the basic human rights are is — especially on the above analysis — one of the long-standing questions of ethics, one might be forgiven for throwing up one's hands at the prospect of trying to answer it plausibly in so brief a space. Nevertheless, I believe that real progress can be made if we bear in mind two major points about the terms of reference of the project. These are, first, that human rights are to be the rights of all humans and not, for example, only of our friends. And second, we speak *to* everybody, as well as *of* them. A corollary of the second, I believe, is that intuitionism will not do. Both points and the corollary require elucidation.

1. Human rights are by definition to be possessed of all humans. But there is, as we know, room for serious argument on the question of just what that class comprehends. Various people have had various intuitions about whether fetuses, human vegetables, newborns, or the feebleminded are to count. But to depend on such intuitions when we do basic theory is, I think, to invite trouble. The proper procedure, surely, is to understand what morality is all about, and thus which properties of putative subjects of moral predicates make them eligible for those predicates. Once we know that, we will of course have cases that do not fall clearly on one side or the other of the lines thus drawn, but they will not then pose critical theoretical problems.

The assumption we will make on this matter now is minimal: that the term "human" as it occurs in "human rights" is sufficiently close to everyday usage that typical adult humans count if anything does. Whether the reasons we can find for granting rights to them are such as to generate a case for rights of the nontypical cases — or even some of the noncases, such as animals — is a question we will not consider in any detail, though it is hoped that what is said will be at least germane to those issues.

We may now make the first of my two points. The class of "typical adult humans" is very wide indeed. Among its members will be found not only our friends, relatives, co-workers, and fellow countrymen, but also aliens, enemies, people who share none of our particular goals, tastes, or aspirations, and people who have never even heard of our country, much less hold it in any affection. When we think about it, in fact, we realize that scarcely any of us would recognize more than, say four thousand individuals at sight. That leaves roughly a million perfect strangers for every person we know. And how many of those unknown billions would we really care much about if we did know them? The moral is clear. Human rights are not the rights of people we like. They are the rights of everyone, including those we detest and those who detest us as well as all those unknown individuals. We will be wise not to be excessively generous when it comes to granting such rights!

2. My second point was that we speak not only of, but also to, all when we erect a theory on this matter. Moral theory is for the guidance of actions, which is a main part of what makes it moral; but it is still theory. Unlike theories in the natural sciences, though, a moral theory is one in which the subjects of the theory, so to say, participate in its construction: those to be guided by it are also capable of addressing themselves to its provisions. Those subjects are, in a word, rational beings, much like the theorists who formulate those theories. Responsible theory must not ignore this: on the contrary, it must appeal to the reason of these beings it presumes to guide. For that "guidance" can consist only in giving reasons that will not be found wanting by those addressed.

Now, to acknowledge a right is to accept a constraint on our behavior: for A to agree that B has a right against him is for A to accept that he has a duty or obligation. To acknowledge rights of all, prior to and independently of any particular special arrangements, is to accept duties toward all—a small matter, on the face of it. We need reasons to accept such responsibilities. And these cannot be moral reasons initially, for it is precisely morality whose content is in dispute. What must make the acceptance of these duties reasonable, if acceptance of them *is* reasonable, must be whatever makes behavior in general reasonable.

We therefore require a notion of practical reason. Do we have a fairly good theory about that at hand? If not, of course, our approach will fare no better than the intuitionists' or any others that lead to irresolvable impasses. (One type of intuitionism might not. That is the type that imposes as a constraint on some putative intuition's being a genuine, acceptable one that literally all persons do, on reflection, share it. It is worth noting, though, that apart from the extreme unlikelihood of there being such universally shared intuitions, it would also seem that our theory will inherit any advantages there would be if such an intuition were to be found. For our theory, as will be seen, will make anything that appears morally reasonable to everyone part of the content of morality. And if something seems indubitably right to someone, how will he also deny that it is reasonable?)

In fact, though, we do have a decent theory on this matter. A rational individual is one who attempts by his actions to bring about as nearly as possible the states of affairs he values most highly, in terms of his considered values. Just what his values are is left open, by and large. It is not our concern to decide what is good for any individual. It is, instead, our purpose to try to decide what are the basic terms on which we are to live with our fellows. In particular, it is to determine when it is reasonable from a nonidiosyncratic point of view to intervene in the activities of our fellow persons, thus overruling that individual judgment about his actions which is the sine qua non of rationality. For it is the office of rights to do just that.

III. THE "SOCIAL CONTRACT"

Justice must consist, on the view we are evidently heading toward, in the observance of those requirements that it is interpersonally rational to accept. It must be obvious, though, that our theory can hardly require the actual acceptance of each person, at the very time his actions are being constrained by the principles arrived at. Some broader perspective is evidently required. But how much broader?

One popular proposal has been that of Rawls, who suggests that we put our value-maximizers behind a "veil of ignorance" that conceals from them their very identities, requiring them instead to reason from the assumption that they could be (i.e., could turn out to be, when the veil is "lifted") just *anybody*. But there is an evident problem in getting anyone who is rational by the general criterion proposed to adopt any such standpoint. Since we are in fact particular persons, reasonably proceeding in the light of the values we do have, and since those values might differ to virtually any extent from those of others, how is it rational for us to proceed as if we could as well be just anyone else? On the face of it, Rawls's requirement is far too strong.[1]

If the perspective of the moment is far too narrow, and that of indiscriminate mankind in general far too broad, then where do we find a suitably happy medium? The natural suggestion is that of the individual's whole life. We cannot fix the beginning point of his reasoning earlier than that, since prior to birth there is no individual with values to reason from, as well as no reasoning ability anyway. Nor can we assume any terminus later than his death—bearing in mind, of course, that one has a certain control over the timing of that terminus.

We should note explicitly that we are allowing each person to reason from a standpoint (namely, that of his actual life) that is both basically and substantially "morally arbitrary." Here we side with Robert Nozick and against Rawls. Some will have had what others regard as great advantages by virtue of having just the parents he does and no others; others, disadvantages. There is no initial presumption against anyone on that score, and it is to actual people, with all their arbitrarily acquired characteristics, that we must show the reasonableness of our proposed set of constraints. We start with a clean slate.

Nor can we fix the beginning point of life, as the perspective of rational valuing, much later than birth. The voluntary doings and forbearances of others as he proceeds toward adulthood are relevant to the "agreement" in which the principles of right consist. Even though it is adults who primarily enter into this contract, they can have an eye for the manner of treatment acceptable from the point of view of their earlier selves.

Much has been said about "fair" starting points for the present purposes. But what is fair in the way of starting points at this level? It must not be supposed that justice is rather like a race, where all contestants start at the same place, and all sorted into more or less equally capable groups. Fairness for the starting points for a theory of justice must be a matter of what we can reasonably expect of individuals as they are. Nor is it to be presumed that there is any common enterprise that we are all in together, any *common* goal we are all trying to reach — unless we account the fact that each has goals of his own which he is trying to reach as a "common" goal.

The envisaged point of view must, however, be independent of changeable institutions and, in that sense, "antecedent" to them. With respect to any institution, we can ask what things might have been like prior to it; and then we can ask what rational beings would agree to in the way of institutions of that kind, if anything. Naturally there will also be questions about the difference made by the existence of institutions that may be found to have deviated from the principles arrived at in the preinstitutional perspective: What, if any, corrections are in order? Important though that kind of question is, however, we shall have to shelve it here, noting only that it is part of the very idea of a right that one who violates it owes compensation to those whose rights he violates.

The idea of "what things might have been like prior to any particular institution" is roughly the idea of the state of nature in the classical theories, and that idea has its notorious problems. Two of those especially assault us. First, since language itself is, no doubt, an "institution," it is hard to see how any agreement could be negotiated prior to it. And second, there is the fact that we enter into the world as infants, not only helpless but also prerational. Yet if we draw our hypothetical starting points at some stage of adulthood, we have not only the question of just how to identify that stage nonarbitrarily but worse still, the embarrassment that anyone reaching it, however identified, will have got there with a very full dose of acculturation from just the kinds of institutions we are trying to think our way beneath. How, in view of these facts, are we to hope for a sensible answer to the fundamental question of how rational people would agree to constrain each other prior to institutions?

Fortunately, these questions are not unanswerable. To begin with, as is well known, the question we raise at the fundamental level is at least partly hypothetical. Thus, that we could not make any agreements in the absence of any particular language is not decisive when the question is what we would agree to if we had been able to make any agreements. (Nor is it to be forgotten that people do communicate without explicit, common languages: travelers in ancient times managed it routinely.) And in the second place, it should be agreed that such facts do make a difference to the substance of these hypothetical agreements. For example, if A and B speak no common language, it cannot be reasonable to impose a requirement that they treat each other in ways that presuppose that they do have one. Again, no reasonable principle could blame someone's parents for rearing him in the manner of their culture: What else could they have done?

A brief excursus into the basics of contract theory is in order at this point. As is well known, there are three apparently incompatible theories of social contract. These are that we are bound (1) by explicit agreements only, (2) by "implicit" ones as well, or (3) by hypothetical agreements, that is, agreements that it would have been reasonable to have made at some relevant prior point. Contract theory has been thought to founder on the shoals of this distinction, for it is argued that purely hypothetical agreements can have no force, that implicit agreements are also not really agreements (besides being too fuzzy to get anything definite out of), and finally that explicit agreements are much too infrequent and specific to cover the ground that moral theory needs to cover. Plainly, we must find our way through these challenges.

We get a good start on them by raising the question of why explicit agreements should be thought to obligate in the first place. Here we can make two observations. First, it must somehow be true that they obligate because that is exactly what they are *for*. Thus, it is sometimes said to be "analytic" that promises obligate. Now, it is obviously not analytic that people do what their promises call upon them to do. Somehow, promises forward, without necessarily bringing about, the behavioral coordination that is aimed at in making them. It is impossible that a reasonable answer to the complaint, "But you promised!" is "What of it?" The obligational force of promises must be some function of their efficacy in bringing about reasonable expectations of future behavior. But if that is so, then why shouldn't there also be obligation when such reasonable expectations are achieved by *non*verbal means? Implicit agreements, just because they are only implicit, are no doubt ordinarily less precise and definite than explicit ones. But they cannot be wholly worthless, a point that is reinforced by a further consideration, namely that no agreement, however detailed and precise, can ever escape limitation by circumstances and tacit understandings that must be admitted to be capable of rendering it nugatory, even though the action in question is clearly covered by its letter. "He could not reasonably be considered to have agreed to *that,*" we say when circumstances intervene between promise and performance; and when that can be made to stick, the contractee is off the hook. So it cannot be true that the obligation-creating force of agreements is entirely due to their explicitness. (Indeed, the very nature of language makes this so: words cannot be learned by definitions *ab initio,* since *ab initio* there are no words to couch them in, and so the conventions of language *must* be tacit at bottom.)

Now the question before us is what principles it is reasonable to advocate and publicly subscribe to concerning our general relations with our fellows. Our answer is that they are the principles which it would have been rational for all to subscribe to from the perspective of their lives, in view of the values held during them. The objection is that such merely hypothetical agreements do not obligate, and so cannot be the source of rights. The reply is as follows:

First, we can agree that the fact that it would have been reasonable for A to agree with B to do *x* does not, taken all by itself, obligate A to do *x*. For one thing, B might be unreasonable or immoral, in fact; and it cannot be rationally obligatory to act as though another person is reasonable if he manifestly is not.

Second, though, what if the other party does give every sign of cooperation? Surely Hobbes is right about this: reason tells us to behave similarly. Or rather, it tells us to support a public rule to the effect that we should do so. But that's what we're after here: a set of the public rules or principles that have the support of reason.

Third, we can argue that as a substantial point of moral theory those fundamental rights and duties on which it is rational to agree include respect for implicit as well as explicit agreements.

We can now suggest in fact that the form of fundamental human rights is that we have, as standard members of the human race, the right to whatever treatment by others is manifestly to mutual advantage, provided that we have observed the correlated duty ourselves. The word "manifestly" is crucial here. For if it is not obvious that a certain type of mutual behavior would be to mutual advantage, negotiation is in order to clear things up. And of course, the arbiter on what is or is not of advantage to A is A himself. A might be wrong about that, to be sure, and if so, then woe to him. But it will not be a failure of justice on the part of anyone if he is. The basis of rights is mutual subjective advantage, not the truth about how to live.

Thus, if nothing is manifestly to mutual advantage from the long-range perspective of each of us, then there are no human rights. We arrive, then, at the crux of the matter: Is there?

IV. THE MAIN OPTIONS

Classical formulations have proclaimed rights to life, liberty, security of person, property, and the pursuit of happiness — among many others. More recently, it has been popular to proclaim rights to minimum or even equal welfare, health, and education, to nondiscrimination in employment, and so forth. And of course procedural rights have also been proposed: the right to a public and fair trial, to certain standards of evidence being used if accused, to equitable punishments that are neither cruel nor "unusual," and to the "equal protection of the laws." Which of these will be underwritten as basic human rights by the foregoing scheme?

I propose to marshal these somewhat diverse candidates under three headings: *negative rights, positive rights,* and *administrative rights.* In the present section I shall explain these and some of their main features and implications. Then in the following section, I shall argue that the case for negative rights is generally very strong, for positive rights generally very weak, and that no separate case is really needed for the third type.

1. It is not typically very clear just what is being claimed when various parties proclaim various rights. What, for instance, is "the" right to life? It might be simply the right not to be killed. But on the other hand, it might be the right to medical attention, food, or other things needed to sustain life in various cases. The right of free speech may be advanced as the (negative) right to say what one pleases to such persons as are willing to hear one out; but alternatively it may be advanced as a positive right that others listen, or that they provide free time on the television channels so that one can have a hearing. These examples surely illustrate the enormous potential for confusion in not observing the distinction between these two sorts of rights.

What I am calling "negative" rights have often been referred to as "liberty" rights, whereas positive rights are frequently called "welfare" rights. There is some justification for this, but it is important to realize that the negative/positive distinction is not the same, as was noted at the outset of this essay. Thus, with regard to liberty of actions, there is a difference between being *allowed* to do as one pleases and being *enabled* to do as one pleases. Negative rights are rights to noninterference.

But in order to be able to apply the concept of interference, we must be able to identify the thing interfered with as being in the sphere which it is proper for the right-holder, rather than some other person, to do with as he pleases. Here is a particular arm, which I have no right to break. Why? Because it is *yours*. Rights entailing duties of noninterference amount to property rights, in that they require that we be able to identify entities of which the right-holder is the legitimate owner or controller. If there were no natural relations that we could appeal to for this purpose, the idea of a basic right to liberty could not get started. One's mind and the parts of one's body obviously belong on any sensible list of things of that kind. What seems to put them there is that they are things one naturally has power over. If a right to liberty is anything, it is a right to use at least those things as one wishes. The right to liberty cannot be literally the right to do whatever one likes. It can't even be that right, limited by the similar right of others. It must instead be the right to do as one wishes with one's body and mind, one's "natural property," limited by the similar right of others.

A right to liberty is inevitably a "historically" based one. One's natural assets — and liabilities — are things with which one simply finds oneself; there is no question of having deserved them. If Jones was born with qualities that Smith wasn't, and Smith comes to think those qualities highly desirable, an agreement to respect liberty entails that Smith has no claim at all against Jones on that account, despite its being a sheer dispensation of the "natural lottery" that this unequal distribution came about. Nor will it be easy to avoid a further implication concerning property in the more usual sense of that term. For if Jones may use his hands, back, and brain as he wishes within only the similar right of others, then he can use things he finds in the world, and others must allow him to do so despite the fact that his only claim on them is that *he* got there *first*. In no other sense need he establish his title to such things on a basis of "desert," if liberty is our guide. "Finders, keepers," and "first come, first served" are the inevitable implications of a right to liberty.[2]

What is prohibited by a right to liberty is a certain class of injuries, damages, and impediments. At the bodily level, these of course include the infliction of wounds, diseases, pains, disabilities, and death — except, of course, in those unusual cases when the right-holder consents to such inflictions. Identifying the class of psychological damages is considerably trickier. If we say that it is the alteration of one's psychological equipment (intellectual and emotional) in ways not wanted by the right-holder, we have to allow for the fact that to have any dealings with others is inevitably to invite some such alterations. To some enormous though unknown extent, our characters, intellects, personalities, and emotional makeups are formed by others, especially during the lengthy period of our upbringing. It is impossible to know with any precision just which of these influences were "unwanted" by the putative right-holder. Nor can we neglect the fact that people are born of others, often as the result of voluntary actions by the latter. A right to liberty must surely give the parents of a person a substantial degree of control over just which influences the child will be subjected to. Yet it seems difficult to accept that that control is unlimited at any stage. Might we need to resort to a theory of natural good to rectify such problems? I think not, but it is an issue we cannot further discuss here. On the other hand, we can less problematically include lying, misleading, and breach of promise. If we are granting liberty to do as one wishes with what is one's own, starting with one's own body and mind, then we may view communications as the act of putting things (namely, ideas) into the minds of audiences. What audiences must generally be presumed to want, in the absence of specific indication to the contrary, is information — not misinformation. To mislead, delude, or lie is thus to invade the domain of someone's mind, using it in ways other than intended by the owner, and would thus be in violation of the owner's right.

2. Positive rights are rights that others help, rather than merely that they refrain from hindering. But although hindering and helping are both matters of degree, it is easier to state a negative right without reference to degree than a positive one, for one can simply assert that any degree of impediment to the acts protected by a negative right would be wrong. The parallel formulation of positive rights, however, would entitle the right-holder to *any* amount of help necessary to achieve the condition to which a right was being asserted, and that would strike us as incredible if not impossible. A's right to be enabled to do *x* is B's duty to enable A to do *x*, and what B might have to do to so enable A is to spend the rest of his life devoting his entire time to that project. Ordinarily, some limit much short of that would be intended: for example, to do as much as one readily can, or to do at least a little. The question of how much is required is obviously of prime importance.

Some think that the sheer idea of a positive right of everyone against everyone is nonsense, on the ground that it is impossible to be so related to everyone, or indeed to more than a very few people. But that is just a matter of care in formulation. The posited duty to help is, of course, a duty to help if one can; if one cannot, that fact will obviously excuse. It plainly can, in principle, be the duty of everyone to help to some specified extent if he is in a position to do so. The question of degree at issue is not that of possibility, but rather of how much that is one's power to do one is going to be required to do. Some will have it that we are to exert ourselves on others' behalf up to the point where they are as well off as we. Others will have it that we must help only when the disparity between A's need for our assistance and our interest in doing something else with our time is very great. A theory of positive rights plainly must declare where it stands on such matters.

Of course the main question for such a theory is just what positive rights exist. The usual answer is welfare, or some aspects thereof, though opportunity for self-development is also a favored candidate. But before we get into that, we shall have to consider whether there is ground for any positive rights at all. We shall take up that issue in the next section.

3. Finally, we have what I call "administrative" rights. They are not in fact a third type, different from either positive or negative rights; indeed, all of them would themselves be either the one or the other. But I list them separately because of their relation to whatever basic rights we end up with. Once we have a basic right, there are rights in regard to the way in which the basic ones are administered. Suppose that we grant everyone the right to a certain kind of treatment, R. Now take A and B, equally eligible for R, yet A gets it but B does not. Someone is then at fault; B has a complaint, one that cannot reasonably be ignored by those who uphold the original right to R. In general, if people have rights, they also have rights that those be fairly and reasonably administered. Or rather, this will be straightforwardly true if the original right is positive; for positive rights are rights to certain types of activities of others, and those activities amount to administration of the right.

Negative rights are another matter, though. My right against X not to be damaged is not a right against all and sundry to help make X avoid damaging me. This further activity will require some system to be established whose purpose is to do such things as promote the likelihood that X won't damage me. We do not automatically have the right to the existence of such a system merely by virtue of having the first right. What we have is the right to establish such a system ourselves, involving any willing others.

Such things as the right of the accused to jury trials and to reasonable rules of evidence may also be considered as auxiliaries, though often very important ones, to the set of fundamental rights proposed. No very special arguments will be needed.

V. THE HUMAN RIGHTS

At last, then, we consider the case for human rights. We look first at the case for negative rights generally. I have suggested that these are all property rights in essence; but it will be urged that we ought to divide these into two classes: rights of the person—liberty and thus security of body and mind and rights of property—in the more usual sense of external property. Let us accept this division, at least for the sake of argument, and see what might issue.

It may seem obvious that our interest in security of our persons will generate the right not to be harmed or coerced, as outlined in the previous section. But can we be certain even of this? Is it certain that there is mutual advantage, among all persons, from observance of such a requirement? Or is a right of this kind only of advantage to the weak?

Here we have a problem, one that deeply infects the theory of social contract and perhaps also the whole subject of rights. Viewed individually, it is obvious that each of us *is* "weak," so that to be "only" to the advantage of the weak is no limitation at all. Not only is each individual helplessly weak in relation to the sum of his fellows, but each of us is, after all, quite helpless for the first several years of his life. Unquestionably we owe our lives to the forbearance of the many adults who for that long period had us completely in their power. None of us can argue, qua individual and taking any longish perspective on the matter, that it would not have been a good bargain to lay down our liberty to damage others in return for their similar nonbelligerance. The snag, however, comes when we consider the matter of united groups, large enough to achieve a fair degree of security in relation to outsiders, but less than the whole group of humans at any time. If we must reckon not only with every individual, acting as an isolated agent in relation to others, but also with any and every grouping of persons, things may be radically different. A large and well-organized group could, conceivably, attain a position of real superiority of power. What then?

It may reasonably be granted that this theoretical possibility is nevertheless not a real one. But it is not clear that that is quite to the point if it is basic, enduring human rights we are after. If there is any solution to this problem at all, perhaps it lies along the lines explored by Plato, who points out that for any group acting in concert, internal justice will at least be essential for successful action of any kind, including nefarious action. But it is not clear that Plato's argument, strong as it is in the abstract, will convince a large and united gang — such as just about any sizable contemporary nation-state. And it may not be true of each such gang that its current viability is due to the forbearance of the other, lesser states with whom it has shared the world up to this point.

This matter of united groups is no trifling issue. But perhaps it is one we can respectably sweep under the carpet. For we might well insist that the idea of justice is essentially individual and that to argue in relation to unreduced groups is out of court. (If so, we could take the view that the question about strong groups is not the question whether

justice must protect the small against the large but instead the different question whether it is necessarily rational to be just.) At any rate,
if the individual point of view has priority, then Hobbes's view would
seem to win the day handily, and the right of personal security be fully
endorsed as a human right (or perhaps *the* human right).

Does this right of personal security extend also to external goods?
Certainly it is widely thought that it does not, or at any rate not to the
same extent. Some think that so to regard it is to slant our conception
of rights in favor of the rich and fortunate — though nothing in the
concept of property rights says that the strength of the right is proportional to the amount of property one has. Indeed, even the utility
of this right is not clearly proportional to the extent of one's property:
If one has little, is it not even more important that one not be deprived
of it? But the question is not who is more favored by such a right;
rather, it is whether there is reason to extend it to all in the first place.

And it does seem that there is. For if we grant a right to liberty of
action generally, must that not mean the liberty to use what one finds
around one? If all have that liberty, then, as pointed out above, those
who get there first have, no doubt, an advantage. Newcomers, re-
specting their liberty, must allow them what they have. They, in
turn, will have to engage in commerce with the firstcomers. Each will
have command over what he finds, makes, or acquires in free transactions with others. No other way can evidently be said to involve a
general right to liberty.

But we are not changing our theoretical horses from Hobbes to
Locke or Kant in the middle of this stream. The argument cannot
appeal to such things as the ultimate intrinsic value of autonomy,
and so forth; nor can it appeal to a supposed natural right. The question is what we can rationally agree on, given our self-assessed rational interests. And it must be asked whether we could do better,
some of us, by resorting to force against those with very much more
than (we think) they need.

Searching questions now arise. In the first place, there is the little
matter of the parenthetical qualification two sentences back. It is obvious that we cannot extend the right to everyone to take from others
just because the taker claims to need the thing taken more than those
he deprives of it. At least, this would require a social procedure for
assessing need. But the problem is far deeper than that: Would beings who are rational according to our characterization necessarily be
concerned about the needs of others anyway? It is far from obvious

that they would. People are generally sympathetic. If confronted with another needy human, most will respond with at least some concern. But do the needy have the right to our assistance, independently of any such sympathetic concern? This is evidently the territory of positive rights, to which we will shortly turn our attention. But it is of interest to ask whether some case can be made out for mutual aid on grounds of the same general type that so strongly undergirds our interest in liberty and security of person and property. Perhaps it could be argued, for instance, that a person assisted now is a person available to assist me later. And that certainly does apply to obligations of assistance to those who have assisted us. But does it generate a right to that assistance in the first place? This is not so clear. For surely there might be some to whom the prospect of such assistance is not manifestly to advantage according to his own reasonable assessment of his life situation; and that is the condition which must be met.

But there is another way of looking at it. Suppose that we were to opt for strong and pure negative rights, a la the libertarians: no right of assistance, and no rights against anyone's property, however vast. Would it be rational for all persons in whatever foreseeable life circumstances to respect such rights? Heroic, perhaps, and even admirable. But is it *rational*? Not obviously. One in great need and capable of satisfying it by some modest depredation of the property of others is surely going to see good reason for committing that depredation. And if that is so, then why would he agree to a program of rights so strong that it will deprive him of any case for even a minimal amount of sharing? Likely he would not. And if not, then perhaps here we have the basis for a modest right of mutual assistance. But we may return to this subject after looking at the general case for positive rights. After all, if we have those to any appreciable degree, they will certainly take care of a right of mutual aid.

Let us, then, see how the argument for positive rights might go. Two popular views are of interest. The first view has it that since the supply of natural resources necessary for human life is finite, and since no one can reasonably claim to "own" them initially, we should consider ourselves to carry an equal right to them. Nobody's claim is better than anyone else's, and so all claims are equal. The second has it simply that there is a basic right of equal or fair treatment, from which various positive rights might proceed. Both arguments are widely used, and interesting. But neither will do.

Against the former view, it must be pointed out that if there are any (nonrenewable) finite natural resources on which people depend for life, then each generation must slowly (or quickly) deplete them. And since generations go on indefinitely, it follows that the alleged equal share we are all supposed to have is a share of indeterminately tiny extent. Where, though, are we to stop short of that? Under the circumstances, no intelligible theory of natural shares can emerge — especially since population size itself is under human control. We had best turn to arguments of the other type, then.

Concerning the second view, the problem in a nutshell is that fair treatment is what I have called an "administrative" right. Fair treatment, in short, presupposes treatment. If there is a duty to treat everyone in way W, then no doubt individuals B and C must both be treated in that way, else one of them has a complaint. But what if there is no duty to treat people that way in the first place? In that case, it is far from obvious that A must treat B and C similarly, no matter how similar B and C may be. Wouldn't A have the right to use his resources as he pleased? And if he pleases to devote many more to B than to C, where is the complaint? It seems, in short, that far from a positive right being founded on a duty of fair treatment, it is quite the other way around.

Perhaps considerations of the nature of social orders and our rights against them will help out? Thus one recent writer: "My first assumption is that there is adequate reason for everyone to want to live under a social order that is distributively just. . . . Social institutions must distribute equally unless there are relevant grounds for differentiation."[3] But of course all this requires that there be institutions that are social as distinct from individual — that is, that encompass all of society, and not just those people who choose to join them. Yet why should there be any such institutions? Institutions, it appears, exist in order to cater to rights rather than being the foundation of those rights.

But perhaps the argument may be taken in this direction. Consider a pure "market society," in which all transactions among people are done either out of motives of private profit or else of private affection. But even in such a society, it might be held, everyone is indefinitely indebted to many others. And it would not have been reasonable for people to cooperate even to that minimal degree necessary for carrying on business had they supposed that those with whom they were dealing would be unwilling to accept at least modest positive duties of care for others.

The argument is credible, and often used. And it may certainly be granted that many people, probably the great majority, will find it in their interest to participate in schemes that promote the likelihood that they and theirs will be educated, adequately fed, medically looked after, and so forth, in case of misfortune. But granting this is really no help toward positive rights, for two reasons. In the first place, if almost everyone is like that, it is equally probable that some are not. And a human right can leave no one out, or at least no rational person out. And in the second place, if almost everybody will find it advantageous to "participate in schemes which promote" the welfare of themselves and those they hold dear, then why won't almost everybody participate in them when such participation is voluntary? How does this argument show that an involuntary scheme is *better*?

Here again the question of the place of group power in contractarian reasoning comes to the fore. If the great majority want X, they are evidently in a position to make the rest fall into line, like it or not. They can certainly ride roughshod over any rights to individual liberty previously established. Do we here have the logic of democracy? But so problematic is that logic as a theory of rights that such reflections raise the question whether any *political* rights can be basic human rights at all.

Once we have public institutions, public spaces, and in general public property, we can deduce many further rights. Those who involuntarily help pay for them, for example, would at least have the right to such benefits as those institutions are supposed to offer. Nor is there any problem about the right to fair consideration in the distribution of such services, since all members of the public are to be catered to as such. But again, since the propriety of such institutions requires that there be basic rights to what they have to offer, rather than vice versa, there is little point in pursuing the implications such institutions would have once they exist.

Our general view is that we have the right to such voluntary actions as would be of manifest mutual advantage, so manifest that no explicit agreement or negotiation would be necessary to establish the behavior coordination in question. The "right" to "maximum self-realization," "development of one's human powers," and the like plainly do not come under that rubric. Have we perhaps set the requirements too high? Suppose that there is real mutual advantage in a certain mutual pattern of behavior, but it is not manifest. Suppose instead that nutritionists or other experts should discern the facts that imply such advantage? Might it not be to the universal advantage to support such experts and establish requirements of the pertinent types of action on the part of all?

But we have but to appreciate the varieties of ways of life to which various people have inclined in order to see the dubiousness of any such supposition, taken literally. And one person's expert will be another's charlatan — one person's doctor another's witch doctor. If the basis of rights is individually held values, then we had best abandon hope of unanimous agreement on such things. The best we could do is go back to basics. There are, we may suppose, certain minimal components of any good life as seen by anyone: enough food to keep alive, for example. But why just food? Presumably, if this is the reason for envisaging a right to minimum food, it must also be a reason for supposing a right to minimum X, where X ranges over whatever might be necessary to maintain life. And then what? It seems we would then get into the question of what constitutes the minimum life our minimum X is to maintain. And that way lie imponderable problems, whose solution could only be political. We would have the right to whatever the political process decrees that we have a right to.

This would not be a promising outcome if what was meant was that our basic rights are whatever the political process decrees them to be. However, the supposed right in question would be not that, but rather, the right to engage in those processes; the further rights we might get out of those processes will be derivative, not basic. But still, the question is whether we have grounds for positing rights to engage in the processes themselves. And that in effect presupposes a right to counteract the workings of the free market in external goods and so on. But insofar as the right to a free market is established, the right to political processes cannot be. We must choose between them and on the line of reasoning pursued in this essay, it is clear that we must prefer the market to politics.

Let us again bear in mind that we are not assuming natural rights. Nor are we assuming that liberty is an intrinsic good, which no rational being would sacrifice any amount of in return for any amount of any other good. The question is only whether every rational being would find himself ahead, in comparison with the other options, by signing into a system that subjects him to the rule of persons selected by a democratic procedure plus whatever benefits this might secure him. This would seem to be possible only if there are literally public goods, in the contemporary sense of goods that none can have unless all have them, *and* unless those goods are so good as to outweigh for all the disadvantages of general enforcement of the system that procures them for us. This is a tall order, and it is hard to believe that it is satisfied in fact, despite current data about the environment, and so on.

Indeed, the latter do not cut in this direction at all. For the right not to be harmed, including harmed by toxic wastes generated in the process of producing goods, is already established in the general right of liberty. We cannot include the absence of toxic wastes as a public good in the above sense.

What we are driven back to is the question of how our native ability to harm others feeds into the system we are exploring. Do those in need get to argue that since it would be rational for them to use force, if necessary, in order to satisfy their minimal requirements, those able to provide for those needs must reckon with the consequences if they don't provide them? If so, it appears that some minimal positive rights might be generated.

Or are they really *rights*? Here we might bring in a distinction often employed in these matters, the distinction between rights in the sense of that which it is (merely) not wrong to do and rights in our more full-blooded sense of that which it is permissible to enforce one's liberty (or, in the case of positive rights, one's ability) to do or have. We might say that people have a right only in the former sense, but not in the latter, to obtain necessities of life by force if need be. Even if they do have only that, however, it may be enough to get the political process going. But it is not entirely clear that they do.

We are left, then, with a strong argument for negative rights, and a problematic argument for positive rights, or rather, for the right to engage in political processes possibly resulting in the acquisition of legal rights of the positive type; plus, of course, such "administrative" rights as are entailed by these.

If this list seems too meager, we can add one more, although it is really the presupposition of all of them. This is the right to be presumed, in the absence of specific evidence to the contrary, to be rational, nonmalevolent, and innocent of the sort of wrongdoing that justifies retaliatory action. In the absence of such a right, no substantive right will be of any use at all, if the account given here is at all correct. For whatever our rights during good behavior, all bets are off during bad behavior, and if bad behavior is presumed to be the norm, then we are well and truly in a Hobbesian state of nature from which there is no escape.

VI. CONCLUDING REMARKS

Many readers will doubtless feel that my list of rights is too meager — though there is enough on it to cause ample concern as is. To such readers, I would put two questions. First, I would ask whether they may not be overlooking the fact that we seek here the basic human rights, those which everybody may be required to observe with respect to everybody. Are they quite sure that there is good reason to include their proposed additions for so grand a roster of subscribers? Do they want to observe these more substantial requirements in respect of people they thoroughly dislike? Do they think it reasonable to insist that those people observe them in respect of us?

Second, what are the alternatives? Are they not all just so many forms of intuitionism? One type would abandon our assumption that we are to consider people in terms of their values, as they see them, choosing instead some notion of human nature more to our liking. But if it is not to the liking of those who disagree or who don't conform to it, then what is the use? Our theory does yield the right to try to persuade all and sundry of any thicker theory, and once persuaded, they will no doubt act on it. Meanwhile, though? Alternatively, there is utilitarianism. This does not abandon our assumption, to be sure. And its insistence on the equality of all in point of the relevance of their interests appeals strongly to many of us. Perhaps, indeed, we could generate agreement that it is better for any person to be happy than miserable. Unfortunately, it is difficult to discern what follows in the way of rights. And more seriously, it is quite unclear how utilitarianism is to be squared with the general conception of rationality adopted above. Why would a rational person, as so characterized, accept the utility of others on a par with his own? If that problem can be overcome, then utilitarianism seems to be the way to go, and I would be the first to welcome it. But I see no way, at present, of doing that; nor any convincing support for an alternative theory of rationality capable of yielding the utilitarian result.[4]

Meanwhile, perhaps the effect of our program is more liberating than might at first be thought. By and large, the conception proposed leaves us about as free as it is possible for all to be in a worldful of fellow humans. Perhaps we can ask for no more.

NOTES

1. John Rawls, *A Theory of Justice* (Cambridge, Mass.: Harvard University Press, 1971). The criticism advanced is especially due to David Gauthier. See "Justice and Natural Endowment," *Social Theory and Practice* (Spring 1974). Gauthier, as will be evident, is a major stimulus of the views expressed here.

2. These points about liberty are brought home forcefully by Robert Nozick, *Anarchy, State and Utopia* (New York: Basic Books, 1974). It will likewise be evident that I owe much to Nozick's work in these matter.

3. K. Baier, "Merit and Race," *Philosophia* (November 1978); 130-31.

4. It will not have been overlooked by readers familiar with my earlier writings that this paper represents a decided sea change in my views about justice. Those interested might compare the account here with the views expressed in my *Morality and Utility* (Baltimore: The Johns Hopkins University Press, 1967).

THE SCOPE OF
HUMAN RIGHTS

11

WHEN DOES THE RIGHT TO
LIFE BEGIN?

KURT BAIER*

(1) That the life of a human being begins at conception appears to be a necessary truth. It is to all appearances (logically) impossible that a given individual should have been conceived at a different time from the one at which he was in fact conceived, or conceived of different genetic materials. But from this it does not follow, though it may well be true, that an individual's right to life begins at conception, for the question of when his life begins is essentially a retrospective one. If the blastocyst after traveling down the Fallopian tube is not embedded in the uterine lining, the woman whose egg has been fertilized may be said to have conceived, but she does not become pregnant and there is no human individual to speak of, only a conceptus. For a conceptus is not simply a (very) short-lived human being or individual. If, after a war, all that remained of humanity were a thousand blastocysts stored in some undamaged research institute, and kept alive for years in some nutrient that also arrested their growth, then humanity would not have survived the war; these would not be the last thousand men and women carrying on the human enterprise for some more years.

Facts such as these give point to my title question. But before it is tackled, an obvious objection should be met. My question presupposes that there is such a thing as the right to life. Now many people, myself included, believe that what is claimed by those who maintain that there is a right to life is highly plausible. However, and that is the objection, the history of the language of rights casts doubt on whether that plausible contention can be correctly stated in the language of rights. It seems, on the contrary, that an imprescriptible, inalienable natural right is a contradiction in terms. "Nonsense upon stilts," Bentham called it. [1]

What is the underlying conception of rights that turns natural rights into a contradiction in terms and why should one hold it? Clearly, the language of rights is not essential to moral language. It does not figure in ancient or medieval ethics. Questions it would now be perfectly natural to formulate in terms of rights—for example, whether a starving man has a right to steal food from someone who has plenty—would have been asked in terms of whether it was right, lawful, just, licit, or permissible for him to do so. Traditionally, these terms and their contradictories cover that part of the moral domain for which English notoriously has no word, but which in other languages is called *ius, Recht, droit, diritto,* and so on. Apparently, the first to give a definition of "*a* right," in the sense of something one can be said to have or not to have as opposed to the mere rightness or wrongness of doing something, was William of Ockham. [2]

Many questions arise. Were there no rights before Ockham? Or were they merely first *noticed* and *recognized* in the fourteenth century? Or were they perhaps always recognized, but no one had the courage to *advance claims for their enforcement* before that? It is worth quoting Ockham's definition, for it draws a distinction, between natural and civil rights, which has proved attractive because, among other things, its acceptance would allow a plausible answer to some of these questions. Ockham says:

> Natural right is nothing other than a power to conform to right reason, without agreement or pact; civil right is a power, deriving from agreement, and sometimes conforms to right reason and sometimes discords with it. [3]

Ockham appears to tie natural rights to traditional natural law and right reason. Insofar as "natural right" is not merely the traditional name (like *ius, Recht,* etc.) of a certain moral *domain* but of an individuated power, it is a "*moral* power," that is, a power grounded in right reason, not in—possibly arbitrary—agreement. By contrast, civil rights are grounded in such possibly arbitrary agreements and therefore may or may not accord with right reason. On the basis of Ockham's definition, then, one could say that natural rights had always existed, though perhaps some of them had not always been recognized, whereas civil rights are an invention of the late Middle Ages, legal devices or instruments that had not previously been available to the subjects of a legal order.

Ockham's distinction ushered in a view that became dominant. The concepts he distinguished were developed in relative independence of one another. Civil rights have been the concern primarily of lawyers, who developed and perfected these instruments and of jurisprudentialists, who analyzed and theorized about them. Natural rights, by contrast, have been the concern of politicians and manifesto writers, who pushed for new ones, and of moral philosophers, who analyzed and philosophized about them. Civil rights became necessarily linked to recognition and enforcement but independent of moral grounds, and natural rights became linked to moral ideals of various kinds but independent of recognition and enforcement. The dichotomy was further sharpened by John Austin and the legal positivists who followed him. Rightly suspicious of natural law theorists who claimed that nothing could be law that ran counter to the dictates of morality, Austin posited two parallel, mutually independent, and differently sanctioned systems of established norms, "positive law" and "positive morality," both of which were open to rational criticism from the standpoint of the moral ideal, which he believed to be utilitarianism. [4]

The problem with Ockham's distinction, and similar ones drawn later, is its suggestion that natural and civil rights are two subclasses or *kinds* of rights and so use "right" in the same sense, whereas the definitions imply that they use two different *senses* of "right," so that having a natural right is a very different thing from having a civil right. Civil rights necessarily have essential characteristics that natural rights do not have. A civil right necessarily can be acquired and transferred or alienated, as well as accorded, abrogated or prescribed; natural rights cannot. If one has a civil right, it follows that normally one can count on its being backed by the appropriate social sanctions if those against whom one has it refuse to honor it; this need not even normally be true of natural rights. A civil right is absolute or at least dominant over most other conflicting claims rather than being merely *prima facie,* merely one claim among others; all or most natural rights are not absolute but merely *prima facie.* [5]

Rejection of natural rights is the logical outcome if one accepts the further premise that the only correct or the primary and full-blooded sense of "right" is that used in "civil right," whereas that used in "natural right" is at best a derivative and watered-down sense. For then we have to say that the claim that there are natural rights is not true at all or not literally true but true only in a derivative or watered-down sense.

This additional premise becomes virtually inescapable once we employ a certain popular method for determining the nature of rights. The *language* of rights, we note, appears at a certain time in the history of a culture, and so we ask, "What are the important differences between a society in which people do not have rights and that society after they come to have rights?" Thus, Joel Feinberg begins an important paper with the following thought experiment: "Try to imagine Nowheresville—a world very much like our own except that no one . . . has *rights.*"[6] But this sort of question prejudges the issue, for it implies that the only or the primary sense of "rights" is that of civil rights. The very assumption that in Nowheresville no one has rights implies that there are no natural rights, for of course if there were, people in Nowheresville too would necessarily have them.

(2) Well, then, what sort of a thing is a right? There are several ways of answering this question. The major currently held theories, the power (Spinoza, Hobbes, Blackstone, John Austin), beneficiary (Bentham, David Lyons), discretionary power or option (H. L. A. Hart), claim (Wasserstrom, Feinberg), and entitlement (McCloskey, Nozick) theories are not, as they are usually taken to be, rival answers to the same question, but (at least in part) compatible answers to different interpretations of the question above. In the next three sections I distinguish three such interpretations and offer my answers to them, relating them briefly—where that is illuminating—to some of the major theories.

(A) One could answer the question above by enumerating one's rights, such as life, health, liberty, property, education, and then ask what sort of thing these are. This sort of answer is important because it draws attention to the fact that the content of a right, what it is a right *to,* is something that is, to the right-holder, a good rather than an evil. Talk about the right to punishment sounds paradoxical because it requires us to construe it as a good to the right-holder. The paradox disappears when it is explained, for instance, that what the culprit has a right to is being punished rather than "treated" and that treatment is degrading. Bentham's beneficiary theory is plausible as an answer to this interpretation of the question above.[7]

The things we can have rights to may conveniently be divided into two main categories: (a) things that the right-holder considers goods (e.g., life, health, property); (b) the necessary and/or sufficient conditions of the right-holder's enjoying these goods. Category (a) mostly comprises states of affairs; for example, the right-holder's being in good health, being exposed to no threats or dangers to his life, being in undisputed control of his possessions, and so on; but they also include the freedom to do things whose performance by himself, and some actions or activities whose performance by others, the right-holder considers a good; for example, other people's doing obeisance or the infamous *ius primae noctis*. Category (b) comprises those doings by the right-subjects that are necessary, sufficient, or necessary and sufficient conditions of the right-holder's enjoying the goods in the first category. Suppose I have a right to health. Then, if I am to realize my right, that is, to enjoy the good that is its content, others must have an obligation not to endanger or undermine my health, and perhaps even to restore it to me when I have lost it. Or suppose I have a right to freedom. Then, if I am to have freedom or to be free, others must have an obligation not to interfere with my doing of those things that I must be free to do if I am correctly to be said to have freedom or to be free.

Thus, the two ways of specifying the content of a right, what the right-holder has a right to, are these. One is to specify a good, interest, or concern for the realization of which by the right-holder there are adequate reasons. The other is to specify the conduct of the right-subjects that is the necessary or the sufficient or the necessary and sufficient condition of the right-holder's realizing this good and thereby his right.

The content of a right, the good to which the right-holder has a right, may be related to the right-holder in one of three ways: (i) it may be the right-holder's freedom to do something he wants to do — an action right, such as the right to free speech or to vote; (ii) it may be the continuation of the control and enjoyment of some good he already possesses — a retention right, such as the right to one's good name or of ownership of land; or (iii) it may be the right to some good he does not yet possess — a recipience right, such as the right to goods contracted for or the right to free elementary education.

For each of these types of right, we may distinguish a stronger and a weaker variety, depending on the strength of the correlative obligation.[8] The weaker variety of right involves only "protective" correlative obligations, which merely protect the right-holder in the exercise of his ability to do, to hang on to, or to induce others to give him something. Such rights impose obligations on everyone else not to interfere with the right-holder's exercise of these abilities. We can call these, following Feinberg, "negative rights." The stronger variety involves "constitutive" correlative obligations requiring specific persons to do whatever is necessary for the right-holder to be able to enjoy the good in question. I shall call these, again following Feinberg, "positive rights."[9] The right to private property or to education can be interpreted as either a positive or a negative right. Aquinas was concerned to prove that it was not contrary to natural law to have private property, that is, that private property was a universal negative retention right. He was not concerned to show that (a certain minimal amount of) property was a universal positive recipience right. Libertarians are concerned to show that education is a universal negative action right, that is, that everyone is entitled to select his favorite school without any interference; egalitarians, that it is a universal positive recipience right, that is, that every society has the duty to provide equal education for its members. The right to free speech is most naturally taken as a negative action right. The right to life is usually interpreted as a negative retention right, but certain samaritan and welfare laws can be construed as imposing obligations constitutive of a positive retention right to life. It is, however, hard to see how the right to life could be a positive recipience right, for who or what could be the right-holder?[10]

It seems that negative rights tend to protect and favor those with greater natural abilities to do, retain, or obtain things, whereas positive rights tend to insure goods also for those who would not be able to secure them through their own efforts alone.

It is important to note that rights are most naturally individuated by what they are rights to: life, health, liberty, property, education, and so on. The correlative obligations are designed to insure this good for the right-holder. A person's rights may therefore remain the same even if the correlative obligations change with changing conditions. The correlative obligations subserving the right to health or education may change significantly as the requirements of health and education change.

That the rationale of rights is the good they help secure for the right-holder is true even of those seemingly least good-oriented rights that Hart calls "special rights," that is, those "which arise out of special transaction between individuals or out of some special relationship in which they stand to each other."[11] In their case, only those can be right-holders or right-subjects who are parties to the special transactions or relationships. Hart contrasts these with "general rights," which do not arise out of such special transactions. In their case, neither right-holders nor right-subjects are determined in this way, and they are necessarily rights against "everyone else."[12] Hart thus thinks of general rights as necessarily negative. Now, it is true of special rights that one comes to have them if one comes under a recognized "generating factor," such as being a promisee or heir or representative. But the reason why such factors are rightly recognized as generative of rights is that their counting as such generating factors promotes a very important good, namely, one's ability to get others to commit themselves and so to plan one's life more effectively. It is true, as Hart says, that in such cases "the right and obligation arise not because the promised action has itself any particular moral quality, but just because of the voluntary transaction between the parties."[13] But this implies less independence of morality than might at first appear, for these generating factors are allowed to operate only in the interestices in the network of nonartificial moral guidelines. Thus, a promise to murder someone does not "take."[14] Indeed, a person being hired for such a purpose, far from acquiring an obligation to kill, acquires instead an obligation to inform the police. It therefore seems to me quite misleading for Hart to represent the notions of a right and obligation as "very special,"[15] and as coming from "different dimensions of morality"[16] than the notions of "ought," "right," "wrong," "good," and "bad."[17] True, the creation of special rights allows individuals to *extend,* at their own discretion, the application of these latter terms to conduct to which they would not otherwise apply, but they operate within the moral framework marked out by these latter notions. In any case, *pace* Hart, even this peculiarity of special rights does not hold of general rights. Since the generating factors of general rights are not, like those of special rights, conventional (e.g., saying 'I hereby promise . . .'), and since their correlative obligations (unlike those of special rights) are universal, it is (by Hart's own showing) at least as natural to say that it is *wrong* for anyone to interfere, as that everyone *has an obligation* not to interfere with anyone exercising a general right. In my view, the peculiarities that Hart and many others thought they detected in rights and obligations are present only in special rights, and even in special rights they are not as morality independent as is often assumed.

(B) The first interpretation of the question raised in the beginning of section (2) was, "What are the sorts of things *to* which we have rights?" But clearly that is not the only possible interpretation. It also seems natural to take it to mean "What are we saying of something when we say that *it* is a right?" and the question implied by it, namely, *"Of what sort* of thing do we say it?" But when we examine this, we find that in fact we never say of anything that *it* is a right. "This is a right" does not appear to have a use, except in the sense explained under (A). There is nothing we pick out by some other term or simply by the demonstrative "this," of which we then say that *it* is a right, as we say of a certain hand movement that it is a hand signal or of certain words that they are (constitute) a promise. Hence, these two questions do not seem to arise.

Nevertheless, this appearance should not be taken too seriously. For there *are* rights, or if in some place and at some time, there are not, there surely *could be.* But if this is so, then there must be something of which it is true that it is a right, even if we have no occasion to single it out *in any way* and call it a right; even if there never is occasion for saying *"that X* there is a right" or *"this* is a right."

Thus, even though we never have occasion to single out something and *say* of it that it is a right, we do speak of there being natural rights and of people having rights. And in doing so we refer or advert to something. I believe what we have in mind on such occasions is a certain sort of moral relationship between at least two people, the right-holder and the right-subject(s), a relationship viewed from the standpoint of the right-holder, and involving a certain good, the content of the right.

(C) We have seen reason to think that we never actually say of anything that it is a right and so have no occasion to ask what it is we are saying of it when we say it. Nevertheless, since there are rights, people have rights,[18] and if people have rights, one can ask what that is that they have. So at least a question arises that is closely analogous to "What are we saying of something when we say that it is a right?" And, of course, the conventional power, claim, and option theories of rights, have given what they take to be rival answers to this question. I believe that these three theories are mistaken both in the details of their answers and, more important, in the point they have in common, namely, that having a right is being in a position to make use of some conventional social machinery, whatever may be its precise details. The mistake involved here is the identification of having a right with having a recognized right. That there are rights to something, *X,* means that *there is moral justification for* a certain sort of social machinery capable of securing *X* for him, and that someone has a right to *X* means that he is or would be morally justified in using such machinery to secure *X* for himself.

In greater detail, the correct answer to our question in this last interpretation would seem to be that rights fall into a certain sort of subcategory of the most general moral category applicable to conduct. That category is what we may call "the morally wanted" or "the wanted from the moral point of view." This is a very broad category ranging from the morally required to the morally ideal. What lies beyond this range is the morally neutral, that which is neither morally wanted (welcome) nor morally unwanted (unwelcome). The moral enterprise is concerned with shaping people's conduct in such a way that what is morally wanted is done or brought about and what is unwanted not done or prevented. It is worth stressing (although I cannot defend this here) that what is morally wanted concerns only conduct (and because of it, dispositions and attitudes), which, in a wide sense, are other-referring, that is, affect others favorably or unfavorably, whether they do so directly, as when one stabs, kicks, insults, or lies to others, or do so indirectly, as when one acts on maxims or principles whose widespread adoption, however natural or expedient such an adoption may be for each individual, would have adverse consequences for all concerned, such as pouring toxic substances into rivers, picking rare wildflowers, or never giving to charity.

The moral point of view, though completely impersonal, has two asymmetries built into it, which distinguish it from some of the other points of view with which it has been wrongly identified or confused. The morally wanted is realized by everyone giving due weight to the interests and concerns of *others.* When one adopts the moral point of view, one thus thinks of each individual as *a self* confronting *others.* The second asymmetry is that between agent and patient. Hence the moral demands can be thought of in either of two different ways: (i) as what is wanted of an agent, that is, what a person is asked to *do* or *refrain* from doing for the sake of another (the patient), as when the agent is asked to give up a seat for an old lady or to refrain from smoking for the sake of sensitive passengers; or (ii) as what is wanted of a patient, that is, what he should, for the sake of another, put up with when it happens in consequence of what that other does for his own sake, as when a person is asked to put up with the smoke of the other's cigarette so that the other can concentrate on his work.

Ethical egoism and altruism recognize the first asymmetry but treat it differently. The egoist ideal demands of every individual that he set aside all the conflicting interests of others unless doing so is detrimental to himself directly or in the long run. Altruism holds the exact opposite. Utilitarians, by contrast, do not recognize the first asymmetry. They sum the utilities of all concerned with a view to maximizing the sum instead of equitably balancing the conflicting utilities of different individuals against one another. Kant ignores both asymmetries, for he bases all moral demands on the symmetrical principle, "you must treat humanity, *whether in your own person or in that of another,* always as an end and never as a means only."

In this essay, I can give only some general idea of how moral demands are correctly worked out. In the simplest case, when people face one another, not as institutional role players, but simply as individuals pursuing their concerns as independent persons, the two major moral questions for them are these: (i) What may I do *to* the other, or, formulated from the other's (the patient's) standpoint, What should the other put up with from me? and (ii) What *should* I do *for* the other, or, again formulated from the other's (the patient's) standpoint, What *may* the other expect of me? The overall principle is that, in determining one's morally ideal conduct, the guidelines or maxims or rules to be used in answering these two major questions must be for the good of everyone alike. For then and then only does everyone have the best possible reason (which *everyone* can have) to follow these guidelines. Hence only then are the moral requirements in accordance with reason.[19]

Summing up, the moral point of view is one from which each of us becomes subject to demands to conform our conduct to guidelines that tell us what we must, must not, may, or need not do, for the sake of the well-being of others, and whose general observance by the moral community is for the good of everyone alike. The demands formulated in these guidelines tell us what is morally wanted of us, from the minimally to the maximally wanted. One's doing the minimally wanted is least appreciated by others; doing the maximally wanted is most appreciated. Conversely, not doing (even) the minimally wanted is more resented by others; not doing the maximally wanted is least (or not at all) resented.

Clearly, rights are moral notions. As we have seen, the concept is developed out of the older concept of *ius, Recht,* and so on. It is also clear that a right is a minimal moral demand. Its satisfaction need be only minimally appreciated; its nonsatisfaction may be maximally resented. We must of course distinguish between what is morally demanded (required) and the demands or claims the right-holder may make on the right-subject. What is morally required is that the right-subject satisfy the demands of the right-holder. Not satisfying it would be wrong. A right-holder may demand something as a right (as opposed to a favor); he need not beg for it, may expect its satisfaction as a matter of course, need not even say "Thank you." Joel Feinberg, in two important papers, considers this feature the essential new element of *the language* of rights, and so also of rights themselves.[20] But I think this is a mistake, for this feature is present in all minimal moral demands. I need not be grateful to my neighbor who could have killed me but did not. I need not say "Thank you" even if killing me was in his interest and he very much wanted to kill me and could have got away with it. If I have to beg him not to kill me, he has already wronged me. Perhaps this shows that I have a right not to be killed, but in that case people had this right before Ockham and presumably they have it in Feinberg's Nowheresville, where no one is supposed to have rights.[21]

It does seem, however, that the characteristic identified most clearly by H. L. A. Hart,[22] namely, discretionary power, is indeed an essential feature of rights. Hart explains his point in terms of Hobbes's image of a legal chain: "so also have they made Artificial Chains, called *Civill Lawes,* which they themselves, by mutual covenants, have fastened at one end, to the lips of that Man, or Assembly, to whom they have given Soveraigne Power; and at the other end to their ears."[23] In terms of Hobbes's model, Hart repositions the chain representing rights to run between the right-holder and the person against whom he has the right. There are not now "two persons bound by a chain, but . . . one person bound, the other end of the chain lying in the hands of another to use if he chooses."[24] Thus, those chains forged by the law or by a morality must be seen "as rules placed at the disposal of individuals and regulating the extent to which *they* demand certain behavior from others"[25] before any of them can be interpreted as conferring rights.

Some writers argue that there are important rights not involving such options. Thus, Geoffrey Marshall claims "that some things to which human beings are entitled we often feel should not be the subject of options. Obvious examples are the right to life and the right to protection from criminal offences that do serious damage."[26] And he goes on to say, tentatively, "that certain benefits and protections are such that all men ought to have them and that men in general cannot properly alienate or deprive themselves of these rights or deem themselves to have no rights. Thus the ability to waive one's rights is seen as one common feature of some — possibly not the most important — rights, rather than as a necessary characteristic of the concept of a right."[27]

It would seem to me clearer, and on the account of rights given here it would be necessary, to put Marshall's point by saying that there are some goods — for example, life or education — that have certain features (importance, irreversibility, irreplaceability) on account of which people not only have the right but also the duty to have them. This way of putting the matter does not pose the impossible task of deducing a duty to live from a right to life, but it does leave the task of showing that in certain matters people have both a right and a duty.[28]

There is, however, a further point that could be made on Marshall's behalf. A right involves correlative obligations. It thus not only grants the right-holder the option of exercising or not exercising as he wishes his ability to do, retain, or obtain something deemed good but also imposes on relevant others the obligation to create favorable conditions for him to have that good. Negative rights impose the obligation not to interfere with his efforts to secure it; positive rights, the obligation to aid him in this or even to provide the good for him. The right-holder thus has two quite different options: (a) the option of exercising the ability just mentioned if he wants to — I shall speak of "exercising" and "not exercising" one's right; and (b) the option of cashing in on these correlative obligations, if he wants to — I shall speak of "insisting on" and "waiving" one's right. Someone may now want to say, on behalf of Marshall, that whereas all rights involve the option of whether or not to *exercise* them, some do not involve the option of whether or not to *waive* them, even when one does not have a duty to do what amounts to exercising the right. I cannot here argue that there can be no such rights, but it seems to me that there is every reason to think that the right to life is not among them. Suppose my right to life is a positive retention right. Then, if I cannot waive this right, bystanders are required to prevent me from committing suicide, perhaps from dying, even when I plead with them to let me die. Or suppose my right to life is a negative retention right. Then, if I cannot waive it, others cannot help me in my attempts to commit suicide when I ask them to help me (suppose I am paralyzed), for they are obligated to refrain from shortening my life. But then if (as we assume) there is no (natural) duty to live, the impossibility of waiving my right to life would violate my right to die, which is implied in the option granted by my right to life. Thus, whether we construe the right to life as a positive or a negative (retention) right, it implies the option of waiving the right, unless of course there is a natural duty to live.

Two other features are often but in my opinion wrongly associated with rights, namely, enforcement and recognition. Let us first note that the two are very different. One cannot come to have civil rights unless there are recognized ways of acquisiton, such as inheritance or contract. But enforcement is a further matter. It involves machinery the right-holder can set in motion if the (or a) right-subject fails to honor the right. But he can still *have* such a right, even in the absence of such machinery, as long as there is *a recognized generating factor.* Such an arrangement may be sufficiently effective to be valuable, even if there is no enforcement machinery at all, or if that machinery does not work in all cases, or if there is no provision for enforcement in some cases. And what is true of legal rights is *a fortiori* true of moral ones, that is, those supported by the characteristically moral sanction. The need for sanctions is a function of the unclarity of the recognized generating factors and the morality of the members of the community. The clearer the former and the greater the latter, the greater the value of unenforced rights. But even if their value is fairly low, it does not follow that there *are* no such rights or that people cannot have rights without sanctions.

Of course, though one may have and be able to realize one's rights even in the absence of social sanctions, clearly such sanctions are desirable to the extent that they improve the rate of discharge of correlative obligations and to the extent that their social "cost," in the widest sense, is not greater than the cost incurred by the violation of rights that would occur in their absence. The social cost of our crime prevention system is so high—it has been estimated that it would be cheaper to provide free college education for every criminal than to keep him in prison, to say nothing of noneconomic costs—that it is not absolutely certain that it might not be preferable to do without it.

At the same time, we must not identify social sanctions with an "enforcement" system, taking this literally. Not all rights are legal rights, and even legal rights cannot and should not always literally be enforced, in the sense that right-subjects should be *forced* to discharge their correlative obligations. Quite often it will be necessary or preferable to force the right-subject to pay compensation. And in the case of moral rights that are not also legal rights, the social sanctions will rightly consist only in the adoption by the appropriate persons of various kinds of negative attitude toward the right-violator, such as expression of disapproval, condemnation, indignation, resentment, and so on.

What about recognition? Clearly, there can be no unrecognized special rights, for what creates such rights is not, as Hart rightly points out, the particular moral quality of the conduct the right allows to the right-holder or requires of the right-subject, but just the special transaction or relationship between the parties involved. Thus, the genesis of the rights is procedural, artificial, conventional. Reason, natural morality, reflection on the prerequisites of the good life could not tell us who held which of such rights against whom: such rights are artificial devices or powers, with the help of which individuals can by mutual agreement improve their lives. But that presupposes the recognition of these artifices.

Not so with general rights. There may be general human concerns and interests that *merit* the sort of protection a general right can give. In these cases, what generates the right is not a recognized artificial procedure but the importance of the protected interest for the good life for everyone. Special rights must be created by two steps. The first is the setting up in a society of the generating factors. The second is the employment of these factors by individuals. Individuals cannot have special rights until both these steps have been taken. General rights, by contrast, can be discovered, for they are grounded in general human concerns or interests, and these are discovered, not created. Life is, of course, one such general interest and concern. But if such rights can be discovered, then they need not be recognized in order to exist.

(3) We can now give an account of a right or entitlement that holds for all kinds of rights, not only for special or for legal or for moral or for human rights. In the first place, it is something that is part of *a* morality, something that *purports* to be morally justifiable. This means that one can *have* a right that is not in fact thus justifi-

able, but this cannot be common knowledge, for if it were, the right would no longer even purport to be thus justifiable. When it is discovered and generally realized that a legal right is no longer justifiable, we need not say that the purported right-holder did not after all have the *legal* right he was generally believed to have, though of course the right *now* ought to be abolished and cannot *long remain* a recognized right without undermining the respect for the law. A right should command respect, but it cannot do so if it no longer even purports to be morally justifiable. Natural law theories affirm too tight a connection between law and morality, since on their view nothing can *be* a law (or a right) unless it is in accordance with natural law or right reason. Ockham, John Austin, and the legal positivists overstate the separation of law and morality, for they allow that laws and legal rights may not even purport to be morally justifiable. But, apart from undermining popular respect for the law, this has the consequence, which we noted in the beginning, of forcing us to give purely conventional accounts of what is law (and legal rights) and so requiring us to say that "right" means one thing in "legal right" and another in "moral right."

That rights, including legal rights, *purport* to be morally justifiable constitutes a halfway house between these two doctrines. It means more than simply that people *say* they think them morally justifiable, or don't say they don't. People must really believe it; they must change their *mind* when they change their tune. They must change their relevant approvals and disapprovals and at least *tend* to change their behavior. In the case of *legal* rights, there must be *machinery* for change when the moral unjustifiability of the law is generally recognized. The existing normative order, whether legal or moral, is not simply a conventionally produced extension into the interstices within the ideal normative order, as is argued by Aristotle and the natural law tradition following him. But it is not completely independent of it either, as the legal positivists think. The connection is more indirect: there must be *machinery* for keeping the existing normative order in conformity with the ideal, and that machinery must tend to be effective.

In short, "M has a right to X against N" means that there is adequate reason to hold that there is a good, X, such that M should, if he suitably indicates to N that he wants X, have N's more or less extensive cooperation in enabling him to enjoy X (positive or negative right) and that this cooperation by N, if M demands it, is minimally wanted from the moral point of view.

Rights differ from favors in not involving correlative duties. One can ask and do favors, just as one can claim what is one's right and honor another's right. The difference is that whereas it would be wrong not to honor a right, it would not be wrong to refuse a favor, though if it does not involve great cost to oneself, one *ought* to do favors one has been asked.

Doing someone a favor differs from doing a so-called act of supererogation in that the latter are (in the typical use of the term) highly meritorious and so beyond even what one ought to do, though of course such acts are still morally wanted (welcome) rather than morally neutral.

Lastly, honoring someone's right differs from giving someone his deserts in two ways. The first is that what a person deserves need not be a good to him: he may deserve punishment. The second is that the deserved is what is *earned*. There could be no merely conventional criterion of desert, as there can be conventional titles. And though natural rights also are nonconventional, they are necessarily based on what is common to mankind, whereas desert is often based on individual differences.

(4) Human or natural rights are those moral rights whose moral ground and generating factor are the same, namely, being human in some relevant sense. They differ from special rights in that the question does not arise of whether it is for the good of everyone alike that a particular generating factor, such as uttering the words "I hereby promise . . . " should be recognized as generating a right. The general framework condition of the moral enterprise as such, which is usually equated with being human, is the only condition of human or natural rights. The expression "natural rights" is therefore preferable, for if there are nonhuman creatures who satisfy the framework condition of morality, then they, too, have natural rights, although one might argue about whether they have human rights. To argue that they don't have natural rights would be to adopt a "speciesist" position about morality. I shall not examine this problem here.

It is a corollary of this position that human rights cannot be acquired, transferred, or in any way lost. They are not alienable, revocable, or prescriptible. Some have argued that rights cannot be forfeited either. Hugo Bedau, in an interesting paper entitled "The Right to Life,"[29] says it cannot be forfeited because "a person's *right* to life is intimately connected to his *being* what he is; to say that he can forfeit this right is to say that he can do (or neglect to do) things which have as their consequence that he *ceases to be a person,* and so can justifiably be killed or left to die because now (on account of what he has done) he no longer merits our consideration, any more than an insect or a stone does, (p. 570). However, even if the right to life cannot be forfeited, execution may not violate that right, for he may have forfeited his life. Still, this does not turn him into an "outlaw"; he has not ceased to be a person; he may not be treated like an insect. It may even be required of society that it restore him to health if he attempts to commit suicide, certainly that it protect him from lynch mobs or fellow prisoners or vicious guards. It does not even follow that the community has a duty or ought to execute him. It follows merely that *if* the community did so, it would not violate his right to life. If he forfeits his life, he loses the protection of that right against the state, though not against anyone else. And even vis-a-vis the state, the individual is not an outlaw but still a person to be treated with respect, not simply to be destroyed like an insect. One can agree with Bedau that "one of the purposes of the notion of natural or human rights must be to discourage, indeed prevent, us from ever thinking about anyone in this way" (ibid.), that is, as an insect, without having to admit that a person cannot, by whatever he does, forfeit his life and with it part of the protection his right to life gives him.

There is, however, also another sense of "human right," namely, a right whose ground is "being human *and* living in a given society." This still excludes the other conditions of having moral rights, such as their having been conferred or transferred or earned. Such rights are still human in the sense that no society can justifiably deny such a right to any of its members, provided they are human, in the appropriate sense. But of course *what such human rights are* will vary from society to society. Such human rights, therefore, should not appear in declarations of universal human rights. I believe certain rights mentioned in the United Nations Declaration are of this sort (e.g., arts. 24, 25), that is, imprescriptible in certain societies. Moreover, what such rights are will be a highly contentious question, since the answer depends on what the society in question is capable of providing for *all* its members, and what goods should have priority over others.

I shall assume, for the sake of the argument of this paper, that normal adult human beings have the natural or human right to life in the earlier sense. I shall assume that it is not a recipience but only a negative retention right, that is, a right that implies a universal correlative obligation on the part of others (but not the right-holder himself) to refrain from certain actions that would endanger or shorten the right-holder's life. I shall assume without argument that it is possible to specify, in sufficient detail to be practically useful, wherein this correlative obligation consists. What I want to examine in the remainder of this chapter is the old question concerning the point in his life history at which an individual comes to have this right and at what point he loses it; what exactly is the sense of "life" in which he has a right to it; and precisely on what grounds he has it.

Let us begin with the sense of "life." It is not, of course, the sense in which we may wonder just when life or human life began on this planet. The object of the right to life is not the phenomenon, life, but *the life of* an individual, and the right-holder is the individual himself. Again, it plainly is not life in the sense in which individuals such as cars, washing machines, or even plants can be said to have a life. For although the life of these things is not identical with their existence — a washing machine may "survive" the end of its operative life and dead trees can stand for years — still there is *nothing that is* their life; hence they cannot *lose* their life and so cannot in any important sense *have* a life, either. We cannot commiserate or rejoice with a car or a daisy. Rains can be good or beneficial (or bad or harmful) for the grass or the wheat but not a good (or evil) *to them,* only *to us* who want it to grow.

A dog by contrast can *have* a life and lose it. Things are goods and evils to it: it may lead a dog's life. Lassie with a large litter may have a miserable sex or family life; a disturbing dream life; and if she is a Seeing Eye dog, an exhausting and cheerless working life. One can write the story of a dog's life. A dog may perhaps have some understanding of someone dying or being dead. It is therefore perhaps arguable that *to a dog his life (i.e. staying alive) can be a good,* something he does not want to lose. In any case, the absence of this capacity, life's being a good to it, would greatly weaken the case for saying that a given being had a right to life. For, as we have seen, what someone has a right to must be good to him.

Clearly, then, we must draw a distinction between the biological and the experiential life of a person. Her biological life does but her experiential life does not begin at conception. Her experiential life may be frequently interrupted during her biological life. And, like Karen Quinlan's, it may end in a coma before her biological life ends in death. It is clear, I think, that there would be no sense in talking of a right to life of beings such as plants, which are altogether incapable of having an experiential life. For such beings could not be said literally to *have* a life; nothing could be a good or evil to them, least of all their life. It seems, then, that what the right to life protects is the individual's biological life and that the ground for it must have something to do with the experiential life, since in the absence of such a life there is no ground for a right to life. It will be granted, I imagine, that it is the experiential life that makes possible the worthwhileness or fulfillingness of the individual's life, all those things on account of which people want to go on living, on account of which they cling to life and would regard being deprived of it as being robbed of an immensely important good, as well as the condition of anything being to them a good at all. There can therefore be little doubt that it is for the good of everyone alike if every society, as far as it is capable, insures for its members the protection of this important good.

I want now to look at the question of when it would be a good thing for this protection to begin. Let us note first that whereas in the case of normal adults the natural right to life can be merely negative — that is, the correlative duty may be simply to refrain from doing things that would endanger or shorten the lives of others — in the case of infants, the disabled, the aged, the sick, and the insane, that duty would have to include assistance and life support if these lives were to be effectively protected. Thus, in a primitive society the right of normal adults to look after themselves and their obligation to look after the incompetent may come into conflict. I believe that in such cases the right of the competent to look after themselves has priority over the duty to look after the incompetent. Here we encounter another sense of "human life," namely, the life (= existence) of mankind. Since human life in that sense depends on the success of the reproductive activities of adults, an adequate supply of new members is of special importance. I say this on the assumption that the continuation of human life in this sense should have priority over the continuation of any particular or every individual life where both cannot be achieved. This is an important point, because it shows that where the right to life involves more than noninterference, the question of what can be due from the society or from individuals to those in need is a function of the sophistication of the relevant social order. Assistance of the long-term incompetent is thus not simply a matter of natural right but one partly dependent on individual and social capacity. This consideration raises another important point, namely, that even where society has the capacity to give life support to its members, the right to receive it will depend not solely on one's humanity but on the priority of one's claim. It will be necessary to establish a set of priority classes, on the basis of which the essentially limited capacities of a society can be justly assigned to the task of giving life support to those who cannot do so for themselves. It will be a very difficult decision, far remvoed from the simplicity of natural rights, to set up such priority classes. Should the forces of the market determine how many kidney machines are manufactured and who has access to them? Or should there be some overall scheme of priorities? Should, for instance, more money be allocated to insuring enough food for all, before some or much is allocated to keeping those with defective kidneys alive?

I want now to ask the question of what society owes to fetuses. Plainly, a fetus cannot survive, at any rate for quite some time in its career, without the life support of the mother. Suppose the mother does not want to give that support. Should she be forced to give it, that is, forbidden to remove the fetus? If not, should society devote its resources to the keeping alive of the fetus? I think it is obvious that if the mother should not always or ever be forced to do so, the question of whether the society should care for the fetus is one that has no simple, society-neutral answer. The claims of the aborted but viable fetuses must compete with those of other classes of human beings who need support. There can be no unconditional, natural right to such support, but only a *prima facie* moral right.

Society may indeed have adequate reason to force mothers to bear this burden if there is a danger of depopulation because of a widespread unwillingness of mothers to procreate. This, too, will vary from society to society and from time to time. I believe it fair to say that nowhere on earth today is there such a danger. On the contrary, the rate of population increase is such — doubling every forty years at the present rate — that we may well be condemning our offspring to life in increasingly undesirable conditions. There may then be no reason relating to species survival for society to force mothers to give life support to fetuses, nor to give such support itself when viable fetuses are thrust into the world.

But what of the interests of the fetuses themselves? Do not their interests require that protection be given to them? It seems to me that of all the classes of incompetent human beings in need of life support, the claims of the fetuses should have the lowest priority, in a time when the interests of normal adults during their procreative period — the prime class of concern for society because they are best equipped to insure the satisfactory continuation of the human enterprise including the survival of fetuses and babies — require a decrease in the numbers of men making ever increasing and competing claims on probably diminishing resources. The main reason for this low priority is, of course, that the fetus, at any rate in the early stages after conception, cannot have any concerns at all, for the fetus would not seem to have any experiential life in those early stages. Perhaps later the fetus can experience pain, and then it is perhaps true that it has a concern not to experience pain. But the fetus as such has no other interests or aspirations. Above all, life is not a good to it. It has no conception of *its life,* the way even a ten-year-old or an adolescent has, for whom death would be the tragic termination of life at its very beginning. It would be absurd to say this of a fetus. Concerns and interests can be ascribed to the fetus only as a potential person. That is to say, they can be ascribed to the fetus only because, unless something happens to it, it will eventually be a person with concerns and interests that call for protection. If we experiment on a fetus without inflicting pain on it but in such a way that the fetus will or may later be deformed or retarded or so sickly that he will live only a short time, then we are interfering with the interests of a potential (in the sense of "future actual") person. For we are allowing such a crippled fetus to become a being who in all probability will have such necessarily thwarted interests and concerns. Life, health, and self-esteem will become goods to this being. But by letting it develop into an adult with such interests and concerns, we are condemning it to a greatly handicapped life, handicaps that will with very great probability be evils to him.

Of course, this leaves open the difficult question of what sorts of handicaps justify the judgment that the fetus, if allowed to come to term, will "in all probability" have such necessarily thwarted interests and concerns. There is here a great deal of room for legitimate disagreement, and I cannot now take up this point in detail. I imagine, though, that a strong case can be made for including in this class of handicaps, say, the case of Thalydomide fetuses without arms and legs, perhaps a somewhat weaker case for deaf-mute blind fetuses, though even there one should not close one's mind to the fairly small likelihood that such a child will have the intelligence, the determination, and the teacher of genius to grow up into a Helen Keller.

We tend to overlook the fact, and this is what I want to stress here, that if a parent knows of the handicaps of the fetus and does nothing about it, he or she must share in the responsibility for running the risk of condemning a future person to a severly handicapped life. The belief in the fetus' absolute right to life, in everyone's absolute duty to see to it that it is born and grows up into an adult, blinds us to the responsibility that putting it into the world involves. Our general ideology of growth alerts us to our responsibility for maintaining the human enterprise, but it blinds us to our responsibility to those on whom we bestow the sometimes dubious benefit of human existence. There is little excuse for this blindness in the case of those who do not believe in God on whom believers tend to shift that responsibility.

Thus, if society's population needs are adequately met by a laissez-faire arrangement of reproduction, then the "parents' " only obligation to their fetus is that of responsible parenthood. In other words, if they are proposing to put him into the world, they must take into consideration the interests and concerns of the potential, that is, eventual, child and adult. Thus, since as a baby and young child, he will (normally) be completely dependent on the parents, at least one of the parents should *want* the child and be able and willing to look after it to provide the minimally adequate preparatory conditions of a fulfilling life, and the conditions into which he will eventually be launched as an adult should not be such as to condemn him to a life not worth living.[30]

It is, however, frequently claimed that fetuses themselves as such have a right to be born. Thus, John T. Noonan, Jr., in a very influential paper, "An Almost Absolute Value in History," [31] claims that they do have such a right, although the genetic materials whose union forms the conceptus that eventually grows into the fetus do not. Starting from the premise, which I myself accept, that normal adult human beings have the right to life, Noonan argues that fetuses, because they develop into persons, must, in the course of that development, acquire that right, and that we must therefore identify that point somewhere in the course of that transformation. So far, so good. But then he goes on to say that we should locate it where there is "an enormous shift in probabilities," namely at conception. Noonan claims that the odds against a spermatozoon becoming a person are two hundred million to 1, whereas those against a conceptus are only 5 to 4. And from this he *infers* that the right to life begins at conception.[32]

However, this is a curious inference. Quite apart from its inconclusiveness,[33] the argument rests on an implicit premise that is highly contentious. Clearly, from the fact that persons have a right to life it cannot follow that beings that are not persons have such a right, however likely they are to become persons. It is only if we rely on the further premise that it is a good thing if these potential persons develop into actual ones, and a bad thing if they do not, that we can infer that these potential persons also have a right to life. But it is precisely this addtional premise that can no longer be taken for granted.

Noonan may, of course, be right in saying that the complex property on account of which we are warranted in ascribing the right to life to normal adults is acquired gradually over time and that we must, therefore, fix a point where the right to life begins, based on our estimate of when the acquisition of this property is completed. But Noonan himself says and it seems to me undeniable that this is not likely to be at conception.[34] What makes us focus on this particular point in the development of an individual is of course the fact that, *if* reproductive material does reach the stage (whatever it may be) at which he or she is a human being with an inalienable right to life, then we must *trace back* his or her beginning to the (usually) unknown moment of conception. But that does not give this moment any other significance. Few people would argue, and Noonan certainly does not, that those reproductive materials that have it in them to reach conception have the right to be conceived. Why, then, should we think that the sperm and egg cells that have become united in a conception have a right to grow into full members of society even if they are parentally or socially unwanted or undesirable? Surely, the mere fact that *if* we allowed this fetus to grow up into a full member of society, its beginning would rightly be traced back to the moment of conception, does not by itself show that this fetus, which has it in it to become a full member of society, has the right to become a full member. The fact that the biological life of *an individual* begins at conception is no reason whatever to think that the right to biological life begins then.

Might it not begin there, all the same? Would it not be a good thing for everyone else if parents or society were saddled with an absolute moral requirement on everyone to *allow* (all?) the reproductive materials at the disposal of its members to unite and so become potential new members of society, or an absolute requirement on everyone to give the necessary life support to *any* conceptus or fetus, whatever the explanation of its existence and whatever its prospects, to enable it *to become a new member?* I can see no reason to think so. The termination of the life of a conceptus or fetus is not comparable to the termination of the life of a young person who has already formed a conception of his life, with its plans, ambitions, expectations, and rewards. As I said before, the fetus has no conception of its life. It is not robbed of anything to which it is already attached. It may be objected that a person alseep or in a temporary coma is in the same position as a fetus. But this is not so. For one thing, a person asleep or in a coma continues to have the interests he has in his waking life. The reason is that unlike a fetus he has already formed lasting concerns by reference to which some things are in his interest, others detrimental. But there is a second and very important difference: the denial that persons have such interests and rights while asleep or unconscious would enormously increase the insecurity and mutual distrust among adult members. People would be afraid to go to sleep or to a hospital. Not granting such interests and rights to fetuses need have no such side effects.

To sum up: I know of no good reason to doubt that it would be for the good of everyone alike if the biological life of normal adults were universally given the sort of social protection we associate with a right. I have therefore assumed that normal adults have a natural right to life. Of course, the extent of this protection must be such that it is compatible with a like protection for every human being. The main ground for saying this is, of course, that his biological, as the condition of his experiential, life is to every normal adult an extremely important good, if not the most important. It also seems clear that, as soon as we extend the protection envisaged by a right beyond that of retention rights to that of recipience rights, we can no longer talk of natural rights, because we make reference to the capacities of societies or its members to provide the goods in question. Thus, when we talk about the right to life of those human beings who are unable to keep alive without assistance, who need life support, we are going beyond the natural right to life. I have argued that where such life support is concerned, we need to draw up classes of need and priorities among these classes and that fetuses are near or at the bottom of the hierarchy of such classes. I have tried to show that there is no good moral reason for singling out conception as the point in an individual's development at which the right to life must be thought to begin quite irrespective of why the conception came about, what life prospects such an individual will have when he is allowed to grow into a member of society, and what impact this would have on the lives of other present and future members.

NOTES

*Earlier versions of this paper were read at the Mountains and Plains Conference, and to a Colloquium on Rights at The University of North Carolina at Greensboro where David Falk gave a very helpful critical response. I have benefited very much from these criticisms and from the comments, objections, and stylistic improvements of Roland Pennock.

1. Jeremy Bentham, *Anarchical Fallacies;* reprinted in A. I. Melden, ed., *Human Rights* (Belmont, Calif.: Wadsworth, 1970), p. 32.
2. For details on this and related historical matters, see, for instance, Martin P. Golding, "The Concept of Rights: A Historical Sketch," in E. and B. Bandman, eds., *Bioethics and Human Rights* (Boston: Little, Brown ed., 1978); also H. L. A. Hart, "Bentham on Legal Rights," in A. W. B. Simpson *Oxford Essays in Jurisprudence, second series* (Oxford: Clarendon Press, 1973), pp. 171 ff., and Eugene Kamenka, "The Anatomy of an Idea," in Eugene Kamenka and Alice Erh-Soon Tay; eds., *Human Rights* (New York: St. Martin's, 1978).
3. Quoted by Golding, "The Concept of Rights," p. 48
4. John Austin, *The Province of Jurisprudence Determined and The Uses of the Study of Jurisprudence.* With an introduction by H. L. A. Hart (London: Weidenfeld and Nicholson, 1954), lect. V.
5. For a detailed discussion of this point, see Joel Feinberg, *Social Philosophy* (Englewood Cliffs, N.J.: Prentice-Hall, 1973), chaps. 5, 6.
6. Joel Feinberg, "The Nature and Value of Rights," *Journal of Value Inquiry,* 4, no. 4 (Winter, 1970): p. 243.
7. For a full discussion see, for example, David Lyons, "Rights, Claims, and Beneficiaries," *American Philosophical Quarterly,* 6, no. 3, (July 1969); 173-185; and Hart, "Bentham on Legal Rights."
8. I here omit consideration of so-called liberties, Hohfeldian privileges, which involve no correlative obligations at all.
9. Feinberg, *Social Philosophy,* pp. 59 f.
10. I borrow the useful terms "action" and "recipience" rights from D. D. Raphael, "Human Rights, Old and New," *Political Theory and the Rights of Man,* (Bloomington and London: Indiana University Press. 1967), pp. 56 ff., and D. D. Raphael, *Problems of Political Philosophy,* (London: Macmillan Papermac, 1970), p. 68, but two differences should be noted. (i) Raphael wavers between treating the distinction as one between two *senses* of "right" or two *kinds* of right (e.g., *Problems of Political Philosophy,* p. 68). He treats it as the distinction both between liberties (Hohfeldian privileges) and claim rights (a difference in sense) and between types of content, doing and receiving something (a difference in kind.) I treat it as the latter. (ii) He treats it as a distinction both between types of content and strengths of correlative obligation. I treat it as the former only. It

should be noted that action, retention, and recipience rights could be either negative or positive. In theory, my action right to travel, my retention right to a good name, and my recipience right to an education *may* involve *positive* correlative duties: your correlative duty may be to *enable* me to travel where I want to; to combat other people's efforts to destroy my reputation; and to provide schooling.

11. H. L. A. Hart, "Are There Any Natural Rights?" *Philosophical Review,* 64 (1955): 175–91; reprinted in A.M. Quinton, ed., *Political Philosophy,* (Oxford University Press, 1967) pp. 53–66; p. 60.

12. Ibid., p. 64.

13. Ibid.

14. For a more accurate formulation of this point, see below, p. 214 ff.

15. Hart, "Are There Any Natural Rights?" p. 60.

16. Ibid., p. 62.

17. Ibid., p. 65.

18. In the case of natural but not of all kinds of rights, this is a straightforward entailment: if there are natural rights and beings of the appropriate nature, then these beings necessarily have (natural) rights. Not so for, for example, legal rights. For suppose that, as of the first of last month, there has existed in our state a valid law to the effect that, on deposits of $1 milllion or more, banks must pay 17 percent interest, but that no one has as yet made such a large deposit. Then, although the right to draw 17 percent interest *has come into existence,* no one as yet *has* this right. The right did not exist earlier but exists now, because earlier people could draw only 12 percent, whereas now they would draw 17 percent. All the conditions of the existence of the right in our state are satisfied, but for someone to acquire and so to have that right a further condition must be satisfied: he must deposit $1 million or more. No such additional condition is needed for "acquiring" natural rights.

It may be objected that I am drawing a distinction where there is no difference. The fact is, the objection continues, that the right which comes into existence, namely, the conditional right to draw 17 percent on $1 million, is also simultaneously acquired by every eligible person in the state. And the unconditional right to draw 17 percent, period, does not come into existence and is not acquired until someone deposits $1 million. Both these claims seem to me mistaken.

The *conditional* right to draw 17 percent on $1 million is not acquired by the whole class of eligible persons when the law is passed. If it were, all these people would have a right, though no one has the appropriate correlative obligation. It may be objected that the correlative obligation is also only conditional. Suppose you promise to pay me, for service rendered, $100 *on demand,* but I never demand—nevertheless I have a (conditional) right and you have a (conditional) obligation, to pay me $100 on demand. But the cases are significantly disanalogous. Here I have a right and you have an obligation because I may insist on or waive my right as I choose. Your obligation is not in any ordinary sense conditional: there is no condition that must be satisfied for you to (come to) have the obligation. What is conditional is merely the requirement upon you to discharge your obligation: you have the obligation, but under certain conditions you need not discharge it. Of course, this is possible only if the condition's satisfaction or nonsatisfaction depends on the person to whom the obligation is owed, not on the person obligated. Otherwise, one could have an obligation whose discharge one could legitimately abort oneself simply by not satisfying the condition. Similarly, there can be unconditional rights that nevertheless no one has unless a condition is satisfied. But that is possible only if the condition for acquiring such rights depends on at least some persons of the appropriate class who can satisfy the condition, say, by depositing $1 million. Note, though, that the condition need not be satisfiable at will: there may exist a right of certain classes of persons to receive an old-age pension *at age sixty-five.*

Similarly, the *unconditional* right to draw 17 percent is acquired by someone in our state *only* when that person actually deposits $1 million, but does not come into existence then. Otherwise we would have to say that the right exists only during the time some bank holds such a deposit by someone. But this would be to misconstrue the existence of legal rights. For, surely, we know whether this right exists in our state if we know whether there is a law to that effect even if we do not know who has deposited $1 million or indeed whether anyone has. Again, our knowledge that this right exists in this state does not depend on our knowing that someone actually has an obligation to pay someone 17 percent interest. It is sufficient if we know that *if* someone has deposited $1 million, then someone has the obligation to pay 17 percent. But knowing this is not sufficient to know that someone has this right. For that, we must know that some bank has the appropriate correlative obligation.

19. I have said more about these questions in my "Moral Reasons and Reasons to be Moral" in A. I. Goldman and J. Kim, eds., *Values and Morals* (Dordrecht, Holland: D. Reidel, 1978), and "Freedom, Obligation, and Responsibility," forthcoming in Morris B. Storer, ed., *Humanist Ethics* (Buffalo, N.Y.: Prometheus Books, 1980).

20. Joel Feinberg, "Duties, Rights, and Claimants," *American Philosophical Quarterly*, 3, no. 2, (April 1966): 137–44, and "The Nature and Value of Rights," 4, no. 4, (Winter 1970): 243–57.

21. Feinberg has recently modified his account of rights in an article entitled "A Postscript to the Nature and Value of Rights (1977)," in Elsie L. Bandman and Bertram Bandman *Bioethics and Human Rights* (Boston: Little, Brown 1978), but the article came into my hands too late to be taken into account in this essay.

22. Cf. H. L. A. Hart, "Are There Any Natural Rights?" in Quinton, ed., *Political Philosophy*, p. 58, and more fully in Hart, "Bentham on Legal Rights," p. 192.

23. Thomas Hobbes, *Leviathan,* chap. 21.

24. Hart, "Are There Any Natural Rights?" in Quinton, ed., *Political Philosophy*, p. 58.

25. Ibid., p. 59.
26. Geoffrey Marshall, "Rights, Options, and Entitlements," in Simpson, ed., *Oxford Essays in Jurisprudence*, pp. 228-41.
27. Ibid., p. 239.
28. Some philosophers, for example, Hobbes (*Leviathan*, chap. 14), hold that one cannot have a right and a duty in one and the same matter. I know of no good reason for accepting this view, but in any case one could make Marshall's point in terms of natural duties. One would then have to say, not that we have an "unwaivable" right as well as a duty to be educated, but only that we have a natural duty to attend school and that officials have a duty to provide schools for us to attend; not that we have a right and a duty to live, but only that *we and others* (or perhaps only others?) have a duty not to do anything to shorten our natural lives, or perhaps even that we have a duty to do what we can (within reason?) to prolong our natural lives as much as possible. But once it is clear that the duty to live cannot be deduced from the right to life by way of the importance or irreplaceability, and so on, of the good in question, it becomes very hard to defend such a duty outside a framework of religious belief in God's ownership of our bodies, and the like.
29. Hugo Bedau, "The Right to Life, *The Monist*, 52, no. 4 (October 1968): 550-72.
30. Joel Feinberg, in an article entitled "Is There a Right to Be Born?, in James Rachels, ed., *Understanding Moral Philosophy*. (Encino, Cal.: Dickenson Publishing Company, 1976), pp. 346-58, argues that fetuses can have rights (p. 354). Indeed, he thinks that there is conceptual room for the question of whether fetueses have *conditional* or *unconditional* rights, including the right to be born. To say that a fetus has a conditional right to X is to imply that someone has an obligation to hold X in case the fetus is born alive. If the fetus dies *in utero* or is stillborn, the right *vanishes* without a trace. An unconditional right of the fetus is not in this way dependent on whether the fetus is born alive. Feinberg then suggests that although a fetus can have a variety of conditional rights, the only noncontingent (unconditional) right it can have is the right *not* to be born. It has that right if before the child is born, "we know that the conditions of the fulfillment of his most basic interests have already been destroyed" (ibid.). Feinberg's main reason for allowing this unconditional right is that "he has it before birth, from the very moment that satisfaction of his most basic future interests is rendered impossible" (ibid.). But, in fact, the cases of Feinberg's conditional and unconditional rights are almost completely parallel. What exists prior to the birth can in both cases be expressed without loss in terms of obligations on the part of others, in light of the real possibility that it will be born alive and of what would happen if it were. We need not allow in either case that a right come into existence *before and unless it is born*. The difference between the two cases is simply that in the former the right may be either respected or violated, whereas in the latter, the right can only

be violated. The reason for this is, of course, that the right not to be born comes into being only if the baby is born alive and if, therefore, the *obligation* to prevent its birth is neglected and so its right violated. This way of characterizing the two cases, (which rejects ascriptions to fetuses of rights, whether conditional or unconditional) preserves the natural parallelism and avoids the awkward consequence that in the case of conditional rights we must retroactively ascribe a right to the fetus if it is born alive but deny it such a right if it is not. If we date the beginning of the right at birth and confine ourselves to ascribing the correlative obligations to other people before birth, we avoid such awkwardness and asymmetries. No substantive moral issues are affected by this terminological one.

31. John T. Noonan, Jr., "An Almost Absolute Value in History." in John T. Noonan, Jr., ed., *The Morality of Abortion: Legal and Historical Perspectives*. Cambridge, Mass: Harvard University Press, 1970

32. Ibid., p. 56.

33. Suppose a young, healthy married couple has intercourse every three days. The chances of a given ovum being fertilized are then rather high, perhpas not very much lower than those of a conceptus surviving to birth. At the same time, the chances of a given spermatozoon turning into a conceptus are astronomically low. Does this difference in probabilities give us adequate reason to ascribe a right to life to an ovum but not to a spermatozoon? What if the couple have intercourse twenty times a month, or every night? Can the question of whether the ovum has a right to life depend on the frequency of intercourse? Can it be true that the better the reason to ascribe that right to an egg, the worse it must be to ascribe it to a sperm cell, or even to a whole ejaculate?

34. Noonan adds a false analogy that gives greater surface plausibility to this contention than it merits. He says that "if the chance is 20,000,000 to 1 that the movement in the bushes into which you shoot is a man's, I doubt if many persons would hold you careless in shooting; but, if the chances are four out of five that the movement is a human being's, few would acquit you of blame" (ibid., p. 56). He thus presents the shift in probability as one concerning *the belief* that the entity in question *is* a human being in the relevant sense. If that were the shift, then indeed a case would have been made for the claim that the right to life begins at conception. But, of course, *that* is not the shift for which Noonan offers evidence. On the contrary, he himself admits that it is quite *clear* that a conceptus is *not* a human being in the sense of having the properties possession of which warrants ascription of a right to life. He admits that transformation into such a being occurs not at conception but at some later stage in the development of this human "enity." So there is no shift of *this* probability at conception.

12

LIBERTY AND WELFARE: SOME ISSUES IN HUMAN RIGHTS THEORY

SUSAN MOLLER OKIN*

Two political initiatives have probably had more effect than anything else in recent years in stirring political theorists to think about
human rights. The first of these is the United Nations Universal Declaration of Human Rights (1948) and the covenants subsequently
adopted. The second is the Carter administration's determination to
make the securing of human rights a major objective of U.S. foreign
policy. The United Nations, on the one hand, after considerable controversy, endorsed a comprehensive list of human rights, classified
into two basic groups — civil and political rights; and economic, social, and cultural rights. The current U.S. administration, on the
other hand — whereas its rhetoric has included reference to both of
these broad categories of rights — has so far confined itself, in its major policies, to a subset of the first type of rights, namely, rights not to
be subjected to violations of one's personal security.[1]

In neither of these two important cases has much philosophical
analysis been offered by the major figures involved, in their central
policy statements, either by way of an argued foundation for belief in
human rights and their importance, or by way of justification for the
priorities chosen among types of rights. In both cases, however, numerous political theorists, either by invitation or at their own behest,
have undertaken to think through and argue out some of the major
issues behind policies adopted or pronouncements made in the political arena. In short, neither the United Nations' nor the Carter Administration's policy has lacked critics, either positive or negative,[2]
and human rights have been a major concern of political philosophers in recent years.

If human rights are to command such a position of importance on the world stage, it is essential to separate them from all those other things that it would be good or desirable for human beings to be able to enjoy. Human rights, it is generally agreed, are a subset of moral rights, and moral rights are claims that have special moral force, for one or more reasons. Some moral rights arise from promises, agreements, or other antecedent actions, the moral content of which is immaterial to the moral weight of the resulting right. Human rights, however, are rights by virtue of their content, that is to say, because of what it is that they are a right *to*.[3] They do not owe their special moral status as rights to previous actions or agreements but are rights that human beings have by virtue of being human. I will argue that certain rights are human rights and should be recognized as such, because human beings have fundamental needs and capacities that make certain goods and freedoms essential to their continued existence as human beings.

A characteristic of human rights that should be noticed from the start is that, unlike most legal and other positive rights, they are rights independently of whether they are recognized or acted upon by either the right-holder or the person, persons, or institution on whom the corresponding duty or obligation falls.[4] Whereas in order to establish the existence of a legal right, or a moral right deriving from prior agreement, we engage in empirical inquiry, the existence of a human right must be established by moral argument. There are countless examples from history, and even in the contemporary world, of persons — slaves, for example, or women in forced marriages — who have not recognized, let alone acted upon, their human rights. Neither have the corresponding duties been acknowledged or acted upon by those responsible for the violation of these human rights. But these facts of history and contemporary life do not lead us to deny the existence of either the rights or the corresponding duties. Indeed, one of the central purposes of moral argument to prove that human rights exist is to get them recognized and acted upon.[5]

I will first address the issue of what foundations are needed for a comprehensive and coherent theory of human rights. Second, I will consider the matter of priorities, which itself falls into two parts: the question whether welfare rights[6] are human rights at all, and the question of how we should go about deciding the ethically proper ordering of priorities among human rights.

A FOUNDATION FOR HUMAN RIGHTS

Any well-founded and defensible argument for human rights must begin with a postulate of some sort of equality among human beings, and any attempt to circumvent this requirement must fail. The equality postulate, of course, may differ considerably from one theory of human rights to another. Both the type and the extent of equality that characterize people have been controversial, but no theory of human rights, however limited, can avoid some initial statement about the equality of human beings.

Alan Gewirth's recent work on rights exemplifies the attempt to repudiate the need for such an egalitarian premise.[7] He criticizes Rawls's and others' moral theories for relying on assumptions of human equality[8] and claims that his own theory, which establishes the equal generic rights to freedom and well-being, has no recourse to such premises. Gewirth claims to derive his substantive normative moral principle regarding equal human rights solely from the nature of human action. By the use of the dialectically necessary method, he argues, one can proceed logically from the necessary nature of agency to the claim, on the part of each human agent, to cerain generic rights. Thence, again by a series of logically necessary steps, one can establish that every other human being, as a prospective purposive agent, has these same rights to freedom and well-being that one claims for one's self.

Gewirth, then, argues that he can derive an egalitarian universalist conclusion — and, moreover, one that no one can deny without self-contradiction — from the simple fact of human agency, and without reliance on any egalitarian assumptions. I will argue that this cannot be done and that if Gewirth's conclusions about the equal rights of everyone to freedom and well-being are to be soundly based, a hidden egalitarianism must be contained within his premises. This egalitarianism, I argue, is indeed clearly discernible: it saves Gewirth's theory of rights, but it is just the kind of premise that he regards as a flaw in the theories of others.

Gewirth has to confront the argument that some people, being superior, should have more extensive rights than others. In order to do this, he argues that, whereas there are degrees of approach to being a prospective purposive agent, there are not degrees of *being* one. Indeed, he states that "If agency itself were to involve various inegalitarian differentiations, this would create problems for the egalitarianism inferred from it."[9] It is in the course of this argument that his unacknowledged egalitarian premises become obvious. For although Gewirth wants to argue that some persons, such as children, the insane, and the mentally deficient, merely approach prospective purposive agency to varying degrees (and therefore should be given only certain restricted rights in proportion to their capacities), he denies that, above the minimum competency level of a "normal" adult, there are any degrees of prospective purposive agency that are relevant to arguments about rights. Even though persons' purposes may vary in number and intensity, he asserts, and even if one concedes that some persons' practical abilities for purposive action are superior to those of others, "in relation to the claim to have the generic rights, actually being a prospective agent who has purposes to fulfill is *an absolute quality, not varying in degree.*"[10] This assertion, however, is nothing but a camouflaged egalitarian premise. What Gewirth is really saying is that *although* in many respects human agents differ—*although* their purposes vary in number and intensity, and *although* they may have varying capacities to pursue these purposes—in one crucial respect, all human beings, *as purposive agents, are equal.* In other words, Gewirth is saying that, above a minimum competency level, the differences among human beings' purposes, and among their abilities to pursue these purposes, must not be taken into account in shaping the fundamentals of a moral theory. In short, Gewirth cannot derive equal human rights to freedom and well-being from the nature of agency alone, but he *can* derive them from the more complex premise that he adopts but does not acknowledge as egalitarian—that, being prospective purposive agents, human beings must be considered fundamentally equal.

The need for some postulate of human equality has long been acknowledged by those whose moral theories revolve around the concept of rights. Neither Hobbes nor Locke (hardly egalitarians in many of their conclusions) thought that a theory of human rights could avoid being founded on some premise regarding human equality. Hobbes's natural rights (which are highly irregular in that they entail no corresponding obligations) are derived from the appetites and aversions taken in conjunction with the fact that human beings are sufficiently equal in strength and prudence that they all *consider* themselves the equal of any other, which gives them "equality of hope in the attaining of [their] Ends."[11] For Locke, the equal right to natural freedom in the state of nature (bounded as it is by the right of others, in accordance with natural law) is founded on the premise that men are "Creatures of the same species and rank promiscuously born to all the same advantages of Nature, and the use of the same faculties." It is this empirical equality, which Locke later warns us must be understood as strictly limited, that leads him to conclude that no man has natural authority over any other. [12]

In twentieth-century discussions of the basis of human rights, despite a post-Humean sensitivity to the fallacy involved in deriving normative from purely descriptive statements, the same types of argument have been made. For example, Gregory Vlastos undertakes to defend, to a Martian visitor from "a strict meritarian community," the ascription to persons of equal human rights, regardless of merit. Vlastos argues that what is at issue, most fundamentally, is one's "estimate of the relative worth of the welfare and freedom of different individuals," and that, in human society, there exists "a concept of value attaching to a person's individual existence, over and above his merit," a concept he calls "individual worth."[13] It is this, Vlastos claims, that forms the necessary foundation on which human rights are based. Although some capacities for experience differ from person to person, there is a wide range of experiences that all are capable of sharing. In regard to well-being, he affirms that the most brilliant and the most nondescript of persons both crave relief from acute physical pain. With respect to freedom, Vlastos asserts: "We feel that choosing for oneself what one will do, believe, approve, say, see, read, worship, has its own intrinsic value, the same for all persons, and quite independent from the things they happen to choose." From the general premises thus established, that (1) one person's well-being is as valuable as any other's and (2) one person's freedom is as valuable as any others, Vlastos claims that it follows reasonably that people have equal *prima facie*[14] rights to well-being and freedom and that these in turn involve many specific rights, including all those listed in the Universal Declaration of 1948.

Although this argument seems fully satisfactory so far as it goes, and avoids the problem of deriving "ought" from "is" by including value terms such as "value" itself, and "worth," in its premises, it does not form a comprehensive argument for equal human rights. What is lacking is that, apart from the two examples cited above, the reasons we regard human beings as of equal worth are not made fully explicit.[15] We must consider whether the suggestions that persons share an equal vulnerability to pain, and an equal capacity for making free choices, can be enlarged upon.

It appears to be generally agreed, even by philosophers who disagree with each other on related questions, that a human right is a claim to something (whether a freedom, a good, or a benefit) of crucial importance for human life.[16] (As I noted earlier, the claim does not have to be made by the right-holder, who might be unaware that he or she has such a justified claim.) I will take this as my working definition. In order to know what is of crucial importance for human life, however, we must try to identify the fundamental characteristics of human nature.[17] This is why the characteristics discussed by Vlastos must be enlarged upon. I will suggest, first, three needs shared by all human beings and, second, three almost universally shared capacities. As I explain below, I think it important that human rights should not be derived from any single human characteristic.

(1) Needs

First, although many human needs differ from one society or period to another, all human beings share the physical need for basic shelter, clothing, and food of an identifiable nutritional value. Second, a shared need that is largely physical but also emotional is the need for physical security. Assault may kill or cause permanent injury, just as deprivation of subsistence needs can, and the close parallel that exists between the two needs has been well argued in a recent paper by Henry Shue.[18] The physical component of this need is obvious. Its emotional component has to do with the fact that it is psychologically damaging, if not immobilizing, to live in a continuous state of fear for one's person. Third, I would suggest, all persons need to be respected, in the sense of being treated as persons by others. What we think of ourselves closely affects our well-being, and our self-perception is to a large extent shaped by the way we grow accustomed to being treated. I would argue, therefore, that being treated as less than equal will have a more or less permanent effect on one's basic well-being.

Using the definition of human right given above—that is a claim to something (some good or freedom) that is of crucial importance for human life—we can logically infer three fundamental human rights from these three needs. The first need, taken together with the definition, leads us to conclude that there is a human right to at least basic subsistence and health care; the second similarly leads to the human right to protection of one's personal security; the third leads to the human right to be treated with the equal respect due to a human being.

(2) Capacities

The issue of *capacities* shared by all human beings is a more problematic one, for it is immediately open to the charge that there are few if any capacities that all human beings share equally. The choice of rationality, or even the potential for rationality, for example, raises problems, for even the latter excludes all permanently mentally deficient persons, and yet we would surely be loath to exclude such persons from holding any human rights.[19]

The dilemma of how human beings with subnormal abilities are to be considered has led me to conclude that it is unsound to base a theory of human rights on any single human capacity. The problem is that a reasonable case can be made that, to the extent to which an individual's capacities are severely limited or lacking (e.g., the small child's or the brain-damaged person's capacity for rationality, or the autistic person's for experiencing personal relationships), any right that derives directly from possession of the relevant characteristic may be either severely limited in the case of such persons or denied them altogether.[20] The only way to avoid the danger of such persons' being denied all human rights, or having all their rights limited, is to perceive these rights as variously founded on a number of characteristics, *and* on basic needs, which would appear to be less variable. It would, then, be permissible to deny to certain groups of people, such as the severely retarded, rights derived from those human capacities they lack, but not those rights derived from human needs, or from those human capacities in which they are not deficient. The basing of human rights on multiple gounds rather than on a single ground therefore appears to be not only desirable but essential, unless some people are to be denied or severely restricted with regard to all human rights.

Acknowledging some exceptions, then, I suggest three capacities generally shared by human beings that are especially pertinent for their holding of rights. The first is the capacity for making choices and, most importantly, choices that affect significantly the characters and qualities of their lives. The second is the capacity to learn and to benefit from that learning, in the sense that their lives are enlarged and their capacity to make rational and informed choices improved. The third is the capacity for having relations, particularly, intimate and psychologically important relations, with each other.

Given our working definition of human rights, recognition of these important human characteristics, like that of the aforementioned needs, leads logically to a number of rights. The capacity for making significant choices forms a basis for rights to a sphere of personal freedom and privacy and to the right to political participation. The capacity for learning requires that human beings have rights to at least basic education and access to information. The capacity for personal relations suggests strongly that the rights to freedom and privacy be made to include those most crucial to the sphere of family and/or other intimate relations, such as the right not to be separated, for example, by force or overwhelming economic pressure, from those with whom one has one's most important connections.

I turn now to the subjects of what rights are properly called human rights, and what priorities should hold among them. I argue against the claim that has frequently been made by liberals — that liberty rights should always take priority over welfare rights.

TWO TYPES OF RIGHTS, AND THE ORDERING OF PRIORITIES

Liberty rights can be generally described as rights not to be treated in certain ways, or not to be interfered with. They include Articles 3 to 20 of the UN Declaration, with problems being raised by Article 15, section 1, the right to a nationality (since, in certain cases, where a person is born stateless, this would seem to be an entitlement right, not simply a right not to be deprived of something one already has), and Article 8, the right to an effective remedy, in case of violation of one's rights. These liberty rights include the rights to speak, move, and associate freely; to be free from slavery, arbitrary arrest, torture, assaults on one's person and the like; and the right to hold property.[21] The second type of human rights, welfare rights, can generally be described as rights to be assured the provision of certain goods or services considered necessary for human well-being. They include Articles 22 to 27 of the Declaration, with the possible exception of Article 23, section 4, the right to form and join trade unions, which seems to be a right of the liberty variety. Examples of rights of the latter type are the rights to employment and to an adequate living wage, to social security, education, rest and leisure, and participation in cultural life.

As I have suggested, the status and relative positions of the two types of rights has been the subject of considerable dispute. Some have argued that welfare rights should not be considered human rights at all; others have acknowledged them as admissible but have stressed the priority of liberty rights. I will take up three major arguments made against welfare rights and will contend that the line between liberty rights and welfare rights is acceptable neither as the division between human rights and nonrights, nor as the division between more and less important human rights.

THE SCOPE OF THE STATE'S AUTHORITY

One of the arguments frequently made against welfare rights as human rights is that they require positive state action, and indeed are very likely to enlarge the state's sphere of activity. Liberty rights, it is claimed, are, by and large, rights against the state, which are much easier to secure, since they require restraint on the part of the state. Cranston writes, for example:

> Since [the liberty rights] are for the most part rights against government interference with a man's activities, a large part of the legislation needed has to do no more than restrain the government's own executive arm. This is no longer the case when we turn to 'the right to work,' 'the right to social security,' and so forth.[22]

That liberty rights can largely be secured by restraining legislation, whereas large amounts of money are required to finance welfare rights, is taken by Cranston to be part of the reason that the latter should not be accorded the status of human rights.

Similarly, though without drawing the same conclusions, Schneider asserts: "There is no doubt that the classical doctrine of the rights of man is concerned in the first instance with the relationship between *individuals* and the *State*." He, too, stresses the complicated bureaucratic apparatus required to give effect to welfare rights.[23] Schochet, also, despite the fact that he acknowledges earlier that liberty rights require not only restraint on the part of the state but also "its restraining persons who would otherwise interfere with them," concludes that welfare rights "surrender all claims to qualify as rights even by extension, for they do not limit the state but they actually enlarge it."[24]

It is of particular interest in this context that the United Nations Universal Declaration of Human Rights, the very document that started the controversy about the two types of rights, is frequently referred to as being addressed exclusively to governments, as potential violators of human rights, and not at all to individual persons. When one reads the Declaration carefully, however, one sees that it is by no means its sole intent to warn governments against their own potential for violation. To the contrary, besides hardly mentioning governments at all, it suggests strongly that at least some of the obligations correlative to the rights it pronounces fall on individuals as well as on states.[25]

The explanation for these views of human rights, as being secured primarily through the state's restraint, rather than positive action, and properly or at least primarily held against states, seems to derive, at least in part, from the historical circumstances in which theories of human (or earlier, "natural") rights have been most appealed to and most influential. In the seventeenth and eighteenth centuries, the struggle against restrictive feudal and/or absolutist states was at its height, and the 1940s and 1950s immediately followed the disastrous experience of fascism and Nazism.[26] The circumstances of such times and, in particular, the identification of the right-infringing state as the enemy, seem to have led to a strong emphasis on rights as being held solely, or at least primarily, against the state. This emphasis, however, both obscures an important and primary part of the earlier theories of rights and neglects the role of government in securing liberty rights in the modern world.

If we turn back to Locke, we see that he would have thought it absurd to discuss natural rights as first and foremost rights against governments, since, as he makes very clear, he considers the whole purpose for which government exists to be the protection of individuals' rights — specifically those to life, liberty, and property — against violation by other persons.[27] Admittedly, and not suprisingly, given the context of his writing, Locke considered governments, once instituted, to be even greater threats to freedom than individuals. This is why he attacks absolutist theorists for thinking "that Men are so foolish that they care to avoid what Mischiefs may be done them by Polecats or Foxes, but are content, nay think it safety, to be devoured by Lions."[28] On the other hand, if the threat of polecats and foxes were insignificant — that is to say, if Locke's men in the state of nature had seen no need to protect their rights from each other — they would have seen no need for civil government. Liberty rights, in liberal contract theory, must be understood as first and foremost rights against other individuals, or else the establishment of government makes no sense.

The argument that rights are properly so called only if they can be secured primarily by constraint by the state and that therefore the so-called welfare rights are not rights suffers from two critical defects. First, the claim that liberty rights require little if any positive action by the state has no foundation. Certainly, liberty rights do require that the state refrain from various types of activity—from arbitrarily arresting, detaining, or murdering citizens, for example, or from seizing their property without compensation. They also require, however, that the state undertake various types of activity, which are frequently complex and require much in the way of expenditure.[29] Since governments were instituted, according to the classic liberal view, primarily in order to protect individuals against the threat of violation of their rights by their fellow human beings, it is incumbent upon them to establish the police forces, judicial systems, and prisons that are necessary to maintain the highest achievable degree of security of these rights. As we are all aware, even the sometimes inadequate protection that is provided by such institutions is enormously expensive and involves the maintenance of complex bureaucratic systems.[30]

Another aspect of government expenditure and proliferation of bureaucracy that vastly enlarges the power and scope of the state's activity, but that is not usually acknowledged to be related to the securing of citizen's liberty rights, is that required for foreign policy and defense. Protection from the threat of invasion or defeat by foreign powers is surely just as essential an aspect of the protection of one's liberty rights as is protection from one's fellow citizens. It might be objected here that the purpose of defense is to protect the polity rather than the liberty rights of individuals. However, since it is the polity that protects the liberty rights of individuals, the defense of the polity itself is necessarily related to this end. In addition, it is clear that one of the acknowledged aims of foreign policy is the protection of national investments abroad, where this phrase clearly refers largely to the privately owned investments of some citizens, that is, the liberty rights of some citizens. When a military budget of more than $100 billion is passed annually by Congress, at least primarily for the purpose of protecting the liberty rights of Americans, it is difficult to see how one could claim that the protection of such rights requires little action but restraint on the part of government and that it is only welfare rights that require the enlargement of governmental powers, appropriations, and bureaucracy.

The second defect of the claim that human rights that deserve the name must be able to be secured at least primarily by restraint on the part of the state would be a problem even if the point just argued were incorrect. This defect consists in the fact that the claim rests on an unargued assumption. In its more general form, this assumption is that human rights ought to have as their correlative obligations *restraints* on behavior, or inaction rather than action. In its more specific form, the assumption is that enlargement of the state's positive obligation or sphere of activity is necessarily not just a bad thing, but *so* undesirable that it precludes the acceptance as a human right of any claim whose fulfillment would necessitate such enlargement. This assumption may be sound, but it certainly requires to be argued. I would suggest, to the contrary, that the conditions of modern industrial society are such that it would be very difficult to prove the intervention of government per se to be necessarily detrimental. To mention just one pertinent issue, it is clear that nongovernmental organizations have grown enormously in wealth and power in the past century. To borrow the terms of Locke's analogy, though the lions have grown, relative to the polecats and foxes, some of the polecats and foxes have grown, too, not only relative to others, but also relative to the lions. Some of the largest corporations' outputs are now bigger than many countries' gross national products. There has been a gradual, though at times clearly reluctant tendency on the part of governments to recognize that the interdependencies and power differentials of industrial society rendered the laissez-faire age's securing of formal liberties insufficient protection for the individual. Gradually with the growth of modern corporate giants has come acceptance of the role of government as a regulator and social service provider, necessary for the welfare of the individual in a society in which technology creates unprecedented opportunity for harm as well as benefit and that permits vast inequalities. Surely it is at least dubious that most individuals would benefit from the substantial shrinking or disappearance of this vast governmental activity. The argument that welfare rights should not be recognized as human rights, or at least not given high priority, since their fulfillment leads to enlargement of governments, therefore, fails on two accounts. First, the vast growth of government during this century has been by no means entirely due to the attempt to guarantee people's economic needs or social welfare. Second, even if it had, a case must be made that such growth is very undesirable.

THE RELATIVE IMPORTANCE OF DIFFERENT TYPES OF RIGHTS FOR THE QUALITY OF HUMAN LIFE

It would be difficult to disagree with the general contention that claims accorded the status of human rights should be claims of paramount importance for human life. The issue of paramountcy, however, has been used in order to justify the wholesale inclusion of liberty rights in, and wholesale exclusion of welfare rights from, this status. These are the arguments that must next be confronted.

Cranston, for example, asserts that the matters with which liberty rights are concerned are of "a totally different moral dimension" from those addressed by welfare rights. He draws a parallel between the two types of rights and the duty to relieve great distress (a paramount duty) and the duty to give pleasure (not a paramount duty). He writes:

> A human right is something of which no-one may be deprived without a grave affront to justice. There are certain deeds which must never be done, certain freedoms which should never be invaded, some things which are supremely sacred.[31]

This account of "supremely sacred" things, I would argue, is inadequate for the very reason that it is confined to defending liberty rights. Although a theory of human rights must certainly provide that persons must not have certain things done to them and must not have certain of their freedoms invaded, it must also provide that persons are never deprived of certain necessary requisites of human life.

First, Cranston defends the paramountcy test in an obviously unfair manner, by comparing the most essential liberty rights with the least essential economic rights. (This, clearly, is no more valid than choosing a very bright yellow and a very dull red to demonstrate that yellow is brighter than red!) The economic right he chooses to emphasize is the right to paid vacations, which seems to be generally regarded by critics of the Universal Declaration as the most questionable and extravagant right in the entire document.[32] With this, he chooses to compare such crucial liberty rights as the rights of Jews not to be exterminated and the right of persons not to be held in prison indefinitely without charge. As Raphael has pointed out, however, the liberty rights enumerated in the Declaration include some that are at least as extravagant as the right to paid vacations.[33] When Cranston's examples are more fairly comparable, such as paid vacations versus the right to take up a scholarship at Oxford, his argument becomes far less convincing. It is by no means obvious which of this pair of rights is more "supremely sacred." For a subsistence level migrant worker, the right that enables him or her to enjoy family life for a few weeks each year might well be far more valuable than the right to do something that he or she is likely never to be in a position to do. To the aspiring black scholar of Cranston's example, on the other hand, the right to a vacation with pay may seem like an extravagence in comparison with the right to take up his or her scholarship.

This point indicates the importance of recognizing, when weighing priorities among human rights, that we are all liable to cultural parochialism and ideological bias when it comes to questions of values.[34] It is by no means self-evident that the identical value is placed on various freedoms or benefits by people of different cultures, or even by people of different groups or classes within the same culture. This may seem at first to place insuperable obstacles in the way of deciding priorities among human rights. However, referring to my earlier attempt to provide a foundation for human rights, it is clear that the value placed on the fulfillment of basic needs — subsistence, physical security, and treatment as a person — is far less variable than the values that different cultures may place on the provision of the requirements for the development of the various capacities. Placing a high value on privacy, for example, or freedom of speech, may be partly culturally determined. But, though what are considered the requirements for subsistence vary from one time or place to another, it would be difficult (for fairly obvious reasons) to find any tradition or people that did not place priority on the continued achievement of their recognized subsistence level. Similarly, physical security would seem to be valued highly by the vast majority of people in all cultures. And, although many cultures have treated people differently, depending on what caste or rank they belonged to, it has never been widely considered desirable to be treated as an inferior type of being.

Bearing this in mind, I will suggest two approaches to determining

priorities among human rights that I consider to be much more reasonable than separating liberty rights from economic and social
rights and giving all of the former priority over all of the latter. One
approach involves the consideration that there are some rights that
are prerequisite to the enjoyment of others. Raphael has argued this,
in the following manner:

> one cannot exercise the initiative of a human being (which is
> what the rights of liberty are intended to protect), or indeed re-
> main a human being at all, unless the basic needs of life are sat-
> isfied, and if a man is not in a position to do this for himself, it
> seems to me reasonable to say that he has a right, as a human
> being, to the assistance of others in meeting these needs[35]

Many types of freedom, education, or access to information are
clearly of little or no value to those who lack such conditions of life as
are necessary to make use of them. Thus this method of establishing
priorities among rights points to rights to basic well-being — at a minimum, the rights to subsistence and to be protected from assault — as
rights that should be high on the list.

Second, while remaining conscious of cultural bias, we might find
it a helpful approach to the problem of deciding priorities, to consider which of various pairs of rights might be valued more highly. by
a person who is deprived of both of them. (This suggestion is reminiscent of John Stuart Mill's argument that the only way of ascertaining
the relative qualities of different pleasures is to ask a person who
knows both, except that my adaptation of the principle escapes the
charge of elitism to which Mill's is subject.)[36] This method would appear to confirm the conclusions of the previous one, for surely it is
unlikely that anyone, faced with the choice between two rights of
which one was necessary for enjoying the other, would choose the latter. In addition, independently of this issue, although people have
sometimes risked their well-being in their struggles for liberty rights,
it is surely unlikely that people would choose to starve or to be con-
stantly exposed to physical danger rather than to be denied the right
to speak freely, to own property, or to be educated.

There are several important related issues that I am not able to address here. The second-to-last question discussed, that concerning
some rights as prerequisites to others, becomes much more complicated, and very interesting, once one takes account of the right to po-

litical participation. For clearly it can be argued that civil liberties such as freedom of speech and of association are prerequisites for the effective exercise of the right to political participation. It can also be held that the right to political participation is ineffective if people are liable to social or economic discrimination owing to their political opinions. The complexities are not endless, but they are numerous.

THE ISSUES OF ABSOLUTENESS
AND PRACTICABILITY

Building on the principle "ought implies can," it has been claimed that, to qualify as a human right, a demand must be able to be fulfilled in practice and without exception in all circumstances and that economic and social rights cannot meet these requirements. I will argue that no human right is absolute and exceptionless and that the problem of practicability can be resolved in several ways other than the drastic one of excluding all human rights to welfare.

No human right is absolutely exceptionless. As E. H. Carr has pointed out, liberty rights have not generally been treated this way.[37] All are considered to be limited by the necessity of preserving the existing social order; declarations of rights frequently include "escape clauses" to this effect; and we would have a hard time pointing to a country that for any considerable period had not limited the exercise of one or more of the liberty rights in some respect or other, when it considered itself to be in danger. It would be comforting to believe that at least some rights, such as the right not to be tortured, are categorical and absolute. When confronted with a hard case, however, in which, say, torturing one person implicated in a plot is extremely likely to yield information that will save a hundred innocent people from being tortured by the other conspirators, one would be hard-pressed to refrain from violating the former person's right not to be tortured, even though to refrain would leave one innocent of having personally participated in the violation of a right.[38] The contention that upholding liberty rights absolutely involves little difficulty seems, again, to be partly due to a parochial view of the political circumstances, histories, and traditions of many countries. Although liberty rights have, of course, frequently been violated unjustifiably, it is surely not impossible to imagine conditions in which allowing what in other circumstances is completely reasonable and generally not dangerous — freedom of speech on all political issues — might be, temporarily at least, as potentially harmful as allowing people falsely to shout "Fire!" in a crowded theater. The recent case of Nazis and the Town of Skokie demonstrated, at least, that this issue remains open. Needless to say, a heavy burden is placed on whoever is in the position of having to judge the claims of free speech against potential danger, and those who decide wrongly are liable to be judged harshly by posterity. However, the issue of categorical absoluteness does not seem to separate liberty rights on the one hand from economic and social rights on the other.

One particular and likely reason that certain rights might not be absolute and categorical is that sufficient resources might be lacking. This argument has been directed against the recognition of economic and social rights as human rights,[39] and several points must be made in answer. First, as I suggested above, some of the liberty rights, too, such as the right to a fair trial or to be defended from attack, require the outlay of resources that may be beyond the means of some governments. As long as resources are limited, choices will have to be made about which rights should take priority. There is clearly a trade-off, in many countries today, between the amounts budgeted for military purposes and those budgeted for social services. In addition, some of the liberty rights, notably the right to legal acquisition of an unlimited amount of private property, clearly affect a society's capacity for meeting all its people's economic and social rights, and without establishing priorities among rights, it is impossible to decide what are the limits of the resources available for the satisfaction of the latter. The struggle for taxation of income, against the absolute right to private property, was clearly a prerequisite for the provision of social services in most existing welfare state systems, and more complete securing of welfare rights has been achieved in many countries that have placed further limits on rights to private ownership.

Second, it is not at all clear why the fact that a claim cannot be met immediately and in full should preclude its being recognized as a human right, so long as it is made clear that the right must be met to the greatest extent that resources permit. Such provisos are clearly stated in the UN Covenant on Human Rights, of which the first article on economic and social rights reads:

The States parties to the present Covenant . . . resolve *to strive*

to ensure that every human being shall obtain the food, clothing, shelter essential for his livelihood and well-being, and . . .
*undertake to take steps, individually and through international
co-operation, to the maximum of their available resources with
a view to achieving progressively* the full realization of the rights
recognized in this part of the present Covenant.[40]

Several writers have argued along these lines that the objection that
welfare rights are impracticable can be met by the acknowledgment
that states must do everything they can, including redistributing
wealth, to fulfill their correlative obligations. Most have assumed,
however, that the obligation to meet persons' economic and social
needs rests solely with the state of which those persons are citizens.[41]
Interestingly, the covenant as quoted above manifestly does not imply acceptance of this limitation of responsibility. It suggests, rather,
that any state that is a party to the covenant undertakes to the maximum of its available resources, both individually and through international cooperation, to take steps to meet the needs of every human
being. Moreover, it has recently been very cogently argued that, because of the extent of contemporary global economic interdependence and division of labor, the reallocation of resources from richer
to poorer states, and not only within states, is required by egalitarian
principles of distributive justice. If this argument is correct, it has
radical implications for the issue of the practicability of the welfare
rights, since clearly a global reallocation of resources would be far
more capable of meeting the needs of the world's poorest peoples
than redistribution within each state alone.[42]

CONCLUSIONS

None of these three objections that has been raised against welfare
rights as human rights, or against their claims to share priority with
liberty rights, can withstand attack. First, liberty rights, too, involve
expensive and far-reaching activity as well as restraint on the part of
the state; even if they did not, a case must be made that enlargement
of the sphere of activity of states is necessarily in itself an evil. Second, it is clear that the criterion of their importance for human well-
being does not separate all liberty rights from all economic and social
rights. This is reinforced by the fact that the enjoyment of certain

basic rights of both types is the necessary condition for the enjoyment of many other rights of both types. Third, no human rights can be regarded as absolute and exceptionless in all circumstances, and the problem of immediate practicability, which can affect both types of rights, need not preclude the admission of a right to the status of a human right.

Since the division of human rights into these two categories seems, therefore, to have hindered rational discussion of priorities among them, it is important to try to understand the foundations of the development of the dichotomy. Liberty rights clearly have their origins in classic liberalism, with its roots in Hobbes and Locke, and have developed hand in hand with capitalism. The history of welfare rights is somewhat more obscure, but is traceable, in the social welfare or socialist traditions, at least as far back as Thomas Paine and Babeuf.[43] In the classic natural rights view, the rights that are given the highest ethical status, by being recognized as natural rights, are all rights to be left alone — not to be interfered with. In this view, the right to life, for example, means the right not to be killed, whether by another individual or arbitrarily by the state. Locke's version of this right has been characterized as a "right to be left free to live (or, if one is unlucky, to die)"[44]

But surely, the representative of the social welfare tradition will object, that is only one understanding of what constitutes the right to life — by no means the most comprehensive, and not obviously the most reasonable. It depends, essentially, upon a view of human beings that is sustained by the concept of the state of nature — independent individuals, primarily seeking protection against each other, rather than living in cooperation with, dependent upon, or benefiting from, each other.[45] It is this mythical view of human beings as self-sufficient and as necessarily potential limitations on each other's freedom, rather than potential co-operators in search of mutual advantage and welfare, that prevents the liberal theorist from focusing on the fact that one can be just as effectively denied life by being so situated in society that one is deprived of the means of subsistence as one can be by being killed. Even in Locke's day, this was the lot of those who, previously subsisting on the land, suffered most from the enclosure movement; in our own day, it is the experience of many — from those in industrialized societies who are unemployed and without access to means of production, to Third World peasants displaced from their means of livelihood by the upheavals of modernization. The abstraction from actual social conditions leads to the failure to recognize that societies sanction and reinforce definite social and economic relations and that, in some cases, these relations result in grave deprivation, which usually does not just happen, as it were, either by chance, or because of some lack of effort on the part of the deprived. The comment of a classic liberal like Cranston that economic and social rights are objectionable because they require people to be *given* something[46] is a clear sign of the persistence in his mind of the state of nature, in which all are free and equal and require only to "mix their labor with the soil" in order to provide for their own subsistence. In a world of ever more complex economic interdependencies and ever more concentrated patterns of ownership of means of production, this is hardly a realistic approach, let alone one that is likely to produce a just social order.

The theory of liberty rights is built on the premise of the equal liberty of human beings, but its egalitarianism goes no further. Many of these rights, once one gets beyond the unquestionably crucial right to personal security, are the rights of persons to be left alone to use their powers and resources (including inherited property and innate talents) as they think fit. This is the issue addressed by Marx in attacking the liberal notion of personal freedom, when he called it the "right to the undisturbed enjoyment, within certain conditions, of fortuity and chance."[47] Obviously, the exercise of equal rights to liberty, when such powers and resources are very unequal, is bound to lead to some people's controlling far more resources than are necessary to live very well and to make the kinds of choices that constitute freedom on a day-to-day basis, and to other people's controlling insufficient resources even to maintain their physical well-being, let alone the capacity to make such choices.

The social welfare tradition — unlike the liberal tradition with its formal "equality of opportunity" — is disposed to view substantive equality, or at least the guarantee of a certain level of well-being, as a positive good. The welfare rights espoused as human rights by this tradition require whatever extent of redistribution of resources is necessary to bring those worst off up to the level of basic well-being, or whatever other standard is established as everybody's by right. At least at the extremes of the spectrum, the inequalities permitted by classic liberalism will be reduced, and if "freedom" includes the unrestrained appropriation and use of unlimited amounts of the world's resources, the required redistribution must involve some restriction of this aspect of individual freedom.

The recent disputes about types of human rights and priorities

among them can thus be seen to be aspects of the larger debates
about freedom and equality, and about different concepts of freedom. In some respects, we are fighting nineteenth-century battles
again, and it seems sometimes as if the earlier critics of classic liberal
theories of rights and freedom, from Marx to T. H. Green, had never
spoken. Clearly, old battles about important issues in political theory
endure. However, I would suggest that new approaches may help
some of the dust to settle. If we approach the subject of human rights
by seeking to establish what are the most urgent of human needs and
the most widely shared of human capacities, and thence to define
what are the rights most essential for the satisfaction of these needs
and the development of these capacities, we may get beyond the old
ways of differentiating types of rights and of seeking priorities among
them. We may conclude that the most paramount human rights, derived from basic human needs, will establish both crucial individual
freedoms—notably personal security—and an essential level of well-
being. Rights to other freedoms, as well as to an extended level of
well-being, derived from human capacities, although still of undeniable importance, may have less priority where choices must be made.

NOTES

*I would like to thank Amy Gutmann, Ann Tickner, the Columbia
University Seminar for Political Thought, and the editors of
NOMOS for their helpful comments on earlier drafts of this paper.

1. Vance's speech, "Human Rights Policy," April 30, 1977 (Office of
   Media Services Bureau of Public Affairs, U.S. Department of State),
   PR 194, defines human rights as including the right to be free from
   governmental violations of personal integrity, rights to the fulfillment
   of vital needs, and the right to enjoy civil and political liberties. However, recent legislation and State Department reporting has been fo-
   cused much more narrowly on the first of these types of rights.
2. See, for example, the articles contained in D. D. Raphael, ed.,
   Political Theory and the Rights of Man (Bloomington, Ind., and
   London: Indiana University Press, 1967), and Peter Brown and
   Douglas McLead, ed., *Human Rights and Foreign Policy* (Lexington,
   Ma.: D. C. Heath, 1979).
3. See the interesting and important discussion of this distinction in
   David Miller, *Social Justice* (New York: Oxford University Press,
   1976), chap. 4, esp. pp. 65–68. Miller includes human rights in the
   category "ideal rights" and concludes that it is not analytically correct
   to consider such so-called rights as rights, except in a rhetorical sense,

since they can be adequately analyzed in terms of desert and need. I do not consider this conclusion justified, but am unable to address the issue directly here. See also James Nickel, "Is There a Human Right to Employment," *Philosophical Forum,"* 10, nos. 1-2, for a fuller characterization of human rights.

4. I use the words "duty" and "obligation" interchangeably. Extended discussion of the question whether rights, and specifically human rights, entail second-party duties, is beyond the scope of this paper. Without being able to elaborate on the reasons for my position, I consider that rights do entail second-party duties, and that human rights are no exception, and therefore do not require to be put into a special category of "manifesto" rights. (See, for example, Joel Feinberg, *Social Philosophy* [Englewood Cliffs, N.J.: Prentice-Hall, 1973], p. 67) It is not always easy to specify whose duties they are, and even when we can so specify, the duties are frequently neither acknowledged nor acted upon by those whose duties they are. However, neither of these factors distinguishes human rights sharply from all other rights.

5. See, for example, Miller, *Social Justice,* p. 66; Rex Martin and James W. Nickel, "Recent Work on the Concept of Rights," *American Philosophical Quarterly,* 17, 1980, 165-180.

6. It is doubtful whether many other subjects analyzed by political theorists or moral philosophers have engendered the degree of terminological confusion connected with human rights. I can safely ignore some of the disputes about terms. However, it is important for the clarity of my argument, in the context of the relevant literature, to note that the two types of rights discussed in the latter section of this chapter have been given almost as many names as there have been political theorists who have addressed the distinctions between them. The first have been called "rights to freedom (or liberty)," "civil and political rights," "traditional natural rights," "old rights," and "option rights." The second have been called "rights to well-being," "economic and social rights," "rights to opportunity," "new rights," and "welfare rights." I choose to call the first type "liberty rights" and the second type "welfare rights." It is impossible to identify briefly and accurately which writers have used all of the above labels, partly because some employ more than one term interchangeably, and partly because some do not classify rights in quite the same way as others, or as I do. Nevertheless, it should be noted that some theorists whose terms are included in the list above are Maurice Cranston, Alan Gewirth, Martin P. Golding, Jacques Maritain, Richard McKeon, and D. D. Raphael.

7. See Alan Gewirth, *Reason and Morality* (Chicago: The University of Chicago Press, 1978), and "The Basis and Content of Human Rights," chapter 6 of this volume.

8. Gewirth, *Reason and Morality,* pp. 19-20; "The Basis and Content of Human Rights," pp. 000-00.

9. Gewirth, *Reason and Morality,* pp. 119-20.

10. Ibid., p. 128 (italics mine). A little later, this is repeated in slightly different words: "In relation to the justification for having the generic rights . . . being an agent is an absolute or noncomparative condition."

11. Thomas Hobbes, *Leviathan,* chap. 23.

12. John Locke, *Second Treatise of Government,* chap. 2, no. 4. The limitations of human equality are spelled out in chap. 6, no. 54. I use the word "man" advisedly, here, since Locke *did* think that there was "a Foundation in Nature" for the authority of husbands over their wives. Locke, *First Treatise,* chap. 5, no. 47. On the inconsistencies and confusions in which Hobbes and Locke involve themselves in order to maintain the subordination of women, see Teresa Brennan and Carole Pateman, "Mere Auxiliaries to the Commonwealth: Women and the Origins of Liberalism," *Political Studies,* 27, no. 2 (1979): 183–200, and Susan Moller Okin, *Women in Western Political Thought* (Princeton: Princeton University Press, 1979), pp. 197–202.

13. Gregory Vlastos, "Justice and Equality," in R. B. Brandt, ed., *Social Justice* (Englewood Cliffs, N.J.: Prentice-Hall, 1962). The arguments I draw on and passages I quote appear on pp. 50–52. Vlastos suggests that the recognition by human beings of each other's individual worth is analogous, in respect to being independent of particular abilities or behavior, to the love a parent has for a child, but claims that the ascription of fundamental worth has a far greater range of applicability.

14. To call a right a "prima facie right" means that its claims may be overruled in special circumstances (ibid., p. 38). Vlastos suggests that no human rights are absolute and unexceptionable (ibid., pp. 36–38).

15. Joel Feinberg indicates that he shares this opinion that Vlastos's argument is incomplete when he writes: "The skeptic's challenge has not been met . . . No skeptic who denies human rights will be easily convinced that there is equal human worth," *Social Philosophy* (Englewood Cliffs, N.J.: Prentice-Hall, 1973), p. 90. See his discussion of various human characteristics as possible bases of human worth, pp. 90–94.

16. For example, David Miller says that to prove that an ideal right (in which category he includes human rights) exists, "What has to be shown is that some benefit or freedom is of sufficient moral value to the individual to be called his moral right" (*Social Justice,* p. 67); James W. Nickel says that one of the arguments for the existence of a universal human right to anything is that individuals have "a very strong or fundamental interest in that thing." "Is There a Human Right to Employment?" p. 16.

17. To undertake such an attempt does not imply adherence to the belief that all aspects of human nature are either unchanging or unchangeable, but only adherence to the belief that there are *some* constant characteristics of human nature, which can be used as the basis of a theory of human rights.

18. Henry Shue, "Foundations for a Balanced U.S. Policy on Human Rights: The Significance of Subsistence Rights" (Working Paper, Working Group on Human Rights, Center for Philosophy and Public Policy, University of Maryland, November 1977). Shue suggests that determining what is an adequate level of subsistence is not as difficult as is sometimes claimed and points his reader to Linda Haverberg, "Individual Needs: Nutritional Guidelines for Policy?" in *Food Policy: The Responsibility of the United States in the Life and Death Choices*, edited and with an introduction by Peter G. Brown and Henry Shue (New York: The Free Press, 1977), pp. 212–33.

19. See Feinberg, *Social Philosophy*, p. 91, on the problems raised by the use of human beings' unique rationality as grounds for the equal human worth on which rights are to be based.

20. See, for example, Gewirth, "The Basis and Content of Human Rights," p. 138 ff.; Vlastos, "Justice and Equality," pp. 52–53, n. 45.

21. The right to own property was not included in the subsequently adopted covenant.

22. Maurice Cranston, *What Are Human Rights?* (New York: 1962), p. 27. See also Cranston, "Human Rights, Real and Supposed," in Raphael, ed., *Political Theory and the Rights of Man*, p. 47.

23. Peter Schneider, "Social Rights and the Concept of Human Rights," in Raphael ed., *Political Theory and the Rights of Man*, pp. 83, 88.

24. Gordon Schochet, "Who Has Human Rights?" (American Political Science Association, 1978), unpublished manuscript, pp. 3, 4, 10.

25. For misperceptions of whom the Declaration is addressed to, see, for example, J. E. S. Fawcett, "The International Protection of Human Rights," p.. 129, and Bernard Mayo, "What Are Human Rights?" p. 77, both in Raphael, ed., *Political Theory and the Rights of Man*. For indications to the contrary, in the Declaration itself, see the proclamation at the end of the Preamble, and Article 1. It should be noted that such misperceptions are by no means universally held. A number of writers on the subject acknowledge that human rights must be understood as rights against other persons or groups of persons, as well as against governments, and that the Universal Declaration recognizes this. See, for example, Gewirth, "The Basis and Content of Human Rights," pp. 000–00; D. D. Raphael, "Human Rights, Old and New," p. 62, and "The Rights of Man and the Rights of the Citizen," p. 108, both in Raphael, ed., *Political Theory and the Rights of Man*.

26. On this issue, see E. H. Carr, "The Rights of Man," p. 21; John Lewis, "On Human Rights," pp. 55–56; and Richard McKeon, "The Philosophic Bases and Material Circumstances of the Rights of Man," p. 39, all in *Human Rights: Comments and Interpretations* (London and New York: A. Wingate, 1949), UNESCO.

27. Locke, *Second Treatise*, chap. 9, nos. 123–24.

28. Locke, *Second Treatise*, chap. 7, no. 93.

29. For an interesting discussion of the weaknesses of labeling security rights "negative" and subsistence rights "positive," which bears on the

following argument, see Shue, "Foundations for a Balanced U.S. Policy on Human Rights," pp. 13-16.

30. Clearly, security of persons and property could be more inexpensively achieved if the rights of the accused were sacrificed, but these are no less important members of the class of liberty rights than is the protection of those who are attacked. It is odd that several writers on the subject of rights claim that the provision of such things as fair trials requires little or nothing in the way of effort or expenditure on the part of government. See Cranston, *What Are Human Rights?* p. 37; Feinberg, *Social Philosophy*, p. 96, where he lists the right to a fair trial as a right to a good that "cannot be in scarce supply." If this is the case, one wonders why the court systems in this country are so backlogged with cases and why so much emphasis is placed on plea-bargaining as a way of avoiding the necessity for trials without obviously sacrificing the rights of defendants.

31. Cranston, "Human Rights, Real and Supposed," pp. 51-52.

32. Its extravagance and/or unimportance is suggested by Raphael, "Human Rights, Old and New," p. 65, and even by C. R. Beitz, "Human Rights and Social Justice" (Working Paper, Working Group on Human Rights, Center for Philosophy and Public Policy, University of Maryland, May 1978), p. 15. I wonder how much this judgment is the result of the world view of the relatively affluent academicians that we all are. Many of the scholars who write on such subjects have probably never engaged in manual or boring labor for any length of time to earn their subsistence needs; surely few of us have been migrant laborers, separated for months by our work from spouses and families; and many of us may be so attached to our generally pleasant form of work that we tend to work during our (paid) vacations anyway. Are we, therefore, in any position to judge whether paid vacations are luxuries or human rights?

33. Raphael, "Human Rights, Old and New," p. 64.

34. These issues are addressed in Beitz, "Human Rights and Social Justice," pp. 9-10.

35. Raphael, "The Rights of Man and the Rights of the Citizen," p. 115. Gewirth similarly recognizes the rationality of setting priorities amongst types of rights in accordance with the degree of their necessity for purposive action ("The Basis and Content of Human Rights," p. 138). Schneider, too, refers to certain "entitlements to benefit" as "creating the conditions under which the individual can achieve self-determination" ("Social Rights and the Concept of Human Rights," p. 92). He adds the significant point that "When these conditions are fulfilled, they cease to be urgently significant," which may well explain some political theorists' refusal to admit claims to the basic needs of life to the status of human rights.

36. J. S. Mill, *Utilitarianism*, chap. 2.

37. Carr, "The Rights of Man," p. 21. See also Vlastos, "Justice and Equality," pp. 37-38.

38. See Feinberg, *Social Philosophy*, pp. 87-88. Feinberg argues that the

right not to be tortured (and several other rights) are categorical and absolute, but he seems to me not to have constructed a difficult enough case with which to test his contention. On this and other aspects of the "dirty hands" problem, see Michael Walzer, "Political Action: The Problem of Dirty Hands," *Philosophy and Public Affairs*, 2, no. 2 (1973): 160-80.

39. For example, by Cranston, *What Are Human Rights?* p. 37, and "Human Rights, Real and Supposed," pp. 50, 53.

40. International Convenant on Human Rights, Article 19 (italics mine).

41. This certainly seems to be implied by Gewirth, "The Basis and Content of Human Rights," pp. 144-55, and is explicitly stated by Raphael, "Human Rights, Old and New," p. 66.

42. C. R. Beitz, "Justice and International Relations," *Philosophy and Public Affairs*, 4, no. 4 (Summer 1976): 360-89; "Human Rights and Social Justice," p. 10; "Disputes over Global Egalitarianism," *Dissent* (Winter 1979): 62-63.

It has been suggested that such worldwide redistribution of wealth, given the relative populations of the right and the poor, would so disrupt the productivity of the presently richer countries that all would end up being worse off. However, while millions have recently died or are presently dying of starvation, is it not impossible to imagine a situation in which *all* would be worse off than they are at present? Perhaps the objection is, rather, that either the aggregate or the average level of welfare in the world would be reduced by such redistribution. But even if this were true, it would not constitute an argument against the right of those who are presently worse off to such redistribution as is necessary to satisfy their basic needs, since one of the central distinguishing features of rights is that persons have them even when the aggregate or average level of welfare would be reduced by whatever actions must be taken to satisfy their rights. (See, for example, Ronald Dworkin, *Taking Rights Seriously*, [Cambridge: Ma.: Harvard University Press, 1977] pp. xi, 190-92.) Needless to say, it is morally desirable to try to avoid, so far as possible, reducing the world's aggregate or average level of welfare while meeting those rights arising from the basic needs of the worst off. Conducting the redistribution of resources and capital in a cautious manner, although as rapidly as is consistent with such caution, may be part of the answer.

43. On the history of the two types of rights, see, for example, Raphael, "Human Rights, Old and New" and "The Rights of Man and the Rights of the Citizen;" Cranston, "Human Rights: A Reply to Professor Raphael," in Raphael, ed., *Political Theory and the Rights of Man;* Martin Golding, "The Concept of Rights: A Historical Sketch," E. and B. Bandman, eds., *Bioethics and Human Rights,* (Boston: Little, Brown, 1978), chap. 4.

44. Raphael, "Human Rights, Old and New," p. 61.

45. See Marx's comments on the liberal view of human beings as "isolated monads" ("On the Jewish Question," in *Karl Marx: Early Writings,* T. B. Bottomore, esp. pp. 24-26.)

46. Cranston, "Human Rights: A Reply to Professor Raphael," pp. 95–96.

47. *The German Ideology,* part I, *Karl Marx: Selected Writings,* ed. David McClellan (New York: Oxford University Press, 1977), pp. 181–82.

13

INTERNATIONAL HUMAN RIGHTS
AS "RIGHTS"

LOUIS HENKIN*

"International human rights" is now a common subject for intellectual as well as popular discourse, but few have written about it in relation to the massive literature on "rights." Are "international human rights" "rights," and what is the source and basis of their authority? Are they moral rights? Are they legal rights and, if so, in what legal universe? Whose rights are they? Are there correlative duties and if so upon whom? What remedies are there when the rights are violated? Are the remedies necessary and adequate to support their quality as rights?

THE INTERNATIONAL HUMAN
RIGHTS MOVEMENT

"International human rights" is a term used with varying degrees of precision (or imprecision) and with different connotation in different context. In wide usage it corresponds to the "international human rights movement," born during World War II out of a spreading conviction that how human beings are treated anywhere concerns everyone, everywhere. That attitude itself perhaps blended several different "statements." An assertion of fact about human psychology and emotion, that human beings cannot close their minds and hearts to mistreatment or suffering of other human beings. A moral statement, that mistreatment or suffering of human beings violates a common morality (perhaps also natural law, or God's law) and that all human beings are morally obligated to do something about such mistreatment or suffering, individually and through their political and social institutions. An international political statement, that governments will attend to such mistreatment or suffering in other countries through international institutions and will take account of them also in their relations with other states. These three kinds of statement combined to support a concept of "human rights" and a program to promote their enjoyment, as implied in declarations like President Franklin Roosevelt's "Four Freedoms" message, in various articulations of the war aims of the Allies in World War II and in their plans for the post war world.

The end of the war saw wide acceptance of "human rights" reflected in two forms. Human rights appeared in the constitutions and laws of virtually all states. Conquerors wrote them into law for occupied countries; for example, Germany and Japan. Departing colonial powers sometimes required them of newborn states as part of the price of "liberation," and many new states wrote them into their constitutions as their own commitment. Older states, responding to the *Zeitgeist,* also emphasized human rights in new national documents.

The human rights movement also took a second, transnational form. Human rights were prominent in the new postwar international order: in treaties imposed upon vanquished nations (e.g., Italy, Rumania); in the UN Charter and the Nuremberg Charter; in numerous resolutions and declarations of the new international institutions, notably, the United Nations and regional institutions in Latin America and Europe. In the United Nations "human rights" was on every agenda, and the dedicated efforts of individuals and some governments resulted in important international political and legal instruments, beginning with the Universal Declaration on Human Rights, and the Convention on the Prevention and Punishment of the Crime of Genocide, both adopted without dissent in 1948.[1] There has followed a series of other resolutions and declarations and an impressive array of other international covenants and conventions, principally the International Covenant on Civil and Political Rights and the International Covenant on Economic, Social, and Cultural Rights, both completed in 1966, and both in force since 1976. Europe and Latin America also developed important human rights law and institutions.

I stress — and distinguish — those two different manifestations of general, worldwide concern with human rights. "Universalization" has brought acceptance, at least in principle and rhetoric, of the concept of individual human rights by all societies and governments, and its reflection in national consitutions and laws. "Internationalization" has brought agreement, at least in political-legal principle and in rhetoric, that individual human rights are of "international concern" and a proper subject for diplomacy, international law, and international institutions.

My subject is "international human rights," that is, human rights as a subject of international law and politics, not individual rights in national societies under national legal systems. But the two are not unrelated in law or in politics. The international movement sees human rights as rights that, under accepted moral principle, the individual should enjoy under the constitutional-legal system of his society. To induce states to arrange their constitutional-legal systems to achieve that result, and to supply any failures to do so, the international system has, *inter alia,* promulgated an international law of human rights. International human rights, then, were born because national protections for accepted human rights were deemed deficient, and can be seen as merely additional international protections for rights under national law. The international law of human rights is implemented largely by national laws and institutions; it is satisfied when national laws and institutions are sufficient. Ambiguities in the content or scope of international rights are resolved (at least in the first instance) by national governments in the light of national standards. The international law of human rights differs little from many national human rights laws. Where there are differences, international rights supplement national rights; in the United States, for example, the two sets of rights would be cumulated and both given effect by courts and other national institutions. In peripheral respects there may be conflict between the conceptions of rights or between particular rights in the two systems, and in most countries national institutions will give effect to the national requirement, placing the country in violation of the international obligation.

THE INTERNATIONAL LAW OF HUMAN RIGHTS

The international law of human rights derives principally from contemporary international agreements in which states undertake to recognize, respect and promote specific rights for the inhabitants of their own countries.[2] There are also older obligations in international law that today fit in the human rights category. Traditional international law imposed on states a responsibility not to "deny justice" to nationals of other states in regard to their persons, probably also to their property.[3] Although that law is now highly uncertain as regards some forms of alien property, it remains otherwise effective and is supplemented, not superseded, by the new human rights law that applies to nationals and aliens alike. There are also old and less old treaties containing undertakings to treat individuals in ways corresponding to respect for some of their human rights; for example, to accord nationals of another state certain rights and freedoms under domestic law (freedom of religion, the right to work) or to provide status and rights for members of friendly foreign forces. Some agreements — for example, those providing protection for minorities, or the many conventions promoted by the International Labor Organization which set minimum labor and social standards — apply to nationals as well as to aliens.

Content

The international law of human rights is contained principally in the International Covenant on Civil and Political Rights and the International Covenant on Economic, Social, and Cultural Rights, which together legislate essentially what the Universal Declaration had declared.[4] In the Covenant on Civil and Political Rights, states undertake to respect and insure rights to life and personal integrity; to due process of law and a humane penal system; freedom to travel within as well as outside one's country; freedom of expression, religion, and conscience; cultural and linguistic rights for minority groups; the right to paricipate in government (including free elections); the right to marry and found a family; and the right to equality and freedom from discrimination — a dominant theme in international human rights.[5] Most (but not all) rights are subject to derogation or limitation "to the extent strictly required," in "time of public emergency which threatens the life of the nation and the existence of which is officially proclaimed."[6] Some rights — freedom of movement, assembly, association — may be curtailed by law as necessary to protect national security, public order, health or morals, or the rights and freedoms of others.[7]

In the Covenant on Economic, Social, and Cultural Rights, states undertake to "take steps" "to the maximum of available resources," "with a view to achieving progressively the full realization" of designated rights.[8] These include the right to work, to enjoy just and favorable conditions of work, and to join trade unions; the right to social security, to protection for the family, for mothers and children; the right to be "free from hunger," to have an adequate standard of living, including adequate food, clothing and housing, and the continuous improvement of living conditions; the right to the highest attainable standards of physical and mental health; to education; the right to take part in cultural life. In this covenant, too, equality and nondiscrimination are a pervasive theme. Derogations and limitations by law are permitted if they are compatible with the nature of these rights and are solely for the purpose of promoting the general welfare in a democratic society.[9] Some rights — for example, trade union freedom — are subject only to limitations "necessary in a democratic society in the interests of national security or public order or for the protection of the rights and freedoms of others."[10]

Remedies

The remedies for violation of international obligations to respect human rights are in principle the same as for other violations of international obligation. A "promisee" a state to which the obligation runs, can make claim and seek redress through diplomatic channels or by agreed-upon international "machinery," or, in some limited respects, by self-help. In human rights agreements the promisee is a state, and the true beneficiary is an individual (and usually a national of the violating state), but that does not detract from the right of any state party to an agreement to seek its observance by others.[11] Particular conventions provide additional "enforcement machinery." Under the Covenant on Civil and Political Rights, states are required to report on their compliance to a Human Rights Committee.[12] As regards states that agree to optional provisions, the committee may also receive complaints of violation from other states, or from individuals.[13] The committee's powers are essentially to inquire, intercede, quietly seek redress, later expose unrepaired violations to publicity. Under the Covenant on Economic, Social, and Cultural Rights, states are required to report on their compliance to the UN Economic and Social Council,[14] which may transmit reports to the

UN Commission on Human Rights "for study and general recommendation," and "may submit from time to time to the General Assembly reports with recommendations of a general nature."[15] The European human rights system has a more complex and more effective system of remedies, combining an active European Commission on Human Rights (which receives petitions also from individuals and nongovernmental organizations), a Council of Ministers, and a Court of Human Rights to which cases may be brought by the Commission or by states. The Organization of American States also has an active commission; the American Convention on Human Rights has just come into force and the Inter-American Court of Human Rights has been established.

PHILOSOPHICAL INQUIRIES

The framers of international human rights were not philosophers, but politicians, citizens. The international instruments do not articulate any philosophical foundations or reflect any clear philosophical assumptions, either for the "human rights" they were recognizing or the international human rights "system" they were establishing. We can only attempt to characterize what we find, deriving—perhaps imposing—a philosophical perspective, and answers to a philosopher's questions. In passing to exploration of international human rights as "rights" I nod to other, related philosophical issues.

Philosophical inquiry about international human rights must distinguish and proceed on two different levels. The international law of human rights creates legal rights and obligations that invite examination in the light of "rights theory." But international discourse, including international law, refers repeatedly to "human rights" apparently as preexisting in some other universe. The individual had human rights before the international system took notice of them, and would continue to have them if the international law of human rights were repealed and the international system turned its back on them. Are these human rights "rights," and how do they relate to the legal rights created by the international law of human rights?

Human Rights in International Perspective
Philosphers properly inquire how seriously the word "rights" is to

be taken in the frequent reference to "human rights" in international discourse. Some will argue that it carries no philosophical "rights" implications at all but is essentially rhetorical. It suggests an affirmative value, a "good," that is universal, fundamental, overriding. Particular reference, too—say, to a "right to education"—means only that it is desirable and important, indeed very highly desirable and important, that every human being be educated.

International reference to human rights commonly indicates also, however, a positive attitude to the concept of individual rights vis-a-vis national societies and largely also to the content of such rights, generally as set forth in international documents. Nominally, at least, this positive attitude is now common to all states, governments, and societies, even those that proclaim allegiance to collectivism and sometimes decry individualism. Indeed, international discourse insists that these human rights exist and that they are rights, although it is not clear what kind of rights they are and in what universe. Most plausibly they appear to be moral rights in an accepted moral order, or even legal rights under some modern version of natural law. Perhaps every human being is "entitled" to essential freedom and basic needs, and has valid "claims" to them against the moral order, or the universe or God; at least, the individual in society has valid claim to them against his society and it is obligated to respect and insure them.[16] In the good society, such rights are also legal rights in the domestic legal order, and valid legal claims, supported by effective remedies, against the society. These rights are human in that they are universal, for all persons in all societies. Some rights—to form a trade union, or to enjoy vacation with pay—of course apply only to workers in industrialized societies, but these too are universal in that they apply to all to whom they are relevant. Perhaps they are human rights, too, in the sense that they are particular expressions of an overall, *a priori,* universal moral principle, that a human being is entitled to what he requires for his "human dignity."

International human rights derive of course from national rights theories and systems, harking back through English, American, and French constitutionalism to John Locke et al., and earlier natural rights and natural law theory. In its American version that constitutionalism included concepts of original individual autonomy translated into popular sovereignty; social compact providing for continued self-government through chosen, accountable representatives; limited government for limited purposes; and retained, inalienable,

individual rights.[17] But the profound influence of that constitutionalism on international acceptance of human rights did not depend
on, or take with it, commitment to all the underlying theory. International adoption of human rights reflects no comprehensive political theory of the relation of individual to society, only what is implied
in the idea of individual rights against society. Human rights are "inherent" but not necessarily "retained" from any hypothetical state of
nature anteceding government. There is a nod to popular sovereignty but nothing of social compact or of continuing consent of the
governed. Retained rights are not the condition of government, and
violating them does not necessarily give rise to a right to undo government by revolution. Inevitably, international human rights also
implicate the purposes for which governments are created, but they
surely do not imply a commitment to government for limited purposes only. Born after various socialisms were established and spreading, and commitment to welfare economics and the welfare state was
nearly universal, international human rights implied rather a conception of government as designed for all purposes and seasons. The
rights deemed to be fundamental include not only limitations precluding government from invading civil and political rights but positive obligations for government to promote economic and social well-
being, implying government that it activist, intervening, planning,
committed to economic-social programs for the society that would
redound as economic-social rights for the individual.

    That there are "fundamental human rights" was a declared article
of faith, "reaffirmed" by "the peoples of the United Nations" in the
UN Charter. The Universal Declaration of Human Rights, striving
for a pronouncement that would appeal to diverse political systems
governing diverse peoples, built on that faith and eschewed philosophical exploration. Because of that faith—and of political and
ideological forces—governments accepted the concept of human
rights, agreed that they were appropriate for international concern,
cooperated to define them, assumed international obligations to respect them, and submitted to some international scrutiny as regards
compliance with these obligations. Tacitly, those who built international human rights accepted individual rights as "natural," in a contemporary sense: they correspond to the nature of man and of society,
his psychology and its sociology. Rights "derive from the inherent
dignity of the human person."[18] Rights are instrumental, leading to
conditions whose value is axiomatic for individuals, societies, and the

international system: "recognition of the inherent dignity and of the equal and inalienable rights of all members of the human family is the foundation of freedom, justice and peace in the world."[19] Respect for and observance of human rights will help create "conditions of stability and well-being which are necessary for peaceful and friendly relations among nations."[20] There is no agreed theory justifying "human dignity" as the source of rights, and we are not told how the needs of human dignity are determined. We are not told what was the conception of justice which human rights would support and whence it came, nor are we given the evidence that, or the theory on which, preserving human rights will promote peace in the world.

Human Rights as Positive International Law

I have suggested that independently of any international law on human rights, international discourse sees human rights as either:

a. "goods," desiderata, that are not rights but that might be translated into legal rights in domestic or international law;
b. moral rights in an accepted moral order (or under some natural law), the individual having "claims" to freedoms and basic needs, seen perhaps as claims upon the moral order, or the universe, or God;
c. moral (or natural law) claims by every individual upon his society; or
d. legal claims upon his society under its constitutional system and law.

The purpose of international political and legal preoccupation with human rights, and of recognizing their quality as rights of some order, is to help obtain for them the quality of legal rights in domestic societies and to enhance the likelihood that they will be enjoyed in fact.

The international law of human rights builds on faith in the validity and desirability of human rights, but it largely avoids the philosophical uncertainties that trouble human rights discourse generally. Whatever the status and character of human rights in the moral order or in some other legal order, for international law human rights are a subject of positive law, conventional or customary.[21]

The positive character of international legal human rights disposes of one part of the debate about economic and social rights. Maurice

Cranston can properly ask whether one can have a right to two weeks' vacation with pay, and whether that is a human right, and he and others (including the governments of the West) argued against treating social and economic aspirations as rights and giving them status as law.[22] But the majority of states did not heed those admonitions, and the Covenant on Economic, Social, and Cultural Rights is now in force.

There are, of course, important differences between that covenant and the Covenant on Civil and Political Rights. The latter is designed for full and immediate realization; the former requires steps only "to the maximum of [a state's] available resources," and with a view to achieving the full realization of rights "progressively." There is even a subtle but conscious and pervasive difference in tone and in the terms of legal prescription. The Covenant on Civil and Political Rights speaks throughout in terms of the rights which the individual has: "Every human being has the inherent right to life"; "No one shall be held in slavery"; "Everyone shall be free to leave any country, including his own"; "Everyone shall have the right to hold opinions without interference." The Covenant on Economic, Social, and Cultural Rights, on the other hand, is couched in terms of the state's action (or obligation), not the individual's right: "The states-parties to the present covenant recognize the right to work"; "the states . . . undertake to ensure . . . the right of everyone to form trade unions'"; "the states . . . recognize the right of everyone to social security," "to adequate standard of living," "to education." There are also important political and practical differences between the two sets of rights, especially in that the economic-social rights tend to be collective, and to depend on national planning and policies, and on their success. As a matter of law, however, I do not think any of these differences critical. The Convention on Economic, Social, and Cultural Rights uses language of obligation, not merely of aspiration or hope. An undertaking to do something "to the maximum of its available resources" and to achieve "progressively" creates a clear and firm legal obligation, subject to those limitations. That a state "recognizes the right to an education" is not different, legally, from "everyone shall have a right to an education." Both create a legal claim against the state for failure to provide what was promised or for not insuring it against interruption ("to the maximum of its available resources").[23] A state's failure to perform its undertakings gives rise to the same kind of remedies as do other international agreements.[24]

RIGHTS UNDER THE INTERNATIONAL LAW OF HUMAN RIGHTS

What has this international law done to human rights qua rights? What new legal rights have the international legal instruments created?

I can only allude lightly to the literature on "rights." In a word, according to the common view one has a legal right only against some other; to say one has a legal right against another is to say that one has a valid legal claim upon him and that the addressee has a corresponding legal obligation in the relevant legal system. Commonly, it is deemed to imply also that the system provides a recognized and institutionalized legal remedy to the right-holder to compel the performance of the obligation or otherwise vindicate the right. It may imply also that the right claimed is, in fact, commonly enjoyed (and "as of right," not by grace), and the corresponding duty is, in fact, generally carried out (and from a sense of legal obligation).

To examine the international law of human rights from the perspective of "rights" theory, it helps to keep in mind special characteristics of international law and of the international legal system. Because international law is made by states assuming legal obligations, the states-parties to international human rights instruments might be seen in two different roles. Acting together, the states-parties are legislators, making law. As a result of that legislation every state-party is an "obligor," having obligations, duties, to respect and insure what are designated as the "human rights" of their inhabitants. After the agreement comes into force, the state as legislator largely disappears (except in the sense that lawmaking continues by interpretation and application); only the state as obligor remains.

Because the international law of human rights is made by states assuming obligations (the state as legislator), the international instruments focus at first on the state's obligations: it is the state's undertaking that creates the law. But under that law after it is in effect, the focus shifts sharply. The instruments are designated as dealing with the "rights" of individuals, and there is reference to individual "rights" in every article.[25] But the state's obligation and the individual's right are not necessarily correlative, or even in the same legal order. There are different possible perspectives on the relation between them:

1. The simple, undaring view sees international human rights

agreements essentially, if not exclusively, in interstate terms. The agreements constitute undertakings by each state-party to every other state-party, creating rights and obligations between them. For violations of the agreement, as for other international agreements, there are "horizontal" inter-state remedies: the victim state can make diplomatic claims upon the violator, request redress and reparation, sometimes may (lawfully) resort to "self-help." Insofar as the victim state has a legal right and pursues legal remedies, the violating state has correlative duties, including the duty, after violation, to provide redress and reparation, and even to accept the victim state's self-help where it is appropriate. The human rights agreements contemplate also special remedies, and a victim state — or the agreed international body — has the right to invoke those remedies and the violating state has a duty to submit to them. [26]

In this perspective, the only rights and duties created by international human rights are the duty of every state-party to act as it had promised, and the right of every other state-party to have that promise to it kept. The individual has no international legal rights; he is only the "incidental beneficiary" of rights and duties between the state-parties. The individual has no international remedies; he is only the incidental beneficiary of the remedies available between states-parties. He stands no better even as regards states that have adhered to the optional protocol to the civil-political rights covenant. A state party to the protocol "recognizes the competence of the [Human Rights] Committee to receive and consider communications from individuals subject to its jurisdiction who claim to be victims of a violation by that State Party of any of the rights set forth in the Covenant." [27] That, it will be argued, does not establish a private remedy for violation of a private right, but only an additional mechanism for enforcing the rights and duties of the states under the covenant, by providing the committee with evidence as to whether those rights and duties have been honored. If a party to the protocol should interfere with an individual's attempt to transmit a communication to the committee, or with the committee's action upon that communication, the state is violating its duty to other parties to the protocol, not any right of the individual, and the only remedies for that violation, too, are interstate remedies.

A fortiori, there are no individual legal rights under the Covenant on Economic, Social, and Cultural Rights. The obligations assumed are by states to other states and even these are collective, long-term;

the individual is not only an incidental beneficiary but a contingent and remote one and has no remedies whatever.

From this perspective, I stress, there are no international legal rights for the individual. When international law speaks of "human rights," it does not refer to, establish, or recognize them as international legal rights in the international legal system. By establishing interstate rights and duties in regard to "human rights," international law indicates its adherence to the morality and moral values that underlie them and strengthens the consensus in regard to that morality; it encourages societies to convert those moral principles into legal rights in their domestic legal order; it creates international legal remedies and promotes other forces to induce states to make such "rights" effective in the domestic legal system; it does not, however, make them international legal rights for individuals in the international legal order.

2. A second perspective would see the international agreements, while creating rights and duties for the states-parties, as also giving the individual rights against his state under international law (in addition to any rights he has under his national constitutional-legal system).[28] The language of the agreements clearly declares these individual rights in every clause: "Every human being has the inherent right to life"; "No one shall be held in slavery"; "Everyone shall be free to leave any country, including his own." The individual has these international legal rights even though they are enforceable only by inter-state remedies, by governments or international bodies acting in his behalf. Under the optional protocol to the Covenant on Civil and Political Rights providing for consideration by the Human Rights Committee of individual complaints, or under the provision in the European Convention that the European Commission "may receive petitions" from any person claiming to the victim of a violation, the individual enforces his own right by his own remedy.

The same argument might apply even to economic and social rights. In the Covenant on Economic, Social, and Cultural Rights, the covenant speaks of rights for the individual in every article. In principle, surely, one can have a legal right to an education, or even to a vacation with pay, and the states assumed obligations to accord these, thereby giving the individual a right — a valid, legal claim — to them. That there are no individual remedies provided, that even the international remedies hardly guarantee that the individual will enjoy the indicated rights presently, may weaken the real enjoyment of these rights but does not derogate from their quality as rights. Every individual has a legal right under international law to have his society "take steps . . . to the maximum of its available resources with a view to achieving" all the enumerated rights.

3. A third perspective, which is independent of but might be combined with either of the two set forth, would suggest that the states-parties, as legislators, have legislated "human rights" into international law giving them status as affirmative independent values. That status is supported and furthered by the rights and duties that were established, whether the rights be those of states or of individuals. Although directly creating status or values, independent of rights and duties, is an unusual conception in international law,[29] since law is made wholly by way of states assuming obligations, one can say, perhaps, that every state-party assumes two different kinds of obligations corresponding to the two roles I have described. Acting with other states (the state as legislator), each state agrees to recognize and give legal status in the international system to "human rights" as claims that every individual has — or should have — upon his own society. In addition, each state (the state as obligor) undertakes to respect and ensure these values for its own citizens, thereby also creating rights in other states, and perhaps in individuals.

Rights, Remedies, and Enjoyment

The different perspectives I have suggested depend, of course, on different conceptions of rights. Immediately, whether the individual can be said to have legal rights in the international legal system depends in large part on the subtleties of "third-party beneficiary." At common law a third-party beneficiary generally had no remedy and had to depend on the remedy of the promisee.[30] The third party was the "true beneficiary" of a binding legal promise; the promise was likely to be kept, and the threat of a remedy by the promisee helped make it even more likely. Did the third party nonetheless have no "right" because he himself had no remedy that he could initiate in his own name?[31] Later, American states began to give the third-party beneficiary a remedy; did that convert a nonright into a right?

International law has moved to recognize a *ius tertii* for another state when the parties intend to accord it.[32] In our context the beneficiary is not a third state, but a mass of individuals. The individual's relation to the promise is not the same as that of third-party beneficiaries generally. The law declares that there is an individual "right." The individual is the true beneficiary, perhaps even the exclusive beneficiary (although one can find indirect "benefits" to the states impelling them to adhere to these agreements). Although the remedies are state to state and international, individuals or nongovernmental organizations and other forces in their behalf often activate those remedies in fact. Under the optional protocol — even more so under the European Convention — the individual himself can formally activate the principal international machinery. As a matter of fact, and as regards some rights also as a matter of law, the individual can waive the obligations and rights created by the international agreements. Can that add up to an individual "right" under international law?

To me, these questions about the rights of individual third-party beneficiaries are aspects of larger issues about rights. What do we achieve by characterizing some claims as "legal rights"? What determines our definition of rights and the elements we require to satisfy it? Why do we ordinarily insist that a legal right must have a formal, institutional, legal remedy and that the remedy must be in the "right-holder"?

Of course, one can define a legal right *a priori* as a valid legal claim supported by a formal remedy that lies with the right-holder. I would suggest, however, that the concept and definition of "right" are not arbitrary but serve a social purpose. In part, the concept of right is descriptive: jurisprudence (and language) developed it to describe legal relations, implying special entitlement, respected by the society with a sense of obligation, and generally enjoyed by the right-holder in fact. In large part, the concept of right is normative: a society develops the notion that someone has a legal right to something in order to assure, or at least enhance the likelihood, that he will enjoy it in fact. Recognizing that a claim is valid, giving it legal status as a right, itself contributes to the likelihood that it will be enjoyed in fact. Usually, however, it is not sufficient. An institutionalized remedy not only enhances the legal quality of the right and its contribution to the likelihood of enjoyment but creates practical "machinery" to help bring about enjoyment. The remedy is more likely to be used, and therefore to bring about enjoyment, if it is controlled by the right-holder.

If the definition of "right" has a purpose, if it is intimately related to probability of enjoyment, one must ask how the requirement of remedy fits that purpose. Even in domestic law, the relation of right to remedy to enjoyment is not simple or perfect. We do not insist that a remedy for violation of a right assure its prompt and full enjoyment. A promise by A to sell B a book is often said to give B the legal right to have that promise performed, but for breach of the correlative obligation the available legal remedy does not assure enjoyment of the book, but only compensation for its value, and only much later. Even when domestic law gives B the remedy of "specific performance," he obtains the object only much later, often after a long proceeding. The remedy for vindicating other legal rights is not necessarily more prompt, adequate, and effective; even when B takes a book A owns and possesses, the remedy will bring prompt and effective enjoyment of it only in rare cases where a policeman is present or A can exercise "self-help." As a practical matter, of course, the real purpose of an available remedy is to deter violation of the right, and often it will be not the right-holder's remedy but the state's penal "remedy" that will serve as the effective deterrent and make enjoyment of the right highly probable.

Some rights in domestic law are even further removed from remedy. Except perhaps for some strict Austinians, constitutional rights in the United States are surely legal rights, yet the principal remedy for violations is judicial review, a limited remedy at best: it may prevent future violations but does not undo the past; for many violations there is not even compensation to the victim.[33] Some constitutional rights moreover have no judicial remedy at all: they are " political questions," not justiciable ones.[34] Judicial review is accepted as an adequate remedy, moreover, although it has unarmed judges dictating to powerful executives, because "it works": rights are in fact vindicated. If so, why not other remedies, other institutions, other forces, which enhance the likelihood that rights will be enjoyed, bringing about some repair or compensation and deterring violators?

A legal right, I suggest, is a claim that the law recognizes as valid, as to which it recognizes a legal obligation on the addressee, and whose benefit the legal system renders likely to be enjoyed. Ordinarily that likelihood depends on the availability of legal remedies in the hands of the right-holder. But in special contexts and circumstances it can be supplied as well by other remedies or other forces — criminal penalties, advisory opinion by judges, an ombudsman, even effective public accountability and other societal deterrents.

Again, except to the eye of some strict Austinians, the international legal system creates legal rights and duties, generally between states. The right-holding state has valid legal claims, but the remedy for its violation often consists only of the right to make the claim, infrequently also to assert it in some judicial or arbitral forum. Yet the remedy "works" to achieve probability of enjoyment because it is supported by political-systemic forces, the general desire to keep the system going, and the particular "right" and power of the victim state to respond in ways the violator would not like.[35] In a word, the sense of legal obligation exists, and although institutional remedies are few and infrequent, there are inducements to comply, creating a likelihood of enjoyment and warranting the character of legal rights and duties.

As regards the international law of human rights too, even the rights and duties of states under the conventions depend on institutional "remedies" that are at best no stronger than those operating in international law generally. But there are, ever waiting in the wings, other forces inducing compliance — political criticism by other states and international bodies (and sometimes stronger reaction, sanctions as in regard to *apartheid*); criticisim by nongovernmental organizations including various activist organizations, and world-press available to mobilize hostile opinion. Might these qualify as well, or in addition, as "remedies" that support the quality of international legal rights because they enhance the likelihood that the rights will be enjoyed in fact?

From this perspective, it may not matter whether one sees the rights created by international human rights law as rights of states or rights of individuals. But seeing them as individual rights may in fact help make it more likely that they will be enjoyed in fact. And especially if the states do not act to vindicate their rights, so that their rights lack effective "remedies" (i.e., effective inducements to comply), it becomes desirable to see the rights as those of the individual so he can mobilize whatever remedies (inducements to comply) are available to him or to nongovernmental organizations in his behalf.

Rights in Theory and in Fact

The relation of rights to remedies to enjoyment raises other questions for the international law of human rights. In principle, whether the human rights agreements are being honored, whether the indi-

viduals are in fact enjoying the human rights promised, is not immediately relevant legally (or philosophically). For the short term, at
least, failure of one or more states to carry out their international human rights undertakings does not vitiate the character of the undertakings as legal obligations, or the rights and duties they create. But
if international human rights obligations fail to make any difference
in fact over an extended time; if the states that undertook these obligations act continuously and consistently as though they had not, or
as if they were not legal obligations; if the promisee states do not seek
to have the undertakings enforced and otherwise acquiesce in violations and act as though no obligations exist — then one would have to
consider whether there are legal obligations and consequent rights
and duties. One might then ask whether, despite the legal forms followed and the legal words used, legal obligations were intended and
were consummated; or, perhaps, whether despite original intentions
to make law, the obligations were ended by implied mutual agreement or acquiescence, or lapsed from "desuetude." (In regard to economic-social rights, in particular, the future may provide evidence
belying the assumption that legal obligations were intended.)

A different question is whether the derogations and limitations
permitted by the agreements are so large as to render the undertakings illusory, especially since they are, in the first instance at least, interpreted and applied by every acting state for itself, and — to date —
no other state (or international body) scrutinizes that interpretation
and application in fact. Those are subjects for fuller exposition another day, but, in a preliminary word, I do not think these and other
"loopholes" render the undertakings illusory or derogate from the
quality of any rights created. In my view the derogation clauses are
not destructive of the obligations (or the rights) so long as they are in
fact interpreted and applied as written and intended, and the other
states and the international bodies scrutinize their interpretation and
application. Similarly I do not consider undertakings to realize economic, social, and cultural rights "progressively" as essentially illusory. The economic-social undertakings were made legal obligations
in order to establish the idea of economic-social benefits as rights and
to increase the likelihood of their enjoyment; it was not clear what
else was expected to flow from making them legal obligations. Even
those purposes may be sufficient to support law and rights; the future
may show whether there are in fact other purposes and consequences

for seeing, and continuing to see, the covenant as law and as creating rights.

*   *   *

I have written about rights and duties and remedies, formally conceived, but have felt impelled to allude to a prevalent skepticism about their reality and effectiveness. If questions of reality are philosophically relevant, they cut both ways. The formal edifice of rights, duties, and remedies is not wholly realistic; in particular, to date the "state promisees" do not commonly assert their rights or invoke their remedies; these may not therefore meaningfully contribute to the probability of enjoyment. On the other hand, there is a network of other forces, including some formal machinery, notably the international committees, and some domestic machinery, whether courts, ombudsmen or something else; and there are informal influences, both international and domestic — the influence of norms themselves, intergovernmental intercessions, "activist" nongovernmental organizations, the effects of publicity by media of information — which combine to achieve substantial respect for the international obligations to different extents in different countries. Some students of law and of politics have learned to ask not only what are the formal rights and remedies and who enforces legal rights but what are the inducements to comply with them and are they respected in fact.[36] If judicial remedies make rights, why not ombudsmen, whether initiated by the individual or self-initiated? And internationally, why not a Human Rights Committee, or — some day — a UN human rights commissioner, especially if they "work" and induce compliance? Does not philosophy have place for these "realities" in its conception of remedies for rights?

NOTES

*In this paper I draw on previous writings: "The Internationalization of Human Rights," in *Human Rights: A Symposium*, in *Columbia University Proceedings of the General Education Seminar*, vol. 6, no. 1, part I: (Fall 1977); *The Rights of Man Today* (Boulder Colo: Westview Press, 1978); "Constitutional Rights and Human Rights," *Harvard Civil Rights—Civil Liberties Law Review*, 13 (1978), 593, and a revision, "Rights: American and Human, *Columbia Law Review* 79 (1979), 405.

1. When the Universal Declaration was adopted, "the communist bloc" (then including Yugoslavia, but not China) abstained, as did Saudi Arabia and South Africa. The European communist states have since accepted the Declaration in various ways, formally by explicit reference in the Final Act of the Conference on Security and Cooperation in Europe, Helsinki 1975. Spokesmen for The People's Republic of China have also invoked the Declaration in the United Nations.

2. It has been suggested that states may have undertaken also to help other states insure the economic-social rights of their inhabitants. See Article 2 or the Covenant on Economic, Social, and Cultural Rights, discussed below. That apart, the international acceptance of human rights is seen in the context of the state system, with obligations only upon an individual's own society.

3. The older law had inspiration different from that for the contemporary international law of human rights. State responsibility in respect of aliens probably did not stem primarily from concern for the individual alien, although the term "denial of justice" might suggest that; it was designed to protect friendly relations between states. The obligation ran to the state of which the alien was a national, violation was an offense against the state, and in principle the remedy also ran to the state. (Denying justice to a stateless person, therefore, was probably not a violation of law; surely there was no international remedy for it.) Contemporary human rights law, on the other hand, is idealistic, not merely political, in motivation, although in legal principle the obligations and the principal remedies run to other states, not the victim. See p. 268.

4. There may also be some customary law of human rights, as a result of continued general practice of states with a sense of legal obligation. Thus, it is widely accepted that slavery and slave trade are now prohibited by customary international law and therefore forbidden even to states that are not party to any formal agreement outlawing them; apartheid may also now be prohibited by customary law and, therefore, binding on the Republic of South Africa, although it is not party to any agreement prohibiting it. Similar argument makes a case that customary international law now forbids torture and other "consistent patterns of gross violations"; some believe that, by a combination of words and practice, some — or all — of the provisions of the Universal Declaration have become legally binding.

    An alternative formulation finds obligations, not in customary law strictly, but in the UN Charter to which virtually all states (including notably South Africa and the People's Republic of China) are parties. In the Charter all "Members pledge themselves to take joint and separate action in cooperation with the [UN] Organization for the achievement," *inter alia,* of "universal respect for, and observance of, human rights and fundamental freedoms for all without distinction as to race, sex, language, or religion." (I have combined Articles 55 and 56.) Although human rights are not defined and the character of the undertaking may be uncertain, later instruments, resolutions, and practices, in particular the Universal Declaration and its aftermath, have realized and concretized the original, inchoate undertakings in the Charter. While this argument would render all the provisions of the Universal Declaration legally binding on all UN members, which most governments would resist, many of them might accept it as regards selected, widely accepted rights—freedom from slavery, from racial discrimination, from torture.

Human rights might come into international law in yet another way, as "general principles of law recognized by civilized nations." See Article 38, Statute of International Court of Justice. Since national legal systems now generally outlaw slavery, racial discrimination, torture, these may arguably be deemed prohibited by international law.

There are also undertakings which the parties agreed would not have binding legal character but which are important "political obligations," like the Final Act at Helsinki, note 1 above. See generally Thomas Buergenthal, ed., *Human Rights, International Law and the Helsinki Accord* (Montclair, N.J.: Allanheld, Osum, 1977).

5. Both principal covenants begin with articles declaring that all peoples have the right of self-determination, as well as economic self-determination, "the right to freely dispose of their natural resources." Western states argued in vain that these are not human rights of individuals.

   The Covenant on Civil and Political Rights also includes group cultural rights. Article 27.

6. Article 4.

7. Articles 12 (3), 21, 22 (2).

8. Article 2 (1).

9. Article 4.

10. Article 8 (1)(a).

11. I state this with confidence and have argued it in an article, "Human Rights and 'Domestic Jurisdiction,' " in Buergenthal, ed., *Human Rights, International Law and the Helsinki Accord,* p. 21. Some others have argued that in human rights agreements that establish special "machinery" and remedies, these are generally intended to be the sole and exclusive remedies and replace the ordinary remedies between parties for violations of international agreements generally. See, e.g., the article by Professor Frohwien in that volume.

12. Article 40.

13. A state may submit to interstate complaints by a declaration under Article 41, and to private complaints by adherence to the optional protocol to the covenant. As of January 1, 1980, 61 states had adhered to the Covenant on Civil and Political Rights; 12 had declared under Article 41; 21 had adhered to the protocol.

14. Through the U.N. secretary general (article 16).

15. Articles 17–23.

16. References to some agreed moral, political, or "natural law" code is implicit in resolutions condemning violations of human rights in circumstances where no international legal undertaking seems in play.

17. I summarize the American conceptions in "Constitutional Fathers,

Constitutional Sons," *Minnesota Law Review,* 60 (June 1976): 1113; see also my article, "Privacy and Autonomy," *Columbia Law Review,* 74 (December 1974): 1410. I compare American and international conceptions in my article, "Constitutional Rights and Human Rights."

18. See the Preambles to both the International Covenant on Civil and Political Rights and the International Covenant on Economic, Social, and Cultural Rights.

19. Ibid. Also the Preamble to the Universal Declaration.

20. UN Charter, Article 55.

21. The positive law may incorporate some morality or natural law by reference, as in phrases like "cruel, inhuman or degrading treatment or punishment," or "arbitrary arrest or detention," or treatment "with humanity and with respect for the inherent dignity of the human person."

22. The argument for treating economic-social benefits as rights is not countered persuasively by ridiculing "vacation-with-pay" as a human right. That may only suggest that this particular benefit is not "right-worthy." Adequate food and other necessities, however, are surely fundamental, and essential to human dignity. The argument against treating them as rights was that they depended on available resources and large national policies and could not be enforced by the means available for enforcing civil-political rights. Treating them as rights, therefore, would only dilute international efforts to obtain respect for civil and political rights. These fears have been realized to some extent, although perhaps in forms different from those anticipated: many states have asserted the priority of long-term economic and social development (even as against present economic-social rights), and the need to sacrifice or defer civil and political rights. Compare UNGA Res. 32/130, Dec. 16, 1977; see my book, *The Rights of Man Today,* pp. 111-13.

23. The United States Constitution contains only limitations on government, not positive obligations upon them; and if affirmative obligations were to be constitutionally imposed, the existing legal system does not readily provide for remedies that would mandate affirmative actions by legislatures, say to appropriate adequate funds for education. See my "Constitutional Rights and Human Rights." But there is no inherent reason why such a system could not be, and legislatures (and officials) who obey judicial prohibitions could also learn to obey affirmative mandates. Compare *Griffin v. County School Board,* 337 U.S. 218 (1964).

24. But compare note 11, above; the argument that interstate remedies were not intended is stronger here.

25. Even in the Covenant on Economic, Social, and Cultural Rights, which is written with the state as the subject. See p. 268.

26. The parties have analogous rights and duties also under the Covenant on Economic, Social and Cultural Rights. Every state-party assumes legal obligations and is also the "addressee" of such obligations by the

others. There are the usual international remedies as well as the additional remedies provided by the Covenant, that is, requirements of reporting to the UN Economic and Social Council, reports and recommendations by the Council.

27. Protocol, Article 1.

28. If international law creates such individual rights against the state some will argue that indirectly the individual acquires rights also against other individuals, since the state is obligated not only to respect these rights but also to "ensure" them, apparently against private interference with their enjoyment. Compare note 33 below. Others will argue that even if an individual is entitled to have the state protect his rights against private interference, the entitlement under international law is against the state only, not against the would-be interferer. Somewhat similarly, the Covenant on Civil and Political Rights provides that any propaganda for war, or advocacy of national, racial, or religious hatred, shall be prohibited. The covenant creates an international legal duty upon the state to prohibit, and a right in other states-parties to the agreement to have the prohibition enacted; there is no international legal duty upon any individual not to publish. Compare American constitutional theory, which also sees constitutional rights as only against the state. The freedom of speech is freedom from official interference. The state is not even constitutionally obligated to protect my freedom from private intereference. If it does so, by tort or criminal law, I acquire rights against the interferer and he duties to me, but these are not constitutional rights or duties. See my "Constitutional Rights and Human Rights."

A different question—a variation on a classic "monist-dualist" debate—is whether the international agreement serves to create (or confirm) legal rights and remedies for the individual under his society's municipal law. Some will say that since international law obligates the state to accord such legal rights, international law effectively puts these rights into domestic law (and domestic courts and other institutions must give them effect). The "preferred view" would have it that whereas the state is obliged by international law to accord such legal rights, it remains master of its domestic legal system, although a state's failure to accord such rights in the domestic legal order would, of course, violate its duties under international law to the other states-parties to the human rights agreements.

29. International agreements have created institutions with international status and character independent of, and going beyond, obligations assumed by states in regard to them. Thus, the UN Organization, created by the UN Charter, is deemed to have status and character in the international system even in relation to states not party to the UN Charter. Compare the Advisory Opinion of the International Court of Justice in "The Bernadotte Case," "Reparation for Injuries Suffered in the Service of the United Nations" [1949] *I.C.J.* 174.

30. In the United States the change came with *Lawrence v. Fox,* 20 N.Y. 268 (1859).

31. Some would also consider relevant whether the beneficiary had the power to cancel the obligation by the promisor.

32. Vienna Convention on the Law of Treaties, Article 36. The consent of the third state is required, but is ordinarily assumed. The treaty does not speak to rights for third "parties" which are not states.

33. See my "Constitutional Rights and Human Rights."

34. See *Baker v. Carr*, 369 U.S. 186 (1962); cf. *United States v. Richardson*, 418 U.S. 166 (1974). See generally, Louis Henkin, "Is There a 'Political Question' Doctrine?," *Yale Law Journal*, 85 (April 1976): 597.

35. Under the traditional view insisting that there can be no right without a formal, institutional remedy, those who claim that the usual interstate remedies are excluded and only those specially provided are available, note 11 above, might even question whether the state promisees have rights under the covenants. The only expressed remedies are reporting to and "follow-up" by the Human Rights Committee (or by the Economic and Social Council). A provision that the committee might consider interstate complaints is optional (art. 41). Even where it applies, is it a sufficient remedy to support a right?

36. See, for example, my *How Nations Behave: Law and Foreign Policy* (New York: Columbia University Press, 2d ed. 1979), esp. chaps. 3 and 4.

14

HUMAN RIGHTS AND
HUMAN OBLIGATIONS
WILLIAM N. NELSON

The most fundamental question about human rights is whether there are any. Assuming a positive answer, the question remains, Which rights are human rights? I shall not attempt to answer either of these questions here. My concerns are more limited: Assuming their existence, against whom are these rights held? On whom do the corresponding obligations lie? If we grant the existence of human rights, to what are we thereby committed? What conclusions do these rights support about the conduct of individuals and nations?

Since I shall not try to offer a general account of what human rights exist, I cannot proceed by enumerating the various rights and asking what obligations are implied by each. Instead, I shall simply ask what coherent answers are available under one or another assumption about morality or about the nature and content of human rights. My reason for asking these questions is that many theorists, politicians, and ordinary people who do believe in human rights seem to make a certain assumption about how the corresponding obligations are distributed. It seems to me worth asking whether this assumption is coherent, or what further assumptions one could make to render it coherent. The question is even more important if, as I suspect, some will probably want to reject this assumption once it is made explicit.

Let me be more specific. A tacit assumption underlying much discussion of human rights seems to be that, although all persons have these rights, the obligations corresponding to a person's rights lie only on his or her own government.[1] I shall refer to this as "the stan-

dard assumption." Once made explicit, this assumption clearly requires discussion. The idea of human rights, after all, is notable
partly because it provides a standard for the assessment and criticism
of established governments. But it presents less of a challenge to the
international order than it would if the standard assumption were
dropped. Cynics might say that this is just what one should expect
from an idea that has found favor primarily in affluent, Western
democracies. The same cynics would expect less wealthy and less
democratic governments, if they speak of human rights at all, to
think of them as imposing significant obligations on the citizens and
governments of all countries.

Disagreements about human rights between affluent democracies
and poorer, nondemocratic countries may sometimes take the form
of disputes about whether political rights and liberties, on the one
hand, or welfare rights on the other, are more important — affluent
democracies stressing the former, others the latter. But it is important to see that this dispute is different from the dispute over what I
call the "scope" of whatever rights we do accept. Thus, whether or
not one belives that human rights include rights to positive assistance
(e.g., to food, medical care, or education), one still must settle the
further question on whom the obligations corresponding to these
rights lie. It is perfectly possible to hold that each person has extensive welfare rights but that the corresponding obligations lie entirely
on his or her own government and fellow citizens. We find an example of this view of human rights in what seems to be a common conception of a human right of free movement. This right seems to be
viewed as a general right to *emigrate* but not as a right to *immigrate*.
Each person is supposed to be free to leave his or her own country,
but any country is regarded as free to set whatever immigration
policy it finds desirable. This seems odd. Isn't a restrictive immigration policy as much a violation of a right of free movement as is a restrictive emigration policy? We could, of course, stipulate a narrow
definition of the right; but we would be left with the theoretical question whether we could provide an adequate *ground* for the right that
justified it narrowly construed, but not broadly construed. [2]

Disagreements about what rights there are and disagreements
about their scope — about who possesses the corresponding obligations — are different but not unrelated. How much one is committed
to if one takes the view that human rights involve universal obligations will depend on which rights one has in mind. If the only human

rights are rights to noninterference, it will make relatively little difference whether we say that everyone has a corresponding obligation
not to interfere, or only that one's own government and fellow citizens have this obligation. Citizens of distant countries will not often
have occasion to violate this right. In the case of welfare rights, on
the other hand, it quite clearly does make a big difference where the
corresponding obligations lie. To the extent that people are reluctant
to grant that universal human rights include welfare rights, it is not
unreasonable to suppose that their reluctance derives from the assumption that universal rights involve universal obligations.[3]

So much for preliminaries. The question I wish to discuss is
whether what I have called "the standard assumption" about human
rights is a reasonable one. Better, under what assumptions about morality, about rights in general, or about specific kinds of rights is the
standard assumption reasonable? Is it possible to offer a coherent account of the nature or source of human rights according to which the
corresponding obligations are distributed as the standard assumption
specifies? If we are unable to offer such an account, this would suggest that a rational commitment to the idea of human rights involves
a commitment to obligations more extensive than is sometimes assumed. Either universal human rights have universal obligations or
they don't exist. If this conclusion is correct, those who are fond of
appealing to the idea of universal human rights when criticizing the
conduct of foreign governments toward *their* citizens will have to re-
think their position. If they reject such rights, they will lack a basis
for their criticism of others, but if they accept such rights and if the
corresponding obligations are also universal, they will have to face up
to the implications of these rights for their own conduct and for that
of their own governments.

In the following sections I shall describe and discuss several views
about morality or about one or another kind of right, each of which
would help make sense of the standard assumption. It is possible to
accept the standard assumption without accepting any of the positions described. None is implied by this assumption. It does stand in
need of support, however, and I shall argue that some of the positions I discuss provide such support and are plausible.

RELATIVISM

It is natural to assume that the existence or distribution of human

rights and obligations has something to do with whether ethical relativism is true. If some form of relativism is true, it might seem to follow that there are no universal rights or obligations at all but only
rights or obligations one has as a member of a particular society.
Standards of correct conduct will vary from society to society, and in
addition, what is appropriate within a given society or culture will be
inappropriate across cultural boundaries. But it is not obvious that
relativism has these consequences. The theoretical issues here are
complex, and matters are complicated by the fact that relativism has
various forms.

If relativism is simply the view that different cultures formulate
different conceptions of what rights and obligations people have,
nothing of much interest for our purposes follows. The mere fact of
divergence among conventional moralities does not rule out the possibility of a single correct moral theory, and it leaves us with the question of the distribution of rights and obligations under this correct
theory. Suppose, however, that the existence of any unique standard
independent of particular, conventional moralities is dubious. Suppose, further, that the basic terms of normative discourse have indexical features so that the truth or falsity of a moral judgment is determined by the specific conventional morality presupposed in a given
discourse.[4] The view resulting from these assumptions seems to me
not implausible. However, it does not determine an answer either to
the question whether there are human rights or to the question
whether the corresponding obligations are universally distributed.
Neither does it make these questions irrelevant or unanswerable. On
the relativistic assumptions proposed the questions can be answered
only relative to some particular morality. So, even if we ask our question from the perspective of a specific morality, and even if the
answer is that all human beings have extensive rights, but that the
obligations corresponding to any person's rights fall largely on other
members of his own society, we are still left with the question whether
a morality asserting this is coherent. But that is just the question I
said we had to answer anyhow.

If what I have said is correct, accepting this kind of relativism does
not commit one to the standard assumption about human rights and
obligations. But another kind of relativism is more relevant. According to this kind of relativism, certain judgments, like "ought" judgments, are *doubly* relative.[5] As above, their truth or falsity depends
on the content of a particular conventional morality presupposed by
the discourse, but it *also* depends on whether the person whose action

is in question has adopted the assumed moral conventions as his own. On this view, whether it is true of anyone that he or she ought to do something, even if this judgment is relativized to a particular set of moral conventions, will not be determined by those conventions themselves independent of his or her acceptance of those conventions. Now, if we accept this account of the truth conditions for judgments of moral obligation and if we make certain natural assumptions about motivation, the consequences are interesting. Specifically, if we assume that people are somewhat self-interested, possessing only limited benevolence, we would expect them to accept moral conventions imposing only limited requirements on them. Whereas they may well grant rights to others and accept correlative obligations, we might expect them to limit their responsibilities largely to other members of their own society.

Given the assumptions in this second kind of relativism about the truth conditions for "ought" judgments, and given the assumptions suggested about human motives, it will not be true of anyone that he has significant moral obligations to members of distant societies. It may be true of most people that, relative to some system of moral conventions, they have significant rights; but it will not be true in any case that the rights are held against everyone. Each person's right will be a right against only some limited range of people. This distribution of rights and obligations is something like the distribution often taken for granted in discussions of human rights. Hence, the type of relativistic theory under discussion is a theory acceptance of which would tend to explain acceptance of the standard assumption about human rights. (The standard assumption, in turn, tends to confirm this form of relativism as an account of our use of terms like "ought.")[6]

The differences between the two kinds of relativism need to be emphasized. It is only in the case of the second kind that relativism *itself* is relevant to the conclusion that a person's obligations to others are limited. It is only in this kind of relativism that what a person ought to do is determined, as a matter of logic, by the intentions that that person has formed. In either kind of relativism, the distribution of obligations will also depend on the substantive content of a morality.

Many will reject the idea that a person's obligations — what he ought to do — depend even partly on what principles he is willing to accept. It seems likely that believers in human rights will reject it. Whether or not we reject it, however, each of us is still left with the question what substantive theory to accept. Acceptance of either kind of relativism discussed does not render substantive moral theorizing impossible or purposeless. In the next section I shall turn to more substantive matters bearing on my basic question.

SPECIAL AND GENERAL RIGHTS

What rights do people have? A sensible response to this question is that it has no general answer. Many of the rights people have are *special* rights. Unlike *general* rights, possessed by everyone and held against everyone, special rights arise out of specific transactions or other relationships. Contractual or promissory rights are an example. The promisee has a (specific) right against the promisor, and the latter has a (specific) obligation to the former. To the extent that we limit ourselves to special rights and obligations, it is clear that one person's rights will differ from another's in both content and number. As long as there are some special rights, there will be no general answer to the question, "What rights do people have?"

What about human rights? According to the standard assumption, human rights are like general rights in being universal but are unlike general rights in that they are not held against everyone. The standard assumption suggests, then, that they might be regarded as special rights that are universal only because, as a matter of fact, everyone is a party to similar kinds of relations. We might say, for example, that each person, in virtue of his membership in a particular society, comes to have rights against other members of that society to share of the benefits of that society. This would give us virtually universal rights to certain kinds of benefit, but the obligations corresponding to any one person's right would not be universally distributed. The question is: How many rights, of what kinds, can be accounted for on this model?

I have suggested elsewhere that rights based on ideals of distributive justice might best be understood as special rights.[7] The underlying idea is as follows. People who argue for the redistribution of wealth often put forth principles of justice specifying an ideal pattern of distribution, like equality, without saying anything about the *context* in which the pattern is supposed to be important. If asked to defend the principles, they can cite examples, like the distribution of doughnuts to members of a Girl Scout troop, in which it seems obvious that an equal distribution is called for. But it always seems possible for a critic to imagine other kinds of situations in which no particular pattern of distribution, or some other pattern, is called for. So it begins to seem implausible that there is any such thing as *the* principles of distributive justice for every kind of distribution. It does not follow, though, that there are no correct principles for the distribution of certain goods among the members of a given society. This distribution may be a distribution of a distinctive type, governed by distinctive principles. These principles would be principles in virtue of which members of a given society come to have rights against one another that social goods be distributed in a certain way. Such rights would be special rights deriving from the relationship that obtains among members of a society and held against only other members of that society.

This proposal requires that one give an account of the nature of the relation that obtains among members of a society and that it be clear why the relation in question gives rise to the relevant rights and obligations. If we could give such an account, it would have definite advantages for the theory of justice. It would show how principles of social justice could be valid even if the distribution mandated by such principles is not appropriate for all distributive situations. Also, it would provide an answer to the question *why* someone who has too much (according to the principles) has an obligation (and, therefore, may be coerced) to give up some of what he has for the redistribution; and, the answer would not refer simply to the abstract attractiveness of some pattern. I agree with the libertarian critics of the idea of distributive justice that some answer to this question is required. What I regret is that, even given space, I can provide no more than a sketch of an answer.[8]

This suggestion shows how it might be possible to ground fundamental rights to positive assistance on social relationships. Such rights, like human rights in general, would be universally possessed if everyone is a cooperating member of some society. Also, although they arise out of social relationships, such rights would provide a standard by reference to which social institutions could be judged: systems of institutions must be designed so that social goods are appropriately distributed. Nevertheless, obligations corresponding to any one person's rights would be possessed only by those other members of his society who benefit from cooperative social relations.

Suppose some basic rights can be understood in something like the way suggested for rights deriving from principles of distributive justice. If an account of rights like this is reasonable, and if it can be extended to cover a fair number of the rights that have been called human rights, we will then have a partial answer to the question raised at the beginning of this essay. We will have a theory of the basis of some human rights compatible with their being virtually universal and also with the idea that the obligation to respect someone's rights falls primarily on other members of that person's society. This suggestion, unlike the suggestion discussed in the preceding section, does not rest on relativistic assumptions.

The question remains whether *all* rights that people accept and regard as human rights can be understood in this way. Rights to life, rights against aggression, and rights to be free from certain kinds of interference or coercion are common examples of human rights; yet it seems implausible that these rights are based on anything like one's cooperative relations with others. The same might also be said of rights to certain minimal necessities. What is the basis of these rights? How are they to be interpreted? What obligations correspond to them and how are they distributed?

THE INTERPRETATION OF RIGHTS

Rights such as the right to life cannot plausibly be grounded in social relations of reciprocity or express or tacit agreements. The right to life is prior to such relations and puts limits on the range of permissible relations. A reasonable account of this right, as of certain other basic rights and liberties, would ground them in fundamental human interests and needs—interests and needs that any reasonable theory ought to recognize. But even if we have a tolerably clear conception of the fundamental interests on which a particular right is based, it does not follow that it is easy to offer what I shall call an *interpretation* of the right. Yet most rights require interpretation. Aside from a few extreme cases (Smith's contractual right to be paid $20 by Jones on or before January 10), the content of most rights is far from clear. It is unclear what kind of conduct is required of others, and, of special interest here, it is unclear *who* is subject to the requirements.

What does the right to life require? One might think it requires at least that we refrain from killing, but even this conclusion seems wrong on reflection.[9] Cases of self-defense, euthanasia, and abortion suggest possible counterexamples; and the category of self-defense, apparently the most easily explicated of these, is in fact far more complicated than is sometimes assumed.[10] Perhaps the only thing we can say in general is that the right to life precludes *unjust* killing. What else does it require? Does it require that we refrain from actions dangerous or risky for others? How risky? Does it require that we aid others when they need aid in order to live? How much aid? At what cost?

If we agree that there is a right to life and that this right includes a right not to be killed (unjustly), we presumably also agree that *everyone* is obligated not to kill anyone (unjustly). The controversial questions about the right not to be killed seem not to include questions about its *scope* but only about its *content*. What about rights to positive aid when such aid is necessary for life? Some might deny that there is any such right, but here I think it is worth distinguishing clearly the question whether a person has any rights against anyone to be provided with necessities of life from the different question whether a person has such rights against everyone.

We can consistently grant that life is valuable and that it is therefore wrong to kill without granting also that everyone has a right to all the necessities of life. In the case of illness, injury, or degeneration, it is sometimes simply impossible to provide someone with everything necessary for life. Moreover, even to the extent that it is possible to provide people with what they need to live, the needs of some can be so great that it is prohibitively expensive for others to provide for those needs; and, being *merely* alive is of little value by itself. We value things other than life, and life largely because it makes these other things possible. The importance of these other things puts limits on the amount any of us would be willing to spend on life itself, even in our own case. It also limits the amount we are willing to spend on the lives of others, even if the expenditures are consistent with preservation of our own life. A reasonable moral theory needs to take these facts into consideration. A moral theory should be intelligently designed to secure human well-being, but it should do so without imposing excessively heavy obligations on individuals.

A system of rules prohibiting (most) killing, but otherwise giving people substantial liberty affords significant protection for individual life, insofar as it is valuable, without imposing excessive burdens on people. Further restrictions or requirements are, to a large extent, unnecessary. People can provide for themselves, either directly or through voluntary transactions, much of what they need to live. But this point can be exaggerated. Small children cannot fend for themselves, and there is no guarantee that individuals, acting independently, will not bring about a situation in which someone, as it were, is left with no room in which to maneuver. How should morality accommodate facts like these? In the case of children, at least, most of us would want to treat the right to life as including rights to food, shelter, and other necessities. Supposing that each child has these rights, who has the corresponding obligations?

It is moderately clear what it means to say that each person has an obligation corresponding to any person's right not to be killed, namely, that each acts wrongly if he kills anyone. What would it mean to say that each person has an obligation corresponding to any one child's right to food? Is each obligated to provide all the food necessary for each child? If there are n adults, is each obligated to provide $1/n$th of each child's food? Most people would say neither of these things but would say, rather, that the child's right to food and shelter corresponds to an obligation on the part of his or her parents to provide adequate food, shelter, and the like. This suggestion is interesting. If we accept it, we have another example of a universal right that does not correspond to a universal obligation. Why should anyone think this is the right distribution of obligations? Can the right reasonably be thought to derive from an agreement between parent and child?[11] Is the obligation something like the moral "price" a parent must pay for the pleasures of sex?

I think it is a mistake to try to explain the respective rights and obligations of parents and children entirely in terms either of the moral basis of the rights or in terms of morally significant properties of the relationship between them. Instead, the distribution of rights and obligations is partly a matter of convention or custom.[12] Morality dictates only a certain range of permissible customs or conventions. The moral right itself is not essentially a right against any specific persons. It is best construed as a right that customs and institutions be so arranged that, in one way or another, the basic needs of children be met. The practice of raising children in the nuclear or extended family represents one possible way of satisfying the demands of the right. Whether it is the best way is not here in question. If it does adequately meet the needs of children, and if it is otherwise consistent with moral rights, then it determines the extent of an individual's obligations. To the extend that it does not, it needs to be supplemented.

I conjecture that something like this approach to the interpretation of rights will be appropriate for many human rights not arising out of special relationships. It is not clear whether, or to what extent, persons have rights, not dependent on special relationships, to positive assistance or benefits. To the extent that they do, however, I think they are best construed as rights that there be social arrangements that will provide people with that to which they have a right. Of course, institutions or arrangements do not themselves literally provide people with benefits or assistance. What is necessary, then, is that customs, laws, and the like assign responsibilities in such a way that, if people comply with institutional requirements, the appropriate benefits are provided.

In the case of some rights, then, the question, "Who has the corresponding obligations?" has no general answer because it is not intrinsic to the right itself that it is held against any particular person or persons. Instead, these rights are simply rights that there be *some* assignment of responsibilities such that, if those to whom responsibility is assigned carry out their responsibilities, people are provided with what they have a right to.

HUMAN RIGHTS AND
NATIONAL RESPONSIBILITIES

It seems to be commonly held by many who believe in human rights that some of these rights are universal but that the responsibilities corresponding to any given person's right fall only on members of his own society. My question has been whether this position is coherent. I have now offered a way of interpreting some human rights designed to make sense of this standard view without relativistic assumptions and without the assumption that all human rights derive from special relations. The position often taken on the distribution of responsibilities deriving from many human rights, I noted, is analogous to the position often taken on the distribution of responsibilities regarding small children. Just as many tend to hold a person's society primarily responsible for that person's well-being, so also we tend to hold a child's family responsible for its well-being. In each case, the assignment of responsibility is not determined solely by an examination of the person's rights themselves. Instead, it is mediated by a conventional assignment, which in turn may be based partly on natural factors. [13] The rights themselves are simply rights that there be some appropriate conventional assignment of responsibility. The scope and content of the corresponding obligations is determined by this conventional assignment, given that it is adequate.

The remaining question is whether the standard assignment of responsibilities to individual nation-states is an adequate one. I will not attempt to provide a complete answer to this question, but I will discuss some considerations that seem to me relevant. To begin with, it does not necessarily count against a particular assignment of responsibilities that people fail to carry out their responsibilities. This problem may arise under any possible assignment. What we must ask is whether the system in question will have its desired effects if people carry out their assigned responsibilities to the extent that can be expected; and we must ask whether alternative systems will fare better.

Even if people have rights that some of their basic needs be met, it does not follow the everyone is responsible for meeting the needs of everyone else. One argument for the institution of private property[14] is also an argument for a more limited assignment of responsibility. No one will have much incentive to work productively unless (1) he is unable to get what he needs without working, and (2) he can reasonably expect to enjoy the fruits of his labor if he does work. Hence, we need not only effective prohibitions on stealing but also limits on what one person is entitled to claim from others as a matter of right. But, if some people are unable to meet their own needs, who is responsible for them?

Morality, I think, dictates no particular answer to this question. In general, though, the units to which responsibility is assigned must have sufficient resources in the aggregate to be capable of meeting the relevant needs of individuals. They also must have a unified structure of authority so they can act as a unit, adopting policies that will move wealth in the direction of need. At the same time, they have to be sufficiently independent of other units that they are secure in the enjoyment of the benefits of their own productive policies. What these considerations suggest, of course, is an assignment of responsibility to sovereign states. To say that individual nations are responsible is to put the burden on nations to make their own, internal assignment of responsibility and to insure that conditions are such that people will be able to carry out their assigned responsibilities. Thus, a society could adopt a system according to which each person is responsible for meeting his or her own needs, so long as it also guarantees an opportunity for everyone to carry out this responsibility. Alternatively, it may provide for many needs through a system of taxes and transfers, so long as it also maintains a sufficiently high aggregate income to make the system effective.

This suggestion is sensitive to the considerations of incentive I have mentioned. On the one hand, if productivity depends on individuals having an incentive to produce, a government can take this into account in designing its own institutions. Moreover, a government will not be foolish if it adopts appropriate internal policies, providing it is not in turn compelled to share the fruits of these policies with other nations, and providing that it cannot automatically expect other nations to subsidize it if it adopts inefficient policies. Still, one might ask whether a government will take its responsibilities to its citizens seriously in the first place. Now, this question will arise for any unit larger than the family. Assuming that families are not always self-sufficient, however, responsibility must be assigned to larger units. What the question suggests, however, is that the best system would be a system in which individual nations are responsible for the welfare of their citizens, *and* in which individual governments are subject to some degree of popular control. Hence, we have at least a sketch of an argument for the conclusion that certain political rights may have a central place in a system of human rights.

My argument assumes that individual nations have sufficient resources to be self-sufficient in the sense that they are capable of organizing in such a way that they can provide for all those needs that people have a right to have met. Whether this assumption holds will depend partly on the nature of international institutions — trade regulations, for example — but it can also depend on noninstitutional factors such as the weather. To the extent that individual nations are not self-sufficient and are not capable of becoming so, the institutional assignment of obligations suggested here needs to be modified — so long as we assume certain basic welfare rights.

SUMMARY AND CONCLUSIONS

I have not attempted a definition of human rights, nor have I assumed that human rights are distinguished from others by their source or ground. (I have not assumed, for example, that human rights are all and only those rights a person has merely in virtue of being human.) The important thing about human rights, I think, is that they are possessed by most everyone and that they provide a standard for the assessment and criticism of social, political, and economic institutions. The question that has concerned me is this: If there are such rights, what is their scope? Who has the corresponding obligations? When we accept the premise that everyone has some such rights, to what are we thereby committed? I raise this question because discussions of human rights often seem to presuppose a particular answer, namely that, whereas everyone has these rights, the obligations corresponding to a given person's rights fall only or primarily on his own society. To assert that everyone has these rights while denying that the corresponding obligations are universally distributed may seem at least disingenuous, and perhaps inconsistent. I have considered various possible ways of rebutting this charge.

To begin with, some forms of ethical relativism, though not all forms, may have the consequence that the range of most people's obligations is rather narrowly circumscribed. But even if we reject these relativistic assumptions, other reasons exist for thinking that the scope of some basic rights is less than universal. Some basic rights, including rights based on principles of distributive justice, may best be construed as special rights arising out of social or political relations and held only by members of a given society against other members of that society. But what about those rights that do not arise out of special relations? These rights, like most rights, still require *interpretation*. Even rights like the right to life do not, so to speak, wear their meaning on their sleeve. Just what they guarantee to their possessor needs to be spelled out, and *who* is obligated to do *what* also needs to be spelled out. Now, in the case of some basic rights like the right to life, some of these questions cannot be answered in the abstract merely by considering the meaning of the right in question. These rights are, in effect, rights against institutions. They require some institutional arrangement with an assignment of specific responsibilities to individuals such that, if people carry out their assigned responsibilities, certain goods will be secured to people. The question what is required of individuals, given that everyone has a certain right, is often settled by appeal to institutional divisions of responsibility. If institutional arrangements are adequate in the sense that, if people carry out their assigned responsibility, rights will be respected, then an appeal to institutional requirements is sufficient. It is at least arguable that a division of responsibilities in which each national government is responsible for certain basic rights of its members is a reasonable division. I have offered considerations in support of this conclusion, though I do not pretend to have established it here.

NOTES

1. In "International Human Rights as Rights," Professor Henkin says, "The international law of human rights derives principally from contemporary international agreements in which states undertake to recognize, respect and promote specific rights for the inhabitants of their own countries" (pp. 259-60).

2. Before assuming a negative answer, we should consider the case of rights to engage in trade. These rights do not include, for example, the right that others be willing to buy the goods we want to sell at the price we want, but neither are they without effect.

3. The assumption that, if someone has a right, *everyone* has a corresponding obligation may make people reluctant to grant that everyone has certain rights. Similarly, the assumption that, if someone has a right against x, everyone has a similar right against x, may lead x to deny that anyone has the original right. This latter point comes up in discussions of rights to a redistribution of wealth. Can we consistently believe that some people have a right to a share of, say, my income without granting that everyone has such a claim against me? I have heard Gordon Tullock raise this question in conversation.

4. The idea that terms like "ought" have an indexical element can be found in Roger Wertheimer, *The Significance of Sense* (Ithica, N.Y.: Cornell University Press, 1972).

5. See Gilbert Harman, "Moral Relativism Defended," *Philosophical Review*, 84 (January 1975): 3-23.

6. Harman (Ibid.) argues similarly that our beliefs in only minimal duties to animals and in a limited duty of positive aid to other people confirm his theory about the relativistic nature of some moral judgments.

7. William Nelson, "Special Rights, General Rights and Social Justice," *Philosophy and Public Affairs*, 3 (Summer 1974). I explicitly avoided drawing any conclusions about international justice in this article, but Charles R. Beitz discusses these implications in "Justice and International Relations," *Philosophy and Public Affairs*, 4 (Summer 1975). He points out, among other things, that my assumptions about justice do not *imply* that there are no international duties of justice.

8. See Nelson, "Special Rights, General Rights and Social Justice," esp. sec. 3.

9. See Judith Thomson, "A Defense of Abortion," in James Rachels, ed., *Moral Problems*, 3d ed. (New York: Harper and Row, 1979), pp. 130-50.

10. Consider the discussion of "innocent threats" in Robert Nozick, *Anarchy, State and Utopia* (New York: Basic Books, 1974), pp. 34-35.

11. Thomson ("A Defense of Abortion," pp. 98–99) discusses possible ways in which a fetus might be regarded as having a special right against its mother, the right deriving from something like the mother's voluntary agreement to care for the fetus. None seems satisfactory.
12. The following discussion is, of course, reminiscent of Hume's treatment of the "artificial virtues" in his *Treatise of Human Nature*, book III, part II.
13. Although Hume is anxious to point out that the rules of justice *differ* from society to society, and therefore concludes that they are conventional, he does not think they are *arbitrary*. One reason for the differences in rules is that natural conditions vary from society to society. See *An Inquiry Concerning the Principles of Morals*, sect. 3, part II.
14. See Allan Gibbard, "Natural Property Rights," *Nous*, 10 (March 1976): 79.

INDEX